THE
BABY BOOMER
BOOK
OF
NAMES

THE
BABY BOOMER
BOOK
OF
NAMES

By Roger Price, Leonard Stern and Lawrence Sloan

PRICE/STERN/SLOAN
Publishers, Inc., Los Angeles
1985

Acknowledgements

The authors would like to extend their appreciation
to L. Spencer Humphrey and Jo McDaniel Cox
for their time, creativity and abiding affection
for this book.

Illustrations and cover: Linda Friou
Design and layout: Tanya Maiboroda
Editorial and research supervision:
L. Spencer Humphrey

Napoleon signatures from *Big Name Hunting: A Beginner's Guide To
Autograph Collecting* by Diane and Charles Hamilton, copyright 1973 by
Charles Hamilton. Reprinted by permission of Simon & Schuster, Inc.

Parts of this book were previously published under the title *What Not to
Name The Baby.*

ISBN: 0-8431-1419-3

TABLE OF CONTENTS

The only child born aboard the Mayflower during its historic crossing of the Atlantic was named **OCEANUS HOPKINS.**

A Foreword

Here is the complete book of names for our times — not just a dry dictionary of nomenclature, but a book which entertains as it enlightens.

You will find complete historical backgrounds on the origin, meaning and variations of thousands of names, plus an unrivaled collection of fascinating and amusing facts.

But this mammoth compendium does much more. It explores to the fullest a startling new theory concerning your name and fate. It reveals that your character and the course of your life were launched, not by your genes or your early childhood, but at the moment you were assigned a name.

This vital theory disproves, once and for all, the ridiculous idea that Heredity, Environment, Childhood Trauma, Television or Lack of Fiber in the Diet could be responsible for our inept and messy Personalities. In other words, this book puts the blame where it really belongs — on Names. If you had another name (such as Takashami or Uga-Ooonga) would you not be a different person?

THE BABY BOOMER BOOK OF NAMES contains a huge catalogue of scientifically unsound examples that fully interpret this important psychological breakthrough.

If you are using this book to choose a name for your baby, we think it is important that your selection be based, not on origin or historical reference, but on what *you* think is beautiful and *you* love to say in combination with your surname. Only then should you use THE BABY BOOMER BOOK OF NAMES to find out the background — whimsical or otherwise — you have chosen.

Happy Naming — or just Happy Reading!

The Editors

YOU ARE
WHAT THEY
NAMED YOU

forgive them...

"Sticks and stones will break my bones but names can never hurt me." Anon.

Due to the unfortunate acceptance of the above couplet as truth, the fields of Name Research and Name Analysis have been overlooked for centuries — until recently when we worked out THE PRICE/STERN/SLOAN NAME THEORY based on the idea that *you become the kind of person your name sounds like you should.*

This section of THE BABY BOOMER BOOK OF NAMES is a comprehensive review of that entire Name Theory. Today we are no longer alone. Hundreds of teachers, scientists and journalists now subscribe to these findings and have, themselves, become "Nomenclaturists." We welcome them.

All babies, when they are first born, are just about the same. Until a baby is given a name it has no personality and to the casual observer, not even any sex. It is nothing but a dampish, noisy lump. But once you give a baby a name, society begins to treat it as if it had the type of personality the name implies, and the child, being sensitive, responds consciously and unconsciously and grows up to fit the name.

Now, just think a moment about the people you know. Don't most of their names fit them? Or, applying the Price/Stern/Sloan Theory, don't most of them fit their names? Naturally, along with other people in the scientific theory game (Galileo, Einstein), we accept the possibility of error. You will at times see flagrant exceptions to the conclusions expressed here. These exceptions merely prove the validity of the P/S/S concept. The theory not only makes as much sense as any other theory about personality, but is easier to explain and much more fun.

PRICE/STERN/SLOAN

ABBEY

is 22 and is having an affair with a 63-year-old man. Everyone keeps trying to find out what sort of sex life they have.

ABIGAIL

needs to discuss everything immediately so she can reassemble her view of life.

ADA

Nothing simple ever happens to ADA.

ADELAIDE

had an interesting operation once.

ADELLE

does things, up to a point. She graduated from law school and passed the bar, but never practiced.

ADENA

is determined to maximize her potential. Her mother wants her to marry HAROLD.

ADORA

is easily moved to tears. She cries at sad scenes in "coming attractions."

ADRIENNE

likes to have her portrait drawn in store windows.

AGATHA

wears pink polyester blouses and is either under- or overweight.

AGGIE

has a couple of neighborhood bars she hangs out in. She has long discussions with the other regulars about how whales mate or can dogs really think, stuff like that. When AGGIE comes to a party she usually leaves alone.

AGNES

wears Oxfords with inch-and-a-half heels and is always complaining about the terrible "smutty" novels they publish nowadays and describing the "disgusting" scenes she objects to.

AIDA

cannot tell a lie. Consequently, she never discusses her age.

AILEEN

can down three martinis at lunch and still return to the office and nobody's the wiser . . . except HOLLY and she won't tell because she works for AILEEN.

AINSLEY

While in the company of others AINSLEY manages to spend the entire evening speaking to a certain man with her eyes.

ALANNA

stops feeling lonely and sorry for herself when her son's marriage breaks up.

ALBERTA

In certain moods she buys pizza and just eats the crust.

ALETHEA

is a musical prodigy — a competition-calibre pianist. She makes a living doing pantyhose commercials.

ALEXANDRA

lives with LINDSAY in an "in" neighborhood and is always trying to talk you into health foods. She has three neutered cats.

ALEXIS

is tall, looks like she is a big time reporter or TV interviewer, but works as a salesperson in a gay boutique.

ALFREDA

has magical fingers. A massage from ALFREDA is more meaningful than a serious relationship with most women.

ALI

holds her high school's record for the 100-meter butterfly stroke.

ALICE

As they get older the other suburban wives get irritated with ALICE because she eats everything and doesn't get fat.

ALICIA

has allergies and a dog with fleas. Her parents are pleased because before she went to therapy it was the other way around.

ALLISON

is blond and broad-shouldered and has the instincts of a mother hen. She has one date with a fellow and the next day she comes around and collects his laundry.

ALMA

is an ex-Army sergeant who owns her own bowling ball.

ALTHEA

isn't quite sure what kind of relationship she's willing to establish with a man until she compares astrological charts.

ALVINA

On applications ALVINA lists her marital status as separated.

AMANDA

is either a plain, friendly girl or a knockout and in show business.

AMBER

undulates even when sitting.

AMELIA

is soft-spoken, quiet. AMELIA always marries the wrong guy.

AMY

always thought she was an ugly duckling. Even now when you tell her she's beautiful, she wants a second opinion.

ANASTASIA

is a big, boisterous MTV star or a witty antisocial doctor.

ANDREAs

are usually dark and look as if they came from some place that hasn't been discovered yet. If they are blond, they are called ANDEE.

ANGELA

is soft all over. Men who get it on with ANGELA experience an Epiphany. If you do not know what "Epiphany" means, don't bother to look it up. It couldn't help you.

ANITA

looks sort of foreign. She's the kind of girl other women use the word "stunning" about. ANITA marries NICKY, but it doesn't last. After that, NICKY falls apart but ANITA looks better than ever.

ANN

is a sort of female version of JIM. She is the one the guys dream of marrying. They dream of jumping into the sack with DARLENE or LILY but when they dream about ANN, there's a license hanging on the wall.

ANNETTE

Never argue with ANNETTE. She has a very selective recall. She remembers every dumb thing you did and stupid thing you said for the past 20 years.

ANNIE

believes she was adopted or that there was a mix-up at the hospital where she was born . . . this couldn't possibly be her REAL family!

ANTOINETTE

once had a torrid affair with a famous person. She won't tell you who it was but she does give clues.

ANTONIA

can make "hello" sound suggestive.

APRIL

is a little person who runs a big business.

ARDITH

has always been composed and together. When she was born, the doctor told her parents they had a six-pound woman.

ARETHA

chants as she mixes exotic drinks.

ARIANNA

Her taste in art is not quite as bizarre and abstract as her taste in lovers.

ARIEL

has four locks on her apartment door. It's tough to get in . . . and once you're in . . . it's tougher to get out.

ARLENE

has big eyes and talks a lot.

ASHLEY

It takes an alarm, a radio, an auxiliary alarm, and a phone call to awaken ASHLEY. Then give her 10 minutes, call back and get her up.

ASTRID

has instincts about people which are instantaneous and almost infallible.

ATHENA

records her identity crises on videotape.

AUDREY

gives the impression she's interested in action. But she isn't. Guys can't understand that the trouble isn't with them — and they keep trying.

AUGUSTA

is a name given only to maiden aunts.

AURORA

forms strange organizations with bizarre objectives.

AVA

Men want to come on to her immediately. However, they back off when she takes out her lipstick and they spot the badge in her purse.

BAMBI

was born 19 years old and will be 19 years old when she's 90.

BARBARA

lives in the suburbs with HOWARD.

BARRIE

graduates at the top of her class. Much is expected of her. She marries RICK and has to support him throughout his college years . . . which number 20.

BEATRICE

has a large bust and is embarrassed by it and wears her sweaters two sizes too large.

BELINDA

is allergic to everything, including her allergist.

BELLE

Her life revolves around her son.

BENITA

redecorates parts of her house each year to boost her spirits. She tells her husband it is to increase the resale value.

BERNADETTE

leads a secret life which demands to be an "As Told To . . ." book.

BERNADINE

reminisces about her cheerleader days whenever she gets together with CONNIE, RUBY and MARILYN.

BERNICE

is an attractive girl's friend or roommate. BERNICE has long hair, wears tight belts and uses depilatory on her arms. She telephones fellows.

BERTHA

includes the three weeks she spent as a waitress at McDonalds on her resume.

BERYL

is pretty and very sweet and has a great job but for some reason or other you feel sorry for her.

BESS

is active in a religious organization. She also reads palms.

BETH

is a rock music aficionado. She suffers from a loss of hearing in the high register.

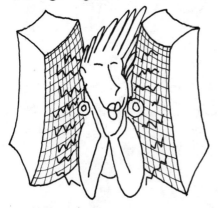

BETHEL

can be an executive, a nurse or a bag lady.

BETSY

is the girl you go out with.

BETTE

is the girl you stay in with.

BETTINA

You think BETTINA wears falsies until you see her in a bathing suit.

BETTY

is maternal and never really understands about making love — but sometimes she wishes she did.

BEULAH

sends gifts to the President.

BEV

is soft-spoken. Men can make out with BEV if they don't rush her.

BEVERLY

tosses her hair and laughs a lot.

BIANCA

has a great sense of style and a throaty voice. At parties she sits on the piano, hikes up her dress and sings torch songs.

BIBI

deserves better from life.

BILLIE

usually has her slip showing, but it doesn't bother her much.

B.J. (BARBARA JEAN, BETTY JO, etc.)

Women called B.J. insist on being called B.J. They are smart and attractive and make excellent executive secretaries. Their bosses say they are "executive assistants." It's hard to get a date with B.J. When you call, she's always just going someplace for the weekend or just getting back, but she says she really wants to see you and please call her again. B.J. eventually marries a nice fellow in the office.

BLAIR

is money-oriented, but a closet decent person.

BLAKE

has long- and short-term goals. Among the long-term goals is getting a steady job.

BLANCHE

is always yanking her kids by the collar and yelling, "Put that down!" and "What's the matter with you?" The kids don't answer. When they get older BLANCHE stops yanking them by the collar and says, "Don't talk to me that way. Who do you think you are anyway?" The kids still don't answer. They're still trying to figure out what's the matter with them.

BONNIE

is a living doll. She smells sensational and the fellows who kissed BONNIE in high school never forgot it. Every so often, for the rest of their lives, they think of BONNIE and wonder what might have happened if . . . . Once in a while one of these fellows looks BONNIE up and before he sees her he tells himself he's foolish, that 25 years have passed, she must be frumpy and ordinary-looking by now and she probably never really was much to begin with. Then he meets her and BONNIE is still the greatest. He feels lousy for a month.

BRANDI

is a name an ambitious, pretty girl makes up to call herself.

BLOSSOM

always looks as if she is about to sneeze.

BLYTHE

becomes a scientist or gets some kind of job using her brain. At work they discover she's got great legs.

BOBBY/BOBBIE

chews gum and saves pictures of Matt Dillon.

BRENDA

becomes an executive in a women's club and organizes charity drives. LOUISE and HELEN do all the work, but BRENDA gets all the credit.

BRIANNA

always passes the "sensuality tests" in her magazines with flying colors.

BRIANNE

can find a cocktail party at 10 in the morning.

BRIDGET

writes a book devoted to the study of women's poetry and sculpture. It's dedicated to HARVEY.

BRIGITTE

has a mother who speaks English with an accent that guys love. BRIGITTE moves away from home at an early age.

BRITTANY

has contemporary hair. Yesterday it was spiked and green ... tomorrow who knows? Certainly not BRITTANY.

BROOKE

is leggy and men can talk dirty to her.

BUNNY

will try anything. She is the first woman to have a nail transplant.

CAITLIN

knows that, of the total membership of the American Institute of Architects, only five percent are women.

CALLA

Half of her life's possessions are in the back seat of her car.

CAMILLE

is warm, friendly and slightly off-center.

CANDACE

is a knockout, but difficult to get to know. Guys who do know her smile a lot.

CANDIDA

is elegant and pristine. She tried pumping her own gas once and decided it was obscene.

CANDY

is either a little kid or a topless dancer.

CARA

resolves at least twice a year to be the women she can be.

CAREY

falls in love with herself. It's an affair that lasts a lifetime.

CARLA

Her taste is middle of the road in music, food and sex.

CARLOTTA

tends to develop an undulating walk and likes to decorate herself with flowers or big jewelry.

CARMEN

is dedicated to RSM . . . Romanticism, Spontaneity and Mystery.

CAROL

Most guys would like CAROL to be more than one of the boys. But she's faithful to . . . that's what most guys are never able to find out.

CAROLINE

is a rarity among human beings . . . she reads and follows instructions.

CARRIE

is big-boned and healthy. She holds down a job, has three children and goes to school three nights a week.

CASEY

is a back-up singer for a rock star.

CASSANDRA

has a few modest fiascos in her love life and one colossal blunder — usually NORMAN.

CASSIE

always has some kind of trouble . . . a disease no one has ever heard of . . . a big weight problem . . . a garbage disposal that backs up . . . it's always something with CASSIE.

CATHERINE

is a name like WILLIAM or RICHARD. Girls named CATHERINE are usually called something else. If your friends call you CATHERINE it means you are sensible, trustworthy and have a small bust.

CATHY

is always sick or just getting over being sick. She leaves early because she has to take some pills and get to bed.

CECILIA

has good posture and a severe hairstyle. She makes a good husband for an indecisive man and raises children scientifically.

CEIL

lives for her eight-year-old daughter who takes dancing and singing lessons. CEIL is always quoting the things her daughter says. CEIL doesn't like the daughter's father.

CELESTE

At age 38 she stops whatever it is she is doing and starts her own business. She does well enough to take care of FRANK until he sells a painting.

CELIA

spends so much time reading the menu you would think it had a plot.

CHANDRA

has a steady occupation ... newlywed.

CHARLENE

marries some kind of minor celebrity, probably in the entertainment field. He calls her "Charlie."

CHARLOTTE

has a good job in sales or merchandising. When a man makes love to her, she watches him every second to make sure he's enjoying it.

CHER

constantly seeks ways to work out all her tensions. This year she's into past-life therapy.

CHERYL

is tall, athletically gifted and can dunk a basketball. It depresses her brother, HAL (who's 5'9"), a whole lot.

CHIQUITA

usually has half a dozen strays in the house. Some of them are animals.

CHLOE

believes in all kinds of fairy tales and men love her for that. They've even been known to make up a few.

CHRIS

is slender and tends to wear tight clothes, even when jogging.

CHRISTINA

Underneath her high fashion shoulder pads and loose-fitting clothing CHRISTINA has a Botticelli body.

CHRISTINE

was the first girl in her junior high class to peroxide her hair.

CHRISTY

doesn't have to do much to her hair or any of her parts. She is the female version of a Porsche.

CICELY

has wonderful taste in clothes and no taste in men.

CINDY

has wonderful taste in men and no taste in clothes.

CLAIRE

does most of the work in the office, but — like Poe's "Purloined Letter" — remains hidden in plain sight.

CLARA

never answers the phone until it rings four times.

CLAUDIA

is the only woman you can call at 2:30 a.m. and chances are her phone will be busy.

CLEMENTINE

names her dog after a television personality.

CLEO

is the one who squeezes all of the chocolates in the box trying to find the ones with soft, gooey centers.

COLETTE

has one favorite picture of herself. It is 20 years old.

COLLEEN

is squeaky clean and has pink, round arms, but if you try to make love to her, she giggles and squirms and says, "Eek, that tickles!"

CONCHITA

has a sex-drenched look that men spend their lives dreaming about.

CONNIE

has more wants than needs.

CONSTANCE

has reached an extremely powerful position in the military, but does not consider herself a feminist.

CONSUELA

is involved in causes. Her central passion is the redevelopment of a downtown somewhere.

CORA

carries a huge shoulder-strap bag that has everything in it from shoes to turtle food.

CORDELIA

has clogged nasal passages all her life.

COREY

Her thoughts are always somewhere else. After you open the door of Corey's car and deposit her in the driver's seat and say good night, do not walk in front of her car or you'll be a memory.

CORINNE

If she's blond, CORINNE is tall and wears pearls. If she's a brunette, she's a deal maker.

CORNELIA

has never recovered from the day in high school when she walked into the boys' bathroom.

COSIMA

has an X-rated glove compartment.

COURTNEY

owns a horse.

CRYSTAL

is a big girl who always seems to be having a good time and is generous with her money, her possessions and herself.

CYBIL

lies about her age before anybody asks her.

CYNTHIA

is very feminine. She marries a fellow she thinks has money — TOM or maybe CHRISTOPHER — and gets up every morning before he wakes up to put on lipstick and tie a ribbon in her hair.

DAGMAR

helps her kids with their homework. They all flunk math.

DAISY

spends most of her life working out her relationship with her mother.

DALE

When you come back from a trip, DALE has stocked your refrigerator with your favorite food and she and her son, GEORGE, meet you at the plane.

DAMITA

is what men hope a blind date will look like.

DANA

Men disclose intimacies to DANA that they wouldn't share with their wives.

DANIELLE

even manages to look sexy in her choir robe.

DAPHNE

acts in an afternoon soap opera. She is in constant fear the producers plan to "kill" her character.

DARCY

is a lifetime member of a Hot-Tub Club.

DARLENE

is a hillbilly who once won a beauty contest.

DAVIDA

has a good life but feels guilty about it. She adopts her friends' abandoned worries ... MIRIAM's husband's dalliance, CECIL's asthma and HENRIETTA's concern about what's happening to the neighborhood.

DAWN

acts like she's the only woman in the world who ever had a baby.

DEANNA

is in her early 30's and is overweight. She was married once but not for very long.

DEBBIE

She's a friend to her father, an ally to her brother and she's still trying to work something out with her mother. She and DAISY consult a lot.

DEBORAH

Her parents drive her crazy. They insist she call home at least once a week. When she does, her parents pick up two extensions and talk to each other, ignoring DEBORAH.

DEE

is born to shop.

DEEDEE/DEEDY/DIDI

has well-to-do parents who buy her a terrific car. After she leaves her second husband she gets mixed up with people who are cult members and have kinky sex.

DEIRDRE

has two little kids and a high-pressure job. She's been known to excuse herself from business meetings by saying she has to "go to the little girls' room and tinkle."

DELIA

is always freshening people's drinks.

DELILAH

There are two DELILAHs, the short one and the tall one. The short DELILAH is a space technician and can drink you under the table. The tall DELILAH is a nude model for a name photographer. The short one is more fun.

DELLA

has not bought anything new in a store for ten years.

DENA

is badgered by in-laws who only want the best for her.

DENISE

is very wholesome. That is, unless she is French. If she is French — well, she's French.

DESDEMONA

has delusions of competency.

DESIREE

moves her lips when she reads. Every language is her second language.

DIANA

gives the impression she is interested in action. And she is. She likes the feeling of power it gives her over men.

DIANE

is the same as DIANA except DIANE is taller and has beautiful hands and is proud of them.

DINAH

Men like to hang around with DINAH. She doesn't threaten them.

DIONNE

Before DIONNE orders anything from the menu, she asks everyone at the table what they're having. She finally orders squid and sends it back.

DIXIE

always takes up with men who treat her badly.

DOLLY

is a very friendly person. She even knows the first name of her mailman, UPS driver and paperboy.

DOLORES

is a vegetarian unless she's taken out to dinner.

DOMINIQUE

From across the table, DOMINIQUE can tell whether it's a genuine Rolex or only a good copy.

DONNA

is a perfect second wife.

DORA

is an executive who's very hard on the people who work for her. She worked her way to the top and expects the same dedication from them. She's constantly disappointed.

DORE

is involved in myriad activities, some of which include her husband.

DOREEN

loves leather and sand.

DORIS

is attractive and friendly, but if you try to kiss her, she perspires and won't stop talking.

DOROTHY

As far back as she can remember, any problems DOROTHY may have had in her life have always been the result of telling the truth.

DOTTIE

is one of the world's great comparison shoppers.

DULCIE

is a "21" dealer at Las Vegas. You can buy her a drink but the casino boss takes her home.

DYAN

is boisterous. She tends to get accidentally pregnant . . . a lot.

EARTHA

is fabulous looking and enjoys knowing that all the men in the office speculate about which one of them might be having an affair with her.

EDEN

is a gardener. Her roses win second prize.

EDIE

can be seen at stop lights bobbing her head in time to the music blasting from the car radio.

EDITH

can't do enough for her daughter. She picks out her furniture, buys her china and her dresses. If the daughter gets mad at her husband and wants to go home to Momma, she's right next door.

EDNA

rides a motorcycle to work.

EDWINA

She would be handsome if her lips weren't so compressed.

EILEEN

is a flirt. She drinks Margaritas and daiquiries and after three she can be talked into ANYTHING.

ELAINE

is dark and intense and is very serious about her group therapy. If a man can convince ELAINE he's off his rocker, or at least "disturbed," he's got it made. But she's pretty sharp and it's best not to try this unless you are a little nutty to begin with.

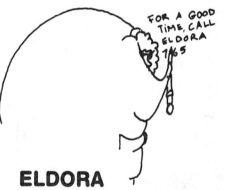

ELDORA

ELDORA's name and phone number are scratched into the wall of a public phone booth. ELDORA did it.

ELEANOR

is quiet and sensual and is usually in love with some fellow.

ELENA

has a poker face and is trustworthy. She knows all the secrets in the office because everyone knows she can be trusted. They never realize how little they know about her, though.

ELISE

always looks like she's on her way to the dentist.

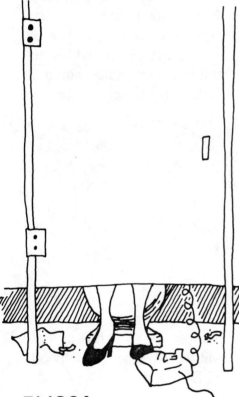

ELISSA

is divorced. When she's on a date, she calls home almost every hour to see how her daughter feels.

ELIZABETH

Like CATHERINE, ELIZA-BETH is usually called something else. If she is tall and round-shouldered she is called ELIZABETH.

ELLA

is pretty and has tremendous energy. She's fun at parties and is always organizing something. When she decides to get married, she picks out someone, and he doesn't have a chance.

ELLEN

has a little kit and makes silk flowers. She tried to sell them but couldn't, so now she gives them to her friends who always say "Boy, these are great. Why don't you sell them?"

ELLY

is always knitting socks for her boyfriend; but, by the time the socks are finished, she's broken up with him. She has a drawer full of assorted woolen socks.

ELOISE

never goes to the movies without having to go to the bathroom at least twice by the end of the film. She's alienated at least 20 people.

ELSA

When she does tip, ELSA leaves exactly 15%.

ELSIE

buys everything in large quantities. She's a firm believer that things are cheaper by the dozen.

ELVIRA

looks like the picture on her driver's license.

EMILY

is an absolutely adorable four-year-old for most of her life.

EMMA

was captain of the field hockey team at school. She charges through life like an Army tank. Later, she may take in foster children.

ENID

Ninety percent of the towels, ashtrays and bar glasses in ENID's home are from hotels.

ERICA

tells everyone PATTY is her younger sister. It drives her daughter, PATTY, crazy.

ERIN

has thin thighs and is sexually aggressive.

ERNA

At 25, ERNA redoes herself by taking elocution lessons and going to movies with subtitles.

ERNESTINE

should buy a new bathrobe.

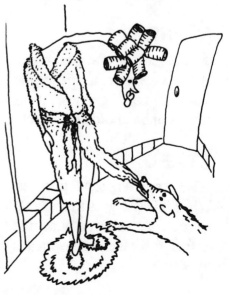

ESMERALDA

Ask TED, LON or BILL and
they will tell you ESMER-
ALDA is the best kisser since
Mary Louise Coucher back in
the ninth grade.

ESTELLE

is a closet blues singer. Once her
kids have established themselves
she "comes out" and amazes
everyone with her success...
including her husband.

ESTHER

is warm, loving and committed
to chicken soup as a cure for the
common cold, cramps, stress
and an unbalanced checkbook.

ETHEL

failed her driver's test four times.
When ETHEL goes to the laundromat, she always jams the
change machine and overloads
the dryer.

EUGENIA

wonders if she turned off the gas
on the stove or, if her apartment
is all electric, she wonders
whether she left the microwave on.

EUNICE

At age 35, EUNICE moves
back in with her parents.

EVE

is a doctor and is so nice that no
one notices she is really a gawky
sort of woman.

EVELYN

wears brown and empties
ashtrays.

EVITA

is obsessed with fitness and
nutrition, but a chocolate
anything is her undoing.

FAITH

fervently prays she never meets
and becomes friendly with
HOPE and CHARITY.

FALLON

fingers her perfectly matched
pearls as if they were worry
beads.

FARRAH

Afraid the contents would shock her parents, FARRAH keeps her diary under lock and key. Twenty years later, she reveals the diary to her parents. They are shocked.

FAWN

has a father who is an international celebrity, but no one knows exactly what he does.

FAY

bleaches her own hair; but not often enough. She likes to ride on the back of motorcycles, and she will lend guys money — if she has any.

FELICE

is graceful, with a long neck and swan-like movements. She can never find shoes in her size.

FELICIA

is involved with a lot of iced tea in her life.

FERN

is intelligent and determined. When her children grow up she goes back to school, gets a degree, practices corporate law and takes vacations to remote places such as Antarctica.

FIDELIA

is warm, friendly, efficient and writes memos filled with mind-numbing detail.

FIONA

appeared in a 1981 magazine as one of the most eligible women in America. The magazine is still on her coffee table.

FLAVIA

Her bedroom is SRO.

FLEUR

Style, albeit glitzy, is a commodity of which FLEUR has an abundant supply.

FLORA

minimizes the anxiety of dating by doing the initial reconnaissance over lunch.

FLORENCE

plays bridge with ETHEL, MARION and MILLY while their husbands, HANK, PETE, FRED and GUS go bowling.

FRAN

is pushing 50, but she smokes marijuana, wears leather sandals, and is "into" macrame and Greek dancing. People always say FRAN is a "character" but she isn't. She's just lonely.

FRANCES

Last summer FRANCES drove to California in a VW with three other women. FRANCES owns 15 shares of GM stock.

FRANCINE

is slightly eccentric, slightly irresponsible and slightly neurotic. All of which leads her friends to think of her as creative . . . or a potential writer.

FRIEDA

is always scrubbing the floors and putting newspapers over them.

FRITZI

is a price shopper's guru.

GABRIELLE

has a sexy phone voice and knows it. She gives great promise over the phone.

GAIL

is graceful and a slow talker who is pleased if people ask her if she's from the South.

GAY

always looks 10 years younger than she is. She considers it a handicap. Her girl friends want to kill her.

GEMMA

Her role models are women achievers who wear jumpsuits to work.

GENA

is four years old and is almost as cute as her father thinks she is.

GENEVIEVE

has bedroom eyes. They ask questions which make men feel uneasy ... but not as much as the answers that come to their minds.

GEORGIA

is the one at the party who makes the other women mad by kissing and whispering to their husbands.

GERALDINE

is a lovely person who always seems younger than she is.

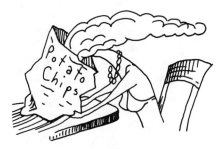

GERMAINE

is on a macrobiotic diet and only eats at health food restaurants, which drives her friends bananas. At home, she sneaks potato chips.

GERRY/GERI

When GERRY was a kid she used to climb trees and play baseball — later she became a top golfer and a killer tennis player. When fellows would try to kiss her she suggested arm wrestling. Somehow she still managed to become a great kisser.

GERTRUDE

When young, GERTRUDEs tend to have too many front teeth and dull hair, but they try to improve themselves. By the time they are 17, they are called TRUDY or GERT, depending on whether they become cute or smart.

GILDA

has been building her body and doing aerobics for years. She marries late in life and carries her husband over the threshold.

GILLIAN

has difficulty delegating duties and would rather do it herself than have someone do it for her. She picks up her dates in a 10-year-old car she repairs herself.

GINA

manages to make "off the rack" discount clothes look chic and expensive.

GINGER

shows up for job interviews dressed in a tennis outfit. If the interviewer is a man, she gets the job.

GINNY

is a kittenish divorcee. She has a lot of pictures of herself around the house.

GISELLE

is currently involved in another permanent relationship.

GLADYS

talks you into coming to a "simply fabulous" party she's having and when you show up, there are seven people there who don't know each other, and GLADYS serves canned spaghetti and garlic bread.

GLENDA

forms a rhythm and blues band with CASSIE, TIFFANY and ERIN, who are all over 30. They call themselves the "Shopping Mall Culture Club."

GLORIA

remodels. Her house is always a work in progress. After the kids leave home, she goes back to work at what she did before she got married.

GLYNIS

has several men in her life, but sequentially, for long periods.

GOLDIE

is an easy mark for a sad story. Three sentences into a tale of woe, she's wiping tears from her eyes.

GOOGIE

All of GOOGIE's friends are wealthy (not rich but WEALTHY) people who spend summers in the Hamptons and winters in Palm Beach or Cap d'Antibes. These people waste the first half of their days planning how they are going to waste the second half.

GRACE

buys nice furniture and puts plastic slipcovers over it. She also keeps the blinds pulled down all day so the sun won't bleach her rugs. Her husband never brings a friend without letting her know 48 hours in advance.

GREER

is at home at a racetrack or dining in a five-star restaurant.

GRETA

is the first woman firefighter to make lieutenant.

GRETCHEN

Her boyfriends are always leaving GRETCHEN to go back to their wives.

GRISELDA

can swear in seven languages.

GWEN

The first thing she reads in the morning newspaper is her horoscope. If it's negative, she gets back into her bed.

GWENDOLYN

is a devoted anglophile who never misses a BBC mini-series on PBS, lives on cucumber sandwiches and has wicked fantasies about Prince Charles.

HALLIE

has her house painted to match her sports car . . . shocking pink.

HANNAH

becomes a lawyer and takes over her husband, MARTY's, business.

HARRIET

tells everyone she still prefers birth control pills. No one cares much.

HAZEL

loves to travel. She and her friend, MARY, spend at least one Saturday night a month reading brochures and planning their next trip. Once they have decided where to go, HAZEL and MARY carefully plan their budget which includes the cost of everything from postcards to dramamine.

HEATHER

has millions of cashmere sweaters and goes to a super private school and is almost a great beauty (there's something about her mouth that isn't quite right). By the time she is 29 she is a financial counselor and taking care of older men.

HEDDA

didn't get married, she struck a deal.

HEDY

was born in Europe, but came here at 10 years of age. She still writes her 7's like this — 1776.

HEIDI

writes a novel. It sells okay and she becomes impossible.

HELEN

goes around telling everyone she just lost 22 pounds, but no one can tell the difference.

HENRIETTA

speaks shorthand. She doesn't finish sentences because she knows what she's going to say and assumes you do, too.

HERMIONE

is chunky. She buys a fox fur jacket that makes her look chunkier.

HILDA

talks to herself. When you catch her at it, she claims she meets a better class of people that way.

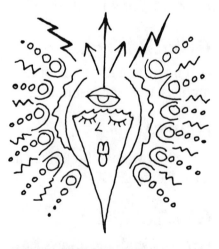

HILDEGARDE

just *knows* she's psychic.

HILLARY

is always saying, "I'm not interested in playing around. I am interested in getting married, nothing else." But she will go out with anyone who calls at six-thirty.

HOLLY

uses her dad's credit card and doesn't tell her mom . . . or her husband, TOBY.

HONEY

is very small and is always running around carrying something that will either melt, spoil or bark.

HOPE

Her mother takes HOPE on a cruise so she can meet an eligible fellow. HOPE meets one and he marries her. The next year HOPE, the fellow, and her mother go on a cruise.

HORTENSE

boards cats.

IDA

loves to bake but her cakes are just awful. However, you like IDA so much you never have the heart to tell her. You always make her think they're great. The next time you come to visit her, you get the same terrible cake because she remembered how much you liked it.

ILKA

can wear a bikini made out of fur and get away with it.

ILONA

Lovemaking gives ILONA a sense of satisfaction like nothing else except knitting.

ILSA

comes from Northern Europe and has a great complexion.

IMOGENE

says it doesn't matter what anyone else thinks, but when she's shopping, takes a poll of the sales personnel before buying anything . . . even pantyhose.

INA

If blond, INA is very elegant, conducts afternoon teas and even though she's given up smoking, she still makes use of her cigarette holder. If brunette, INA is exotic looking and has done something courageous in her life . . . something more than marrying WALTER.

INEZ

always asks the waiter what there is for dessert. She listens intently as he describes in detail the complete list. She never orders anything because she's on a diet.

INGA

and lingerie are synonymous.

INGRID

doesn't have a mean bone in her body, but has some muscles that are suspect. She can bench press 70 pounds. Although he won't admit it, that's what is keeping JOE from asking her to marry him.

IOLANTHE

is never quite sure who she happens to be at the moment.

IRENE

was a buyer for a big store, but she quit and married DICK. She dyes streaks in her hair, is long-legged and well-groomed. IRENE is a good cook but a bad housekeeper.

IRIS

takes two hours with her makeup every day and spends over $200 a month at the beauty salon. Naturally, she always looks great. She used to wonder why she did it because she has only slept with two men in her life and has absolutely no desire to go for three. For awhile she became a secret drinker, but it made her face break out, so she stopped and now she chants with a group of Buddhists.

IRMA

Tall IRMAs have broad shoulders and good posture and marry someone like ED. Then there is a small, skinny, skittery IRMA. This IRMA never looks you in the eye and makes faces when she talks, and combs her hair all wrong. She spends eight years in a second-rate state college and finally marries a guy who never looks you in the eye, makes faces when he talks, and combs his hair all wrong. They are much happier together than the tall IRMA and ED.

ISABEL

has a round little figure and is maternal. Everyone loves ISABEL except the guy she's hung up on. He's a fool.

ISADORA

is a pop singer who depends more on her visual arsenal than the way she sounds.

IVY

is a single parent whose kids do not approve of any of the men she dates.

JACKIE

is small, sparkly and neat. She wears ribbons in her hair, likes to go out with tall men, and if they make love to her, she is very noisy.

JACQUELINE

has an out-of-this-world body. She jogs every morning on heavily trafficked streets. The guys in the office carpool (GUS, MAC, DAVE and MARIO) who drive past her on their way to work are usually late for work because they circle the block for a second look.

JADE

breaks away from her family and searches for her identity . . . at least twice a year.

JAMIE

works out every day. She enters three 10K's a year and finishes all of them.

JAN

is a rebel who is a closet mother. She will go out with anyone as long as he isn't successful, well-to-do, or well-dressed.

JANE

Everyone likes JANE. As she gets older she will get a bit heavy around the hips and will wear the same hairdo she did in high school. She will be friendly rather than flirty because people expect JANE to be that way. After her first marriage to a nerd, she gets into finance and is very successful.

JANET

was a camp counselor, goes to church, and is a Girl Scout leader. She wears thick glasses and has a great complexion. No one is quite sure whether JANET sleeps around or not. She is very cool about it.

JASMINE

writes three times a year to "Miss Manners" seeking advice.

JEAN

must have been a 10-month baby . . . she's never on time.

JENNIFER

Blond JENNIFERs are angels only perkier. Blond JENNIFER tilts her head, lowers her eyes and has an angelic smile. A dark JENNIFER, however, is something else. All her friends are convinced she's dating a married man because she knows the addresses of small, off-the-beaten-path restaurants.

JESSICA

can never go out because she just this minute finished washing her hair.

JEWEL

feels her eyes are too close together, her thighs are too thick and her nose is too long. She won't accept the fact that she is a jewel.

JILL

is something like BONNIE only more athletic and less virtuous. If you have a video recorder, JILL will bring over the porno tapes.

JO

Her life is a series of regularly scheduled crises.

JOAN

wears powder blue and pearls and is the one the fellows always want to marry.

JOANNA/JOANNE

is a natural blonde who comes on big with any fellow who seems to be showing an interest in another woman. Once she gets the fellow's attention, she dumps him and starts up with someone else. JOANNA doesn't have many girl friends.

JOCELYN

calls the restaurant to tell whomever she's meeting she'll be there in a few minutes. She arrives an hour later.

JODY

confides her innermost secrets in public places where she has to shout to be heard.

JOHANNA

In 15 years of driving, JOHANNA has never once exceeded the 55 miles per hour speed limit, failed to stop at a marked intersection or made a turn without giving the proper signal. Even so, she always panics and breaks out in a sweat when she catches a glimpse of a police car in her rearview mirror.

JOSEPHINE

is the big center on the women's basketball team. She compensates for her size by being what ELAINE would call "Easy" — but only if the guy is six inches shorter than she is.

JOY

belongs to so many organizations and is involved in so many causes, she has difficulty fitting a job into her schedule. Somehow she survives.

JOYCE

has seniority in the office typing pool.

JUANITA

has more energy than any of her three teenage children.

JUDITH

has good looks and a great sense of style. Every August, JUDITH gets her apartment in order and her life together for her parents' September visit. After her folks leave, JUDITH spends the first night unwinding at a friend's apartment. Usually HERB's. HERB is the only true beneficiary of JUDITH's parents' visit.

JUDY

has long hair and never gets over being a cheerleader. She marries a guy who worships her.

JULIA

A girl called JULIA will be delicate or at least look delicate. There are a lot of things JULIA can't eat, and no one is quite sure she will be around. She lives to be 96.

JULIE

had the lead in a school play and goes to California to have a career in show business. She gets a job as a production assistant for $200 a week and works 12 hours a day every day with no overtime pay. At first, she identifies with the actors and the director. But after a few years, she realizes she has never been invited to their homes and starts hanging around the technical people. She winds up getting married, having a baby and living in the Valley. When the kid gets old enough she drops by the studio occasionally and works as an extra.

JULIET

has a flirtation quota she meets each and every month.

JUNE

is pretty. Some women are handsome, some beautiful, some striking, some exotic, some cute. But JUNE is pretty and knows it, She looks like she stepped out of a 1925 advertisement for face powder or chocolates. She smiles a lot without showing her teeth and dresses to call attention to her shoulders.

JUSTINE

uses the restaurant knife as a mirror to check her lipstick.

KAREN

is a handsome, humorous female person who is a steadfast supporter of the ERA. She thinks of sex as a form of therapy.

KATE

is KATIE up to 11 . . . KATI until 19 but from then on she's KATE — and watch out!

KATHERINE

warns her dates not to roll over on the dog.

KATHLEEN

takes adult courses at the university in such subjects as "Religious Life for Women in Northern France During the Central Middle Ages."

KAY

is tall, nervous and always trying to stop smoking. She likes to wear suits and chews on her false fingernails. She marries HAROLD or ALEX.

KEELY

dresses as if her hobby was raising eyebrows.

KELLY

is great looking. She teaches a class in backpacking. More men sign up than women.

KELSEY

studies seashells studiously.

KIM

hasn't gotten over the fact that Bruce Springsteen got married.

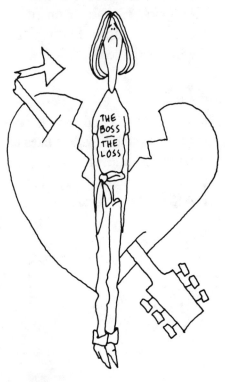

KIMBERLY

has "dates" with her daddy. She is daddy's girl. She and daddy are "real pals." Daddy tries to be jolly with them, but you can see he doesn't care too much for the fellows in KIMBERLY's crowd.

KIRSTEN

An evening with KIRSTEN is similar to reading a good mystery. You never expect it to end the way it does.

KITTY

is a plump woman who owns her own successful public relations company. She is 53 (no one has really been called KITTY since the '30s) but she has a flutey "girlish" voice and flirts with all the men clients. She is always buying new clothes and adding things to them. She gets a dress and sews on a little pocket or some cloth flowers. When she gets a scarf she sews sequins all over it.

KRISTIN

is blond and blue-eyed. Somehow she finds places to ski in the summertime.

LACEY

is someone who schedules sex on her daily reminder pad.

LANA

Her clothes are a series of mismatches which somehow set fashion trends.

LAURA/LAURIE

was NOAH's girl friend in high school. The night after he gets married to REBECCA, he cleans out his desk drawer. He finds a picture of LAURA ... and keeps it.

LAUREL

is very feminine, soft-spoken, generous and smart. No one can understand why she isn't married.

LAUREN

is at odds with herself. She loves her independence but doesn't like being on her own.

LAVERNE

is a gossip.

LEAH

Twice a week LEAH talks to an all-night disc jockey who knows her by her first name. Her neighbors, GOLDIE, HANNAH and NATALIE, consider her a celebrity.

LEE

has a successful career. She is stunning and a lot of married men are in love with LEE. They never get anywhere but they keep hoping.

LEIGH

is tall and has freckles. Eighteen guys are in love with her at all times.

LENA

eats chicken soup for breakfast and thinks gravy is a beverage.

LEONORE, LENORA & LEONA

are lonesome. Men take them out, but never bring them presents.

LESLIE

is nearsighted but won't wear her glasses and people think she is snooty.

LIBBY

used to telephone at 2 a.m. and say, "Guess who this is?" But people say she's no fun since she quit drinking.

LILA

has a lot of girl friends and is always having them over for lunch or coffee or a drink and getting them to contribute to some cause.

LILITH

is a great planner with a flair for both large and small dinners. Her husband hates to entertain. She compensates by giving frequent luncheons for the ladies.

LILLIAN/LIL

LILLIAN tells her troubles to everyone. However, if she is called LIL, everyone tells their troubles to her.

LILY/LILLY

is considered sexy by a lot of people including herself. She has an exotic, ultra-feminine bedroom. LILY never goes to a man's place, but if she likes him she will ask him up for a "nightcap." The way LILY figures it, if anyone is going to get dressed and go home, it isn't going to be her!

LINDA

is married to a businessman who is older and shorter than she is. He has trouble getting her to leave parties.

LINDSAY

went to EST twice a couple of years ago. She sends food back in restaurants a lot.

LISA

is a girl who spends a lot of time saying ": . . with an S not a Z."

LIZ

is beautiful, sensual and a good sport, which is quite a parlay.

LIZA

marries a computer freak. She leaves him . . . but it's a week before he's aware of it.

LOIS

You know if she just digs deep enough into her overburdened purse, she'll come up with something out of the past, such as Lucky Strike Green cigarettes.

DO THIS DO THAT

LOLA

is the ultimate authority on raising children. She'll tell anyone who'll listen how to raise theirs. LOLA has none.

LORELEI

is impressed by people. She keeps talking about the time she once met Waylon Jennings' daughter.

LORETTA

has a lot of curly hair and works in the office with JOYCE, ELEANOR, MARGE and DONNA. Once a week they all have dinner out together and get into a friendly argument over the check. They all wear expensive blouses, buy sling-back shoes at a chain store, and try all the new shades of lipstick and nail polish. After dinner they often go to a bar. LORETTA is the best-looking in this group.

LORI

makes an excellent secretary if you don't mind a considerable amount of "white out."

LORNA

remains friends with all her ex-husbands who get to know and like each other. They wear T-shirts with "Lorna's Exes" emblazoned across the front. They hope they like LORNA's next husband so they'll have enough hands for a poker game.

LORRAINE

Her husband is a workaholic. In his absence, LORRAINE takes guitar lessons and goes to workout classes. In 13 years, she is never absent once!

LOUISE

When LOUISE is young, she has one ambition: to get married. She gets married and still has one ambition: to get a divorce.

LUCILLE

usually looks like she is smelling something and is trying to figure out what it is.

LUCRETIA

is heavy and voluptuous and is always putting blue polish on her nails or wearing adhesive tape instead of a bra or sprinkling glitter in her hair or showing up in a slit-to-the-waist blouse. She scares the bejesus out of most men, but AUGIE likes her. But then, AUGIE likes everyone.

LUCY

still wears a page boy hairdo. She is willowy and girls think she's attractive but guys never take her out more than twice.

LULU

wins a contest in which she and a companion can spend eight days and seven nights in Nassau at a fabulous beach hotel. She cannot get anyone to go with her. She takes her dog.

LUPE

has a temper. She's usually the victim of it.

LYDIA

Her Christmas cards are photographs of trips she has taken . . . Caracas, Madrid, Oslo, Cincinnati.

LYNN

is an executive secretary who always sleeps with her boss . . . most of the time he's her husband.

MABEL

When the fellows get together in one corner of the room and tell dirty jokes, MABEL gets close enough to hear them. Then, when the other girls giggle and say "Aren't they awful. What did they say?" MABEL says "Never mind, I'll tell you later."

MADELINE

is a worrier. She practices dialing "911" in the dark.

MAGDA

is a great cook who obligingly gives you her recipes. Unfortunately, they consist of a "little bit of this, a touch of that and just a pinch of the other."

MAGGIE

hides her sensuality behind the lowered lids of freckle-faced innocence.

MARCIA

Life is a serious business for MARCIA. She thinks before she laughs.

MARCIE

is an executive. Her second in command is a man. They work a lot at night. They really work.

MALVINA

There isn't a thing on her back that does not come from a garage sale . . . with the exception of GARY.

MARCELLA

found her husband, JOE, in the yellow pages.

MARGARET/ MARGUERITE

is someone's aunt. However, if she pronounces it Marga-REET with an accent on the last syllable she is a dingbat.

MARGE

is a working woman and expectant mother most of her life.

MARGO/MARGOT

has a space between her two front teeth but it doesn't matter. She's still a knockout.

MARIA

is dark and deep-bosomed and determined. She is getting her MBA and reads the *Wall Street Journal* every day.

MARIAN

is extraordinarily bright and well-informed, but worries so much about what people think about her that she regrets having opinions.

MARIE

doesn't believe in women's movements. Her ambition is to be a sex object.

MARIETTA

looks like the old-fashioned girl whose suitors would bring a nosegay, but after 9 p.m. when the moon is full, there is quite a transformation.

MARILYN

is a pretty divorcee for whom everyone feels sorry.

MARJORIE

has very inflexible opinions on how to make love. Whenever her husband disagrees, she says "I'm sure Leo Buscaglia would back me up on this."

MARLENE

is stuck with three kids when her husband disappears. She goes into real estate and works 80 hours a week and looks 10 years older than she is.

MARSHA

still wishes her mother understood that she didn't go to law school to meet boys and she isn't a practicing attorney as a steppingstone to marriage.

MARTHA

Guys are crazy about MARTHA, but her commitment to astrology frustrates them. She won't do anything if the stars aren't right. JEFF wanted to marry her but she told him she couldn't possibly give him an answer until Mercury went out of retrograde which would be Friday at 9:27 a.m. So JEFF ended up asking her best friend to marry him. MARTHA feels no jealousy toward the happy couple. She is only concerned because she is sure they are astrologically incompatible.

MARTINA

No matter the time of day or where you run into MARTINA, she looks as if she stepped out of a shower. She probably did.

MARY

is calm, efficient, sweet, honest, clean and courageous.

MARY LOU

lives with her mother and brother and goes steady with BILLY BOB.

MATILDA

Although she's capable of handling everything, MATILDA is smart enough to seek her husband's advice about things she doesn't care about.

MAUD/MAUDE

All she has to do to dominate a room is enter it.

MAUREEN

has broad shoulders and skinny legs and freckles on her back and chest. She is very big with kissing.

MAVIS

spends a great deal of time trying to define feminism to her men friends.

MAXINE

is the only girl in high school who went out with a married man. Later she got married herself. Then she started going out with a single guy.

MAY

wins an all expense paid trip to Europe and breaks her leg boarding the plane.

MEGAN

keeps telling people she meets that her name is "Meg" "an" not "Meeg" "an."

MELANIE

is an assistant editor of non-fiction in a publishing house. She writes sappy romance novels under a pseudonym.

MELBA

If her date is persistent, MELBA's threshold "no's" soften into an invitation for a nightcap.

MELINDA

sublets her apartment illegally. The landlord finds out and dispossesses her. She had never been able to stay in one apartment for more than three months ... until JEREMY became her landlord.

MELISSA

is blond and tries to prove that blondes have "more fun."

MELODY

can't carry a tune.

MERCEDES

If you are dissatisfied with the treatment you receive from an employee and ask to speak to his or her boss, the person you get is MERCEDES. After 30 seconds you wish you had never made the request.

MEREDITH

is a judge. Women admire her intelligence and beauty. Men who come up before her wonder what she wears under her robe.

MERLE

keeps marrying up.

META

always eats her husband's dessert because she thinks he should watch his weight.

MIA

makes 407 different pastas. She's always on a diet.

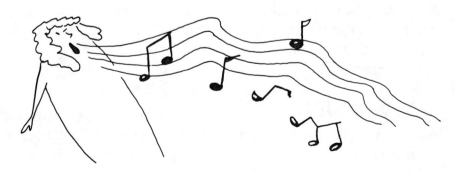

MICHELLE

likes men, which makes her automatically sexy.

MICKEY

is small and laughs a lot.

MILDRED

gets hay fever every September.

MILLICENT

is civically involved. She shows up at your door twice a year with petitions for city improvements, such as sewage systems.

MILLIE/MILLY

suffers, but seldom in silence.

MIMI

is afraid of nothing and helps keep things in perspective for her friends.

MINA

avoids first-hand experiences. She even rents her dreams.

MINDY

has soft eyes and a long neck and lots of guys go for her; but, actually, she's not interested. She's always trying to change her name to ONDINE, but everyone keeps calling her MINDY.

MING TOY

is a Pekingese.

MIRA

Nothing ever really pleases her. In a restaurant she sends food back before she's tasted it.

MIRANDA

coughs too much, seems to be afraid someone will notice her.

MIRIAM

tidies up the doctor's reception area while waiting to see him.

MISSY

helped her mother raise her four younger sisters. She was "Mother's big helper." MISSY is getting married to LEO and does not want children.

MITZI

is dark and has short legs and is always hiding things. She marries HERB or someone who is a friend of HERB's who discovers that one of the things she's been hiding is MARTY.

MO

has a wicked tennis serve.

MOIRA

is a rare breed of fashion designer. Her clothes are inexpensive and they fit.

MOLLIE/MOLLY

sends gifts to her grandchildren who live out of town. She never receives "thank you" notes. She blames her daughter-in-law.

MONA

If she can't take a class in it, she doesn't consider it worth learning.

MONICA

is an artist who makes her living as a numerologist.

MURIEL

is always telling you about men following her on the street. She keeps her windows locked at night and carries a screwdriver in her bag for protection.

MYRA

is a competent whirlwind. She is a den mother, a fund raiser, a hospital volunteer, a surrogate wife and still has time for her family and making chicken soup.

MYRNA

is everybody's good friend. Most of her male friends reluctantly have to settle for that.

MYRTLE

started keeping a diary, but after three years the only things she had in it were notes on movies she'd seen and her appointments with the dentist to have her braces adjusted. So, she burned it.

NADINA/NADINE

If she could find a job for her husband, NADINE would spend all her time at the beach drinking diet soda and reading fat, trashy novels.

NAN

has lunch at least once a month with GLORIA, PHYLLIS and SHIRLEY. NAN gets the check because she takes the least time to include the 15% tip and divide it into four reasonably equal parts.

NANCY

lives in a nice suburb and has a nice husband, and a nice barbecue pit, a nice den and a nice station wagon. She's the prettiest wife on their street and the other husbands have eyes for her, but NANCY never cheats. She flirts a little, but she never cheats. Or at least if she does cheat, no one ever knows about it, which, from NANCY's point of view, is the same thing.

NANETTE

was a firecracker in 1944. Since then nobody has been called NANETTE.

NAOMI

has a master's degree in worrying.

NATALIE

is a talker. You ask how she is — she always tells you.

NATASHA

dresses marvelously but is sort of out of it. She has a lot of homosexual friends.

NEDRA

is mildly upset when her boy-friend sends her picture to *Playboy,* but is greatly disappointed when there is no follow-up from the magazine.

NELLIE

Guys feel comfortable with NELLIE. They don't mind when she sits in for her husband, ARNIE, in their poker game. If a vote were taken, it would reveal they prefer NELLIE to ARNIE.

NEVA

is the ultimate executive secretary. She is a perfect grammarian, can write great letters, and within a month, copy her boss's signature perfectly.

NICOLE

If you are a woman who has been in love with this perfect guy, JIMMY, since you were both in the seventh grade and you are seniors in college and are living together and plan to get married and have three children ... Well, when JIMMY wins this marvelous trip to Europe, NICOLE is what he brings back. She is dark and has shiny skin and a funny accent. JIMMY makes a big thing about how you and NICOLE are going to be great buddies and she can help you learn French (or Italian or Pakistani). You say "Oh, sure, JIM. Yes, of course." What's surprising is that it turns out to be true. Eventually, you and NICOLE open a business together and JIMMY feels left out.

NINA

is full of zip and bounce with a sweet face unmarred by thought.

NITA

is tired of being told by men that she reminds them either of some woman they love or one they can't stand.

NOEL

runs things ... herself ... her business ... her husband.

NOLA

Nothing can be said about NOLA that hasn't already been said by the *National Enquirer.*

NORA

models fashions during the noon hour in a restaurant.

NOREEN

can't hold her liquor but can hold her men.

NORMA

marries many times. She maintains her third husband's name.

NYDIA

is twice divorced and living abroad with a handsome Peruvian worker many years younger than she is.

OCTAVIA

has a beautiful but totally indecipherable handwriting.

ODELIA

is heavy into barbecuing.

OLGA

is a lady mud-wrestler.

OLIVIA

shows up at a party with a dress that is cut too low and keeps asking the guys if they think her dress is cut too low.

ONA

The last person she meets is always her best friend.

ONDINE

is very apprehensive. If you ask her for the time, she gives it to you, but adds worriedly "Don't quote me."

OPHELIA

is a harpist, but when she travels with her instrument she wishes she were a flutist.

ORIANA

has learned to speak English but her body still gestures in Italian.

PAIGE

takes a lot of time with her makeup but she is always insecure about the way she looks ... HENRY, who works for her, thinks she looks great.

PALOMA

Her life is an ongoing opus, with appearances all over the world.

PAM

goes out a lot with her mother. PAM's mother has bleached hair and is almost as much fun as PAM, which isn't much. PAM's father tries to be a good guy — he's a lot older than PAM's mother — and he invites the fellows in the gang to come over and use the pool table in the basement. He doesn't really want them there, though.

PAMELA

somehow manages to combine the best qualities of both the Virgin Mary and Mata Hari.

PATIENCE

has been learning to play the piano for 20 years.

PATRICIA

is a lot of people. A PATRICIA who is tall and dark and has good posture is called PAT. If she is blond and bouncy, she is PATSY or PATTY. PATSY and PATTY are a lot like JACKIE, only they have wider hips. If she is called PATRICIA, she is elegant and has impeccable taste.

PAULA

keeps rescuing dogs from the pound.

PAULINE

On the day her cleaning woman comes in for three hours, PAULINE gets up at five in the morning to polish the silver, dust the furniture, scrub the floors, vacuum the rugs and puff up the pillows. She doesn't want the woman telling her neighbors she isn't a good housekeeper.

PEARL

is shy and quiet, unless she comes from a farm. Then she's shy and noisy.

PEGGY

likes physical contact. PEGGY is always punching men in the ribs and she likes to arm wrestle to see who has the strongest grip. No matter how hard you squeeze, PEGGY never winces.

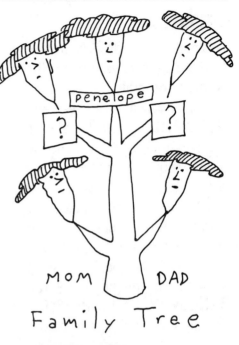

Family Tree

PENELOPE

is the legitimate daughter who has several siblings about whom she knows very little or nothing.

PENNY

About eleven o'clock, PENNY's father telephones to remind her that it's getting late and she goes home. PENNY's father is the kind of man who keeps whiskey in glass decanters labeled "Scotch" and "Bourbon." Every once in a while he holds one of the decanters up to the light, looks at it and then says "Mother, we'd better get another bottle of bourbon." They buy one bottle at a time.

PETULA

is slender and dresses herself from garage and yard sales. She is assistant editor of a trade magazine called *Foot Digest* and makes $223 a week. She is always about to marry someone in television, but it never comes off. Men can sleep with PETULA if they take her seriously for two dates, but she is a problem. You know how it is with some people, if you sleep with them, you are sorry the next day. Well, with PETULA you are sorry while it's going on.

PHILIPPA

If she manages to find a kitchen, all she can make are leftovers.

PHOEBE

can never get her husband to dance with her.

PHYLLIS

is the last girl in town you'd ever expect to get "in trouble." She manages somehow. Later she marries someone weird.

PILAR

decorates her apartment in shades of pale green, peach and beige. It serves as a background for her exotic looks.

PIPER

There's a predictability to her nonconformity.

POLLY

There was a time when everyone thought POLLY was the greatest thing that ever happened. It's still true but the numbers of her admirers have dwindled to a precious few ... ERWIN, TONY and ART.

PORTIA

exists in a time of her own.

PRISCILLA

enjoys those activities she won't allow people to discuss in her presence.

PRUDENCE

Girls named PRUDENCE, CHARITY or PATIENCE are pushovers. For anything — causes, sex and kittens no one else wants.

QUENDRA

felt hideously different until ALEX told her he loved her name. She now tells everyone her full name is QUENDRA TAMARA ZENA.

QUERIDA

is the oddball in her family.

QUINLAN

has an innocent passion for gossip.

QUINN

married BILL or GREG when she was 21. They have a pleasant suburban life and QUINN seems like Miss Prude, but she is getting it on with the mailman.

RACHEL

is a dark, nice person who is a good cook and is maternal with her children, husband, boss and lover.

RAE

Most of her pantry is filled with cat food.

RAMONA

wonders why fortune tellers aren't all rich.

RANDY

is a credit card junkie.

RAQUEL

is someone who left the party right before you got there. You keep hearing about how great she is "built," and what a wild dresser . . . but you never get to meet her.

REBECCA

is beautiful and her voice is as soft as a summer wind. BECKY is someone's cranky grandmother.

REGINA

Her pregnant pauses seem to take nine months.

RENATA

Her voice can fill a room, but so can her figure.

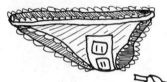

RENEE

buys weird, erotic lingerie. It scares the hell out of her husband.

REVA

Her photo album is a collection of blurs. Her specialty is out-of-focus floral arrangements.

RHODA

wears a flashy hairdo and pastes beauty marks on her cheek. She thinks she is exotic, but her bust is too big and too much of her gums show when she smiles. RHODA goes out with bald, older men who take her to expensive restaurants. She marries several of these men and the high point of her life is when she gets her picture in the newspaper during one of her divorces.

RHONDA

hates the way she looks from the rear . . . most men don't!

RISA

has a lifelong supply of misinformation.

RITA

is a troublemaker.

ROBERTA

is tallish and dark and makes noises when men touch her. The men get pretty impressed at first, but then they begin to wonder if she's putting them on.

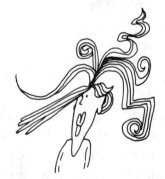

ROBIN

can't remember *what* her hair looked like before they invented styling mousse.

ROCHELLE

has her ears pierced when she's 11 years old.

RONA

tells you her mother drives her crazy but she still drops over on Tuesdays and Thursdays.

RONNIE

dyes her hair every year or so. She makes good grades and comes from a broken home. RONNIE is okay up until she is 35 when she disappears into an obscure cult in Oregon.

ROSALIND

says she wants a "man who will dominate me," but she never finds one. A lot of guys make it with ROSALIND on the second or third date; then she won't see them anymore. Makes the fellows pretty nervous. NICKY was the only one who didn't figure there was something wrong with him. ROSALIND finally marries someone who is scared of her, and manages his life.

ROSE

double dates with EVELYN. Halfway through dinner they go to the ladies' room and compare dates. They often wish there was a back door to the ladies' room.

ROSEMARY

is very female. She is the kind of woman men should marry, but they don't realize it until they're trapped with CYNTHIA or AUDREY.

ROXANNE

is named as a correspondent in three different divorces.

ROZ

has a good job and an apartment. She has a long-time romance with MAURICE. He never gets there until after ten o'clock and never takes her out.

RUBY

follows a fellow clear across the country and marries him. She spends the next five years writing a novel about it and surprises everyone by getting it published.

RUTH

wears suits and puts her younger sister through college.

SABINA

Each succeeding love affair is both surprising and inevitable.

SABRINA

Whatever the occasion — a marvelous party, a fund-raiser, a dedication — SABRINA keeps telling you she had nothing to do with it, until she's sure you know she did.

SADIE

The price of dinner at SADIE's is a commitment to call her as soon as you arrive home and assure her you're safe and sound.

SALLY

Every six months SALLY has either a new job, a new apartment or a new man in her life.

SALOME

always sends cards with quotes from the Bible on your birthday.

SAMANTHA

is a photographer for a magazine that features high-class dirty pictures.

SANDI

worries about getting too much sun.

SANDRA

has to have her own way or she gets mad. SANDRA has one plain-looking friend who is very loyal to her.

SANDY

whispers throughout the entire movie to her friend, ELOISE, about how Jack Nicholson looks like her brother-in-law. Then, if anyone near her talks, she turns around and says, "Shhh!"

SARAH

gets along with her mother, father, brother and sister. Nobody is able to figure out what is wrong with SARAH.

SELENA

is a high school drop-out who becomes well-known as a singer of songs with a political bent.

SELMA

always has a hard-luck story.

SHANA

has great intelligence. She starts to use it in the third year of her marriage and the marriage falls apart. SHANA becomes a success . . . at everything but relationships with men.

SHANNON

is the leader of the gang at school. She marries a guy she can handle.

SHARON

went through a stage where she rode motorbikes and wore leather. Then she got into pills. Now she is in her late 20s, fixes her hair like Brooke Shields, is the best dressed girl in Georgetown and an influence in the House of Representatives.

SHEENA

swears she will have a face-lift as soon as she's 21.

SHEILA

likes to read Russian novels and go to sad movies. Unless she is from Britain or Ireland. In that case she marries a dynamite guy, goes into business and becomes a corporate vice-president.

SHELLY

is on the latest fad diet.

SHERRY

is cute as a kitten and has a lovely figure. She is friendly and goes out of her way to do favors. She never flirts or acts like she is interested in sex — but she makes the girls in those porno movies look like trainees.

SHIRLEY

Her parents named her after Shirley Temple. She has been frumpy for the past 10 years. She still has a secret hope that maybe Eddie Fisher and Debbie Reynolds will get back together.

SIGRID

is so busty, you wonder if it's her or a state-of-the-art bra.

SIRI/CIRI

is a former Las Vegas showgirl who is 6' tall. She is happily married to a musician who is 5'9".

SIS/SISSY

has to take care of her mother, so she becomes a grade school teacher.

SONDRA

puts all her boyfriends' telephone numbers in her personal computer.

SONIA

is intelligent, funny, disorganized and not quite sure who she's supposed to be.

SOPHIA

likes to be a pal to her male friends and wears heavy black glasses.

SOPHIE

Don't talk sexual mores in front of SOPHIE, if you're not prepared for a lot of sighing and head shaking.

STACY

has 23 cats. She belongs to five different organizations for saving animals and yells at women on the street who wear fur coats. Her analyst tells her all of this is healthy because she is expressing herself.

STELLA

never lets you forget that she is a Phi Beta Kappa. She never lets her husband forget it either.

STEPHANIE

organizes everything but her own life.

STOCKARD

is "au courant." Ask her and she'll tell you which European mineral water is trendy this month.

SUMMER

is always late.

SUNNY

after a few drinks tells you her real name is SUNSHINE.

SUSAN

writes lists to herself, plays piano and bakes cookies. SUE, on the other hand, beautiful at age 18, becomes startlingly so at 40. Her friends suspect she has an aging portrait of herself in the attic. SUSIE is perky and doesn't make many mistakes.

SYBIL

is a compulsive volunteer. She's on the board of 27 different charities. She has awards placed all over the house. People drop ashes in half of them.

SYDNEY

is precise. When you ask SYDNEY what time it is, she never says "Around five o'clock." She tells you it's "five-oh-three."

SYLVIA

is very hippy, but you don't notice because she has excellent posture and great taste in clothes. SYLVIA has silver-blond hair and no one makes out with her. It's not because SYLVIA isn't sexy. It's just that she doesn't want to get mussed up.

TABITHA

makes funny faces. She marries a teacher who calls her TABBY.

TALIA

If she is Italian she is okay. If not, she is called TAL or TAL-LY and is short.

TALLULAH

When you call TALLULAH, you hope she's not home so you can listen to the current kinky message on her answer machine.

TAMARA

has or used to have some mysterious connection with show business. She wears two beauty marks. One on her cheekbone and the other . . .

TAMMY

drives all night to get to a ski resort and sleeps through the weekend's skiing.

TANNI

organizes everything, including her leisure time.

TANYA

comes from someplace else. She is a friend of some celebrity.

TARA

is a pretty girl who goes around with schnooky guys. Even after she's married a third husband (with settlements from the first two) the old schnooky husbands keep calling.

TERESA

is ANTHONY's sister. She has thick, bushy hair and is the only one who never cheats in school. When the teacher leaves the room and says "No talking while I'm gone," TERESA is the only one who doesn't talk.

TERRY

is divorced and supports a small child by working in a restaurant or nightclub. Men only ask TERRY for a date if they're desperate. Not because she isn't pretty, but because you have the feeling that she won't show up. They're usually right.

TESS

is good-natured. Friends without a place of their own stay with TESS . . . too long.

THEA

is very much in control of her career, but feels like a bystander in her personal life.

THELMA

orders hot fudge sundaes with whipped cream and then puts artificial sweetener in her coffee.

THEODORA

Small men do not know that THEODORA is a tall woman. She accommodates their egos by wearing flats, bowing her head and standing with her knees bent. By the time DONALD discovers she's 5'10", he's already married her.

THORDIS

whistles at hard-hats.

TIFFANY

gets to a party and before she meets anyone she runs into the powder room and combs her hair for 10 minutes.

TINA

Her figure is what aerobics are all about. She starts as a student and ends up as a teacher. TINA marries a man who considers getting out of bed excessive exercise.

TOBY

is someone's kid sister. The boys always treat her like a sister. At a party she decides she'll get drunk and maybe something will happen. But she just gets sick.

TONI

tap dances. The tenants below, whose ceiling is her dancing floor, although personally very fond of TONI, do not care too much for her feet.

TRACY

Girls who have been given family surnames for first names, like TRACY, HUDSON, TYLER, STANTON, etc., can use bad language and no one minds.

TRISHA

can never find her contact lenses. Sometimes she's looking for them when she has them on.

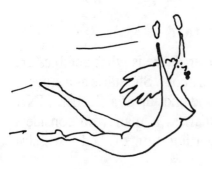

TWYLA

is bright, brisk and cheery. She goes through life as if it were a TV commercial — all problems can be solved by a deodorant.

TYNE

has an infallible sense of what to keep and what to throw away at the office. At home — she's still with HARRY.

URSULA

is elegant and sensitive. She feels uncomfortable at parties where there is "too much ambition in the room."

VALENTINA

runs errands on a moped.

VALERIE

uses men to get ahead.

VANESSA

embraces many causes and very few people.

VEDA

Tired of the self sacrifice required by long relationships with not-so-wonderful guys, she settles for MORT. They live happily most of "ever-after."

VERA

is jealous of her husband and puts him down in public.

VERNA

Lots of men wonder what VERNA looks like in lingerie. Most men will never know. Except CLAY, ADAM, JASON, STEVE and PETER.

VERONICA

has more hair than she needs and a high energy level. If there are men around, she insists on being the center of attention and rotates her hips when she walks. Often she stops walking but her hips don't.

VI

She and her husband never miss Rev. Oral Roberts on Sunday morning television.

VICKI

was afraid of her husband for 20 years, then his business failed and she realized he didn't know as much as he thought he did. And what he did know wasn't right. So she starts her own business and in three years has a chain of stores. Her husband manages one of them.

VICTORIA

has a first-rate mind, a first-rate figure, but always winds up with second-rate guys.

VIOLET

Pantyhose never last more than a day with VIOLET.

VIRGINIA

washes her hair every morning and puts on a baseball cap and goes shopping. VIRGINIA's conversation consists mostly of complaints about her permanent, or discussions of television shows or movies. She may get plump, but she never seems to really grow up. VIRGINIA isn't unhappy. She has a couple of loyal friends, AUGIE and STAN, and it never occurs to her not to let them stay over.

VIVECA

is warm and gregarious. Men find it easy to talk to VIVECA. Consequently, she's seldom alone unless she wants to be.

VIVIAN

is lively but choosy. She is a selective swinger and picks out fellows she likes. Old boy friends are always trying to start up again with VIVIAN, but she hates reruns.

WALLIS

wears flats so she won't dwarf her date.

WANDA

has a refrigerator filled with doggie bags.

WENDY

enthuses more about everything than her friends do about anything.

WHITNEY

always orders anything on the menu that she can't pronounce.

WILHELMINA

has intimate talks with her poodles.

WILMA

Day and night she wears T-shirts with suggestive slogans.

WINIFRED

had parents who weren't too well off but she makes a "good marriage" and spends the rest of her life complaining about the maid.

WINNIE

is a grounded flight attendant. She's at home with almost anyone. When your male friends from out of town say "Hey, you know a lot of girls? . . ." WINNIE always comes through and makes you look good. If you know WINNIE, keep on her good side and don't louse it up by making a pass at her. She's a godsend.

XENIA

Her walk creates fantasies for most men.

YETTA

complains a lot. Especially about her name.

YOLANDA

has no qualms about introducing herself to anyone at a party.

ZELDA

picks out a famous person to look like. When she was 16, it was Twiggy, then Jane Fonda. In 1972, it was Jacqueline Bisset. At 32, it was Lady Di. Now she is 35 and has settled for Meryl Streep.

ZENOBIA

Her accent is charming, but her English is a series of verbal misfortunes.

ZOE

If you look up "hypersensitivity" in the dictionary, there will be a picture of ZOE.

ZORA

is always the last name in a book listing women's names. Unless the book is printed in Russia.

YVETTE

You only meet once. She is great and you make appointments to see her again, but you run out of courage and cancel.

YVONNE

In the beginning her latest fellow is her nirvana ... then she gradually discovers him to be human ... and in a month or two, he's just okay — or maybe not even that.

AARON

always has something wrapped up in a blanket in the back seat of his car.

ABBOTT

belongs to a wine tasting society which meets more often than it should.

ABEL

stays thin all his life. And lives longer than his grandchildren.

ABNER

The first thing ABNER does in the morning is read the obituaries in the newspaper . . . then he is off to the bathroom.

ABRAHAM

is a beloved attendant in a hospital. He is more successful with the patients than most of the doctors.

ADAM

is a cute three year old. As a grown-up, he is some kind of an academic.

ADDISON

subscribes to avant-garde literary magazines. They stack up on his coffee table, unread. Eventually he throws them out.

ADLAI

is a very nice name, but not for a Presidential candidate.

ADOLPH

is the man most likely to walk up to a woman at a dance and ask her for the next march.

ADRIAN

is shorter than his mother. He becomes an executive in a large corporation.

AL

knows all the angles, has contacts, can get great seats for anything — the Super Bowl, World Series, opening nights, early Mass.

ALASTAIR

is a weather forecaster who never gets rid of a summer cold.

ALBERT/ALFRED

If you call your son ALBERT or ALFRED, chances are he will develop an interest in science or math and get a job that requires using his brain. But if you call him AL, he will be a salesman (and get you tickets to the Super Bowl).

ALDEN

His desk and his life are in constant disarray. Once a year he tidies up his desk.

ALDO

is big and good-natured and clean. He marries a smart girl and never cheats on her.

ALAN/ALLEN

If a discount house doesn't sell it, ALAN doesn't own it.

ALDRIDGE

is the good-looking young guy at the bank who straightens out your checking account for you.

ALEC

is smart and has connections. He's AL's contact for great seats.

ALEX

is a hard worker who never bothers anyone. He always gets invited to parties, but no one notices if he doesn't come.

ALEXANDER

is a con man. And that's not all bad. He can talk his way in or out of anything but marriage.

ALGER

embraces tradition. He keeps in touch with all members of his family, including the ones he doesn't like . . . which is most of them.

ALGERNON

is much loved . . . for short periods of time.

ALPHONSE

leads you to tables or up mountains.

ALVIN

has his outfits styled by Ralph Lauren, his outlook by Leo Buscaglia.

AMBROSE

forgets things. He bought a book on Improving the Memory but forgot where he put it.

AMORY

knows everything there is to know about stock acquisitions and corporate takeovers. You don't learn this until you're stuck with the lunch check.

AMOS

jogs while listening to his "walkman." He is hit by a car at least twice a year.

ANATOLE

His parents hate diminutives. They chose ANATOLE because it could not possibly be shortened. At six, ANATOLE's friends started calling him ANNIE.

ANDREW

When ANDREW has a date, he makes suggestive remarks and tries to proposition her right away. When the girl turns him down he feels he's done his duty, so he can relax and be pleasant. Once a girl took him up on it and he started sneezing and broke out in hives.

ANDY

worked his way through school. If you are in trouble, ANDY is a good one to ask for help.

ANGELO

is really handsome with curly black hair and big blue eyes. He could have married a rich society girl, but she found out he had a tattoo.

ANGUS

is someone's uncle who sends nice presents on Christmas.

ANSEL

is an artist who carves birds out of wood. They are commercially reproduced in plastic. ANSEL wouldn't own one.

ANTHONY

is nothing like TONY. ANTHONY has large beautiful eyes, used to be an altar boy and always hangs a flag outside his house on Columbus Day.

ARCHER

acts like a tough private detective. It works, more often than not, with girls.

ARCHIBALD

is picked on by all the kids at school. At age 47 he becomes a school principal and then the kids really go after him.

ARCHIE

makes you feel good. That's the business he's in.

ARLEN

is always chatting with the receptionists at work ... he never tells them he's married.

ARMAND

has very thin calves and is always pulling up his socks.

ARNIE

usually has someone he takes care of all his life, but he doesn't complain.

ARNOLD

acts superior when you light a cigarette. He tells you how long it has been since he stopped smoking. He feels great and his appetite is better and he doesn't cough in the morning and ... he keeps talking long after you have left him.

ART

works for a big company and dresses neatly, but he's secretly a leftover hippie.

ARTEMUS

collects friends with first names such as ALDRIDGE, BALD-WIN and COURTNEY.

ARTHUR

is 46 years old and is planning to get married as soon as he's ready to settle down. He buys *The New York Times* every Sunday but never reads it.

ARTIE

always has shined shoes. He's something like AL, only not as successful. ARTIE can get you home computers, electric blenders and watches at a discount — not wholesale, but at a discount. This way, ARTIE makes a little profit.

ASHLEY

will spend time with just about anyone rather than go home to his empty apartment.

ATWATER

likes to see his name in print.

AUBREY

earns his living as a professional arbitrator. He's been divorced five times.

AUGIE

used to be a guard on a football team and is always breaking things or stepping on the cat. AUGIE likes DORIS, but she once saw him wipe his nose on his sleeve and won't have anything to do with him.

AUGUST

comes between July and September.

AUSTIN

is the fellow who takes your car when you park it in a lot. The guys he works with call him a name based on the state he came from, like TEX (or MISSISSIPPI). He has short blond hair and when he takes off in your car he guns the motor and spins the wheels and you have the feeling he's not going to stop until he gets to Fort Worth. When there's a dent in your fender the boss says "TEX musta did that," but TEX is gone now. The fellow who replaced him is called ARKY.

AVERY

calls up disc jockeys with requests.

AXEL

is the guy who runs the school where you go to learn how to ski.

BAILEY

doesn't particularly like ASHLEY, but ASHLEY's the only person who will hang out with him.

BALDWIN

is the president of the bank where ALDRIDGE, ARTE-MUS and COURTNEY work.

BARCLAY

wishes he were someone else.

BARNABAS

is a glutton for punishment. When his wife isn't around to yell at him, he visits his mother-in-law.

BARNABY

doesn't diet, jog or exercise. He says he doesn't have to ... he has someone come in and do it for him.

BARON

is a killer Hollywood agent who handles big stars. Other agents hate him because he dresses great, speaks French and has really super manners.

BARRY

asks girls to pick him up at his apartment. When they get there BARRY is in a bathrobe and says "I got hung up on the telephone, Honey. Still haven't had time to shower. Make yourself at home." Then, when he gets into the shower he keeps hollering out "Hey, how'd you like to wash my back?" This makes the girls sore and they leave. The only one who doesn't leave is VIRGINIA.

BART

was in an airplane crash once.

BARTHOLOMEW

is always called BART by everyone but his mother.

BASIL

teaches English literature at a private girls' school. He marries Miss Markham, the vice principal. They raise Persian cats.

BAXTER

Life begins for BAXTER in the backseat of a limousine.

BAYARD

takes naps a lot.

BEAU

has a crew cut and wears T-shirts under a jacket with only the bottom button done. BEAU still talks about when Johnny Unitas was quarterback for the Baltimore Colts.

BELDEN

is his Momma's pride and joy. His nose runs a lot.

BENEDICT

looks like his car.

BENJAMIN/BENNIE/ BEN

BENJAMIN is skinny. BENNIE is plump, but if you are called BENJAMIN you are skinny and women consider you sexy. BEN, however, is an anonymous nice person.

BENNETT

is a dentist who loves to play the game of waiting until you've had a shot of novacaine, your mouth is stuffed with cotton and a tooth is being extracted before asking "How's the family?"

BENSON

is secretive. He has a really good job but no one is sure what it is he does.

BENTLEY

is probably an automobile.

BERKELEY

has a problem with his feet. He's on a first-name basis with three chiropodists.

BERNARD

never seems to have much fun.

BERNIE

is a creature of fixed social habits. He never leaves a party without breaking something the hostess cherishes.

BERT

is a natural salesman who talks to everyone. He can turn an elevator ride into a party or an airplane trip into a convention. The only person he can't think of anything to say to is his wife.

BERTRAM

would like to shed his timid-soul image and be as adventurous as his buddies, AL and CHUCK, but the most audacious thing he can do is order black pasta in a nouvelle cuisine restaurant. He talks about that meal for the rest of his life.

BEVAN

is able to sit up straight on a down-cushioned sofa.

BILL

is beloved and treated like a puppy by women ... they pat him on the back and take him for long walks.

BILLY

has a cute grin and a lot of older brothers and sisters.

BJORN

When AXEL makes enough money from his ski school, he opens a health club and hires BJORN as a masseur.

BLAIR

usually has another name of some kind by the age of 16. If not, he's in trouble.

BLAKE

establishes early that he's in charge. If you question anything he does, he quits and sues you.

BO

is a telephone line repairman who has been on a permanent high since he appeared as himself in a beer commercial two years ago.

BOB

is important enough not to worry about not being called ROBERT.

BOMBO

likes bananas. If he isn't a chimpanzee, he's in trouble.

BOND

To broaden his social life, BOND joins the Automobile Club of America.

BOOTH

Women think BOOTH looks anemic until they see him in his shorts ... BOOTH tries to be seen in his shorts.

BORDEN

BORDEN's father is wealthy. BORDEN had a car when he was 14 and, by now, has been married three times.

BORIS

never volunteers to get anything or help out; but he makes wisecracks when some good-natured person does volunteer.

BOYD

tells you he's a banker. His fingernails contradict him.

BRAD

invites you to a party at someone's house. When you get there, they don't seem happy to see either of you.

BRADLEY

writes rude things on walls in public places. (No one ever sees him, but you know he's the one.)

BRAMWELL

is a walking medicine chest. If you empty his pockets, you can fill any prescription.

BRANDON

constantly claims his integrity has been impugned.

BRENDON

always has a beer in the "fridge."

BRENT

is a good-looking, partially bald guy who runs some kind of exotic business.

BRETT

is a junior partner in a law firm with 63 general partners and 17 attorneys-of-counsel. Each year he keeps hoping that his name will appear on the stationery.

BREWSTER

is the only person to have lost money selling a condominium in the 1970's.

BRIAN

is the great-looking guy your wife used to have a relationship with before she married you. She puts him down now but you know she doesn't mean it.

BRICE

perseveres. He places 1,739th in the city marathon, but unfazed, he enters again next year. He doesn't do as well.

BRICK

played drums one summer in a local band, so he thinks of himself as a musician. He accompanies jukeboxes by drumming his fingers on the edge of the table.

BROCK

is very dependable. He will never let you down.

BRODERICK

is 35 and still afraid of his father.

BROOKE

is very prissy about sex because he claims to be afraid of herpes. Everyone thinks he is gay except GAYLORD and LLOYD. They know he is neutral, just like his clothes, which are charcoal gray.

BROTHER

Anyone over the age of eight who is called BROTHER, SONNY or BUDDY takes pills a lot.

BRUCE

used to spend all his free time working on his car, but since his namesake, Springsteen, came along, he can't keep the girls away.

BRUNO

is the $4000-a-week chef at a 10-star restaurant. He inspects every dish that leaves his kitchen and yells a lot . . . an awful lot.

BUBBA

is 6'5", weighs 200 pounds, has imposing biceps and, to everyone's great relief, smiles a lot.

BUCK

is a good ol' boy from Amarillo who likes to give Northerners the impression he's an oil tycoon. Actually, he owns a gas station.

BURGESS

is always called by some other name. Sometimes even he forgets his real name.

BURTON

is the leading figure in many civic organizations. He suffers from gout.

BUSBY

is the stage manager of the local theatre group. He keeps wanting to act, but those who have seen him perform convince him he's more important backstage.

BUSTER

is beefy and doesn't smoke. He voted for George Wallace and carries a picture of Jerry Falwell in his wallet.

BYRON

When your sister brings a girl-friend home from school, you get the girlfriend a date with BYRON. He looks okay and he won't make trouble.

CAESAR

runs a little cafe in Chicago, Baltimore, or some other big city. The counter top hasn't been cleaned properly in four years.

CAIN

There's nothing CAIN's parents can do to convince him he isn't adopted.

CAL

When CAL has to make a decision, there's a lot of throat clearing and mumbling before he arrives at what is usually a negative response.

CALDWELL

writes instruction manuals for computers. It's a steady job because they are obsolete three weeks after he's finished.

CALEB

Even though he doesn't wear glasses, CALEB looks as if he just took them off.

CALVIN

remains in a funk throughout his teens. He is 6′5″ and has no basketball skills whatsoever.

CAMERON

dates your ex-girl friend ... sometimes before she's your "ex."

CANUTE

was captain of the football team in a Nebraska college.

CAREY

owns a van. He washes it three times a week and polishes it twice a month. His wife hates that van.

CARL

sweats a lot.

CARLTON

isn't very big but tall girls think he is cute.

CARROLL

used to teach his dates to shift gears so he could kiss them at stop lights. He no longer does this, not because he's changed, but because his new car has an automatic shift.

CARTER

cannot remember the date of his wife's birthday, but remembers that Joe DiMaggio struck out on July 17, 1941, after hitting safely in 56 consecutive games.

CASEY

can't help but be cheerful at all times. This is something that depresses his friends no end.

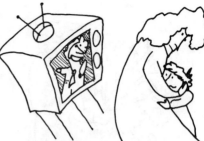

CASPAR

is always getting on Public Access TV and embarrassing his family.

CASSIDY

will find a way of working his ancestry into any conversation.

CECIL

is the only fellow who can find a way to get a drink at a PTA meeting.

CEDRIC

has never dropped food on his clothes, stained anything or missed the urinal in his life.

CHAD

looks good but he really doesn't know anything. If he doesn't marry a girl whose father will hire him, he's in big trouble. He usually does though (marry the girl with the father) and ends up making the business a huge success.

CHANDLER

is a wealthy hypochondriac who wears designer Band-Aids.

CHANNING

is very social. Keeping up with the restaurant scene is his major preoccupation.

CHARLES

likes to hang around with his father's friends. He uses dental floss, twice a day.

CHARLTON

You ask CHARLTON how to get to a bus stop. His response is a soliloquy in rich, sonorous tones. When he finishes you feel you should applaud.

CHASE

believes in reshaping his family's attitude at least twice a year.

CHAUNCEY

wears garters and Bermuda shorts.

CHESTER

is very active in Alcoholics Anonymous.

CHET

plays practical jokes that backfire. At his wedding, when the minister said "You may kiss the bride," CHET replied "I don't feel like it." CHET's first marriage was the shortest on record.

CHICO

is a bilingual, bicultural, bicoastal musician.

CHRIS

has a personal computer, a video recorder, a quadraphonic sound system, a laser disc recorder, wears a cap, and likes to make salads.

CHRISTIAN

is always called CHRIS. He is a hard worker and a real team player. He willingly sacrifices personal glory for the good of the company. He'll either be punished for this or rewarded with a gold watch.

CHRISTOPHER

If CHRISTOPHER weren't directing his energies for the good of society, he would be a master criminal . . . or lawyer.

CHUCK

is athletic and keeps playing touch football and skiing with kids 20 years younger. He gets banged up a lot but he never says anything about it until one day he comes into the office and his knee goes out and he falls into the wastebasket.

CLARENCE

wears double-breasted suits. When CLARENCE goes to a restaurant he always orders the same thing.

CLARK

writes magazine "pieces." He brings a six-pack to BRENDAN whenever he visits.

CLAUDE

has a baritone voice and wears ascots whenever he can.

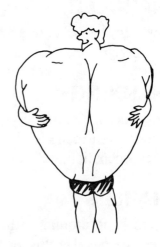

CLAY

is a big blond guy at the beach who spends a lot of time applying sun oil and examining his tan for flaws.

CLEMENT

is related to someone important and keeps reminding you.

CLEVELAND

gets along with everyone's parents but his own.

CLIFF

goes to a hair stylist twice a month and talks loud. He likes to tell you how much he paid for everything he owns.

CLINT

grinds his teeth in his sleep.

CLIVE

travels a lot. He sends a letter to his brother-in-law BASIL at least once a week. CLIVE's writing is quite florid. He overtaxes his metaphors.

CODY

is a musician who won't eat anything but Mexican food.

COLBY

wears a cowboy hat with a pin-striped suit.

COLE

becomes a doctor and drinks a lot, not necessarily in that order.

COLEMAN

is a New Yorker who comes to California and gets a job writing jokes for a late night television show.

COLIN

is compulsively neat. He puts a cover on his car each and every night, even when it's in the garage.

COLLIER

Women feel comfortable with COLLIER. He's often included when the ladies have lunch.

CONAN

His occupation and preoccupation is women.

CONRAD

is an engineer-type who wears odd hats. He goes bald when he is 26, starts drinking at 30, and demolishes several cars before 40.

CONSTANTINE

is a good husband. He was afraid of his mother and it carries over to his wife.

CORBETT

is quick and everyone thinks he is charming.

CORDELL

No one knows what happened to CORDELL after he joined the CIA.

CORNELIUS

makes long-winded speeches laced with lofty phrases such as "our last preserve of freedom."

CORY

can't help but dress funny.

COSMO

wears codpieces.

COURTNEY

is a retired one-star general.

CRAIG

is always putting his arm around your girl and giving her little hugs.

CREIGHTON

loves to find offbeat restaurants in strange neighborhoods where they serve cafe au lait for under a buck.

CROSBY

Despite considerable girth, CROSBY maintains a three handicap in golf.

CULLEN

looks good in tweeds and seems to be a natural leader. He's actually the most henpecked guy in the neighborhood.

CURT/KURT

has only been in the country a year. He says "Ja" instead of "Yes" and keeps telling you he's Swiss, even though you haven't asked him. CURT always tries to make out with your girl and even asks her for her phone number right in front of you — makes you feel like two cents.

CYRIL

is immaculate. You feel he's dusted twice a day.

CYRUS

is born an octogenarian.

DALE

atones for the way he lives his life by writing a religious column for a weekly paper.

DALLAS

has a van with sheepskin seat covers, a mega-buck stereo and fully stocked bar. Unfortunately, he's always stuck driving while his friends party in back!

DALTON

likes to hike and spend days camping and fishing. His wife encourages him to do it often.

DAMION

is a wedding consultant.

DAMON

puts on weight. He's jolly around the boss or customers, but he's miserable to waitresses or people who work for him, until something mystical happens to him at age 37, and he becomes a "9," if not a "10."

DAN

Once DAN accepts you as a friend, he commits to you for life. You've got him even if you don't want him.

DANA

You don't know DANA brought a date to the party unless you ask him. At 30, he marries JUDY and then you don't know he brought JUDY to the party unless you ask him.

DANIEL

even has his little black book custom designed.

DANNY

has a wife who is smarter than he is.

DANTE

opens a bistro. The food isn't very good, but DANTE remembers everyone's name. The place is a big success.

DARCY

is an unsuccessful womanizer.

DARRELL

can be fun if you're willing to hang out with him on his terms.

DARREN

is a second-string guard on a basketball team. The first time he plays he pulls a hamstring and is out for the season.

DAVE

shakes your hand and tells you how glad he is to see you, while his eyes are busy searching the room for important people.

DAVID

When you meet DAVID you think he's a snob, but everyone says he's really just shy. They're wrong. He is a snob.

DEAN

wears jockey shorts until he's 35 and develops a paunch. Over the succeeding years he wears his boxer shorts higher and higher until there are elastic marks across his chest.

DELBERT

keeps reminding you that the "good life" could kill you. He knows all about cholesterol, polyunsaturated fats and low sodium diets. He always has a cold.

DELL

graduates from cinema school, raises a million dollars and directs a contemporary "film noir." It loses money so he takes a job as a camera operator for rock videos.

DEMETRIUS

is a designer's designer.

DENNIS

always has to leave early to drive his mother someplace.

DEREK

is big on sprays. In his desk at the office, he has mouth, nose and hair sprays. Sometimes he reaches for the wrong one. He's been known to have hair with a touch of mint in it.

DERMOT

is a character who usually shows up in Irish novels.

DESMOND

is a tango master with a toupee.

DEVIN

is a friend of DERMOT. He usually picks up the tab for whatever they eat or drink, even though he makes less than DERMOT.

DEWEY

looks like AUSTIN only he has a bigger Adam's apple. DEWEY is the night cook in a diner, and when you go in, he's always talking to the waitress who's just leaving. Her name is NOREEN and no matter when you get there, she's just getting dressed in the little back room full of soda cases. You can almost see into the room, but not enough. She comes out and stands in the door with her coat on and talks to DEWEY while she's waiting for a red-headed guy in a clunker to pick her up. DEWEY never looks at her while he's talking. He keeps scraping the hot plate.

DEWEY likes to make milk shakes, and when he opens the refrigerator to get the milk, you can see one steak in there — a real steak, not a minute steak. You figure DEWEY is saving that one for himself. He waits until the right time to fix it. DEWEY doesn't ring everything up on the cash register and, finally, one day you find out they've fired him; the new cook is an older, thinner fellow named LES. Sometimes you wonder if DEWEY ever sees NOREEN anymore.

DE WITT

reads *Penthouse* with a bookmark.

DEXTER

tells you he's given up smoking whether you ask him or not.

DICK

sends his wife flowers from time to time and takes her to lunch at least once a month. His wife's friends are crazy about DICK. Their husbands hate him.

DIGBY

Everybody likes DIGBY. Sometimes it makes him nervous.

DIRK

has the kind of eyes women describe as soulful. He's myopic.

DMITRI

wonders why his parents (who are third generation Iowans) named him that.

DOMINICK

has an "in" restaurant with sawdust on the floor. If DOMINICK doesn't know you personally, you don't get in.

DON

is a friend of HOWARD's. DON pats his wife on the back when he gets home instead of kissing her. He has a power lawn mower.

DONALD

was once a 4-H Club winner. He walks like he's not quite used to pavement.

DOOLEY

is constantly trying out new material in local comedy and magic clubs.

DORIAN

is a gifted artist without malice or temperament. He has a tough time succeeding.

DOUG

is an executive type. He was big in school politics and likes to hold the telephone with his shoulder and sign letters while he's talking to someone.

DOUGLAS

smokes a pipe and does exercises with barbells. He marries JUDITH. They were high school sweethearts, but JUDITH wanted "to be sure" so they decided she would go to the city for a year. By the end of the year, she realized she couldn't do any better so he came and got her.

DREW

is a business school graduate who has no interest in literature, sports, sex, food or music. He becomes the Programming Director for a TV network.

DUDLEY

is a woman's first date after her divorce.

DUKE

Has long, straight black hair and wears a leather jacket and jeans. DUKE always looks like he crashed the party, even when the party is at his house.

DUNCAN

has a vicious subconscious. It gives him a nightly assortment of terrifying dreams.

DURWARD

is named for a wealthy uncle who has no immediate family. Uncle DURWARD lives to be 103.

DUSTIN

starts out in high school chasing women, gambling and drinking. He finally gets his act together in college, graduates first in his class and goes on to make a fortune designing computer software. DUSTIN spends the rest of his life chasing women, gambling and drinking.

DWAYNE

hates to be alone. Although he doesn't drink, he joins Alcoholics Anonymous . . . for the company.

DWIGHT

is attractive to women, but he is like a Chinese meal, an hour after he leaves they have forgotten all about him. (Remember President Eisenhower was called "IKE" by one and all. Those of you who cannot remember President Eisenhower may leave the room.)

DYLAN

has parents who used to be hippies.

EARL

is a small fellow with a small chin and a deep voice who marries a big woman.

EBENEZER

is one of only seven people in America who uses his car wash rain check.

ED

is active in a veterans' organization and is always telling you what he read in the *National Enquirer.* Don't argue with ED. It's a waste of time.

EDDIE

is an assistant something. He buys porno magazines and owns a tape of *Deep Throat.*

EDGAR

inherits all his father's money. His brothers resent him for the rest of their lives.

EDMUND

has a phone with a built-in memory that can store 100 different names and numbers. So far the only ones he has entered are his mother and his podiatrist.

EDSEL

If your last name isn't Ford, be careful using this name. It's probably copyrighted.

EDWARD

When your mother is unhappy with your behavior she always uses your cousin EDWARD, your friend EDWARD or even an EDWARD you don't know, as an example of a boy who is going to succeed in life because he respects his parents. Whenever you meet an EDWARD later in life it takes great effort on your part to like him.

EGBERT

won't admit he hates his name, but signs everything, including letters to his wife and children, with his first initial and middle name.

ELDON

leads two lives. The only thing extraordinary about this is that they are both ordinary.

ELDRIDGE

is a contradiction in terms . . . a thrill-seeking accountant.

ELI

finances successful gross-out movies. He is much respected in the film industry.

ELISHA

The trunk of his car has more junk in it than you could find at three neighborhood garage sales.

ELLERY

has difficulty explaining his inability to communicate.

ELLIOTT

wishes he could get a job in London. He quotes Winston Churchill and wears suspenders but calls them "braces." He gets very peeved if you write his name without the last "t."

ELLIS

is the older son who runs the family business and constantly complains about his brothers who don't contribute.

ELMER

No one is ever really named ELMER.

ELMO

never has the right change for the bus.

ELROY

puts dumb bumper stickers on his car.

ELTON

is either with NBC, IRS or CIA.

ELVIS

has a voice that arrests women and eyes that frisk them.

ELWOOD

Everyone says ELWOOD is a good listener. Unfortunately he is a terrible understander.

EMERY

is agreeable. He agrees with anything anyone says to him. He runs the biggest insurance agency in the state.

EMIL

looks sort of sleazy and no one knows what he does for a living. When some of the guys want to meet a hooker they always call EMIL to see if he knows any. But, he only knows one, and he's married to her.

EMMANUEL

is a Talmudic scholar and never takes off his hat.

EMMET

belongs to a chess club and knows the names of all the openings and gambits, but if you play with him, he never wins. He doesn't get upset, though, and he will explain at length why you beat him. He also explains to girls why they don't love him. In time, he may explain to the doctor why he can't be cured of his addiction.

ENOCH

is a speech writer for government officials. ENOCH cannot resist adding touches of humor and ethics to their speeches. He's fired.

EPHRAIM

is gentle, well-mannered and civilized. And in all probability a creation of Somerset Maugham.

ERHARD

You just know somewhere in his desk drawer is a monacle.

ERIC

wears expensive shirts and combs his hair a lot. He comes to parties without a date and confuses the women by flirting with all of them.

ERNEST

fails miserably trying to live up to his name.

ERNIE

was an officer during the war and hasn't been the same since he got out of the service. He has a collection of insignia and will show you color slides he took overseas. On Saturdays, ERNIE wears his officer's shirt — the one with the epaulets.

ERROL

is handsome, intelligent and considerate. But apart from that his friends think he is okay.

ERSKINE

has personalized license plates on all his cars.

ETHAN

runs unopposed in an election . . . and loses.

EUGENE

still wears undershirts.

EUSTACE

is an all-purpose ethnic undertaker. He can work in any neighborhood, any race, religion or color.

EVAN

is known for living dangerously. He cheats on his wife in public places.

EVERETT

has such a dazzling smile you don't think of him as homely.

EZEKIEL

wears sandals, everywhere.

EZRA

mutters and shuffles papers before he gives you a noncommittal answer.

FABIAN

just spent four and a half days watching MTV without sleeping. His ambition is to get into the *Guinness Book of Records.*

FARLEY

On most mornings FARLEY is dispirited. The best he can say is "Have an all right day."

FELIX

belongs to the "Give us this day, our daily croissant" crowd.

FERDINAND

manages to remain friends with all of his former loves.

FIDEL

is the highly efficient warehouse manager for Price/Stern/Sloan Publishers.

FIELDING

is a two-star general who can't find a publisher for his memoirs.

FLETCHER

cuts uncanceled stamps off envelopes and saves them.

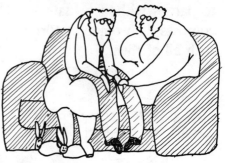

FORBES

has contemplated marriage from time to time, but the thought of leaving his mother is too painful.

FORD

attends meetings and makes voluminous notes, but they're of little use because he can't read his handwriting.

FORREST

is really a cad. He takes a date to his own wedding.

FOSTER

has spent the last 11 months painting "Sunset Over Grand Canyon" on the door of his RV.

FRANCIS

is either a historian or an art director, or he could operate the third booth in a beauty salon.

FRANK

When girls want to redecorate they always get FRANK to come over and help them put up wallpaper. He's good at it and doesn't get fresh afterward. He drinks up all the beer, but he never gets out of control. FRANK is always agreeable and polite, but don't get tough with him. He'll kill you.

FRANKLIN

is very disarming. Even though you didn't plan to you usually end up telling him the truth.

FRAZER

His ambition is to write the ultimate and definitive book on something. To keep himself alive, he writes romance novels using a female pseudonym.

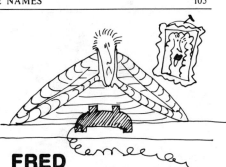

FRED

is skinny and gets his hair cut too high on the sides. He wears striped shirts and works in the same office with JOYCE. FRED had a two-week romance with VALERIE and never got over it.

FREDDY

is always saying "Where's the action?" He usually asks GORDIE or DICK. They don't know of any action, but pretend they do. JIM is the only one who knows where the action is, and he's there.

FREDERICK

is the head buyer for a chain of toy stores. He is the world's foremost authority on stuffed Norwegian Trolls.

FULTON

is a stock broker who rushes home as soon as the market closes, puts on blue jeans and heads for a fern bar.

GABRIEL

has quite a brood and broods a lot.

GALE

quits practicing law to become a plumber. He needs the money.

GAMALIEL

spends half his life on the telephone spelling his name.

GARDNER

is as intelligent as he is modest. He does everything well . . . and quietly.

GARETH

writes the subtitles for foreign porno movies. He can grunt and groan in many languages.

GARFIELD

is either a rich cat or the cat of a super rich cartoonist.

GARRETT

is the Number Two man on the Tenants Committee. He has spent three years trying to get the landlord to heat the jacuzzi.

GARY

No matter what time of day it is, GARY answers the door with a towel around his waist.

GASTON

spends a good deal of his life telling people he is American born.

GAVIN

always says "We must get together for lunch." He's never in when you call.

GAYLORD

Women think Gaylord is either weird or wonderful because he is so sensitive and is a perfect gentleman and never makes passes or asks them up to his place.

GENE

is a bachelor who has his TV set in the bedroom and no chairs. Nothing much happens though, because he always gets too interested in the programs.

GEOFFREY

You never meet any of the women GEOFFREY dates.

GEORGE

People start imposing on GEORGE as soon as he gets old enough. He is good-natured. He puts on a little weight, and when he's 32 he marries the sister of a friend because everyone seems to want him to. Later on he loses a lot of money and his wife's father gives him a seat on the stock exchange.

GERALD

is a clergyman's son who likes to think he is wicked. He has a closetful of old *Penthouse* magazines.

GERARD

is quiet and smokes a pipe and has three different women writing him love letters.

GIDEON

is a tuba player with a recurring hernia problem.

GIL

At parties GIL waits until he catches a woman's eye, then he looks her slowly up and down with a cute, little smile as if to say "Why, hell-oo there." If he gets her alone, all he can think of saying is, "How long have you been in town?" and "Do you like it here better than there?"

GILBERT

After years of vainly trying to improve the system, GILBERT gives up teaching to work at the Department of Water and Power and makes a living at last.

GILES

is the most important critic on the biggest newspaper in Wheeling, West Virginia.

GINO

is DINO with more muscles.

GLENN

goes out with girls and lectures them into bed. Afterward he criticizes them and tries to change the way they act, dress and think.

GODFREY

Ever since health clubs replaced singles bars as the best place to meet women, GODFREY is in the best shape of his life . . . but still lonely.

GORDIE

fancies himself a Casanova. When he goes out on a date, he always tells his friends all the details of what happened. If nothing happened, which is usually the case, he lies about it.

GORDON

has straight blond hair. He reads a lot and joins a liberal political group in hopes of meeting "an intelligent woman with whom he can have a mature relationship."

GOWER

isn't interested in athletics but reads the sports pages every morning so he can have something to talk about with the other stockbrokers in his office.

GRADY

In a crisis GRADY becomes unglued and sometimes unbuttoned.

GRAHAM

GRAHAMs are always raised by a nanny.

GRANT

is a successful wolf in custom-made clothing.

GRAYSON

has secret thoughts that could give perversion a bad name.

GREG

His body is his temple. He worships there twice a day.

GREGORY

His presence and great speaking voice make all his dumb statements sound profound. He's elected to high office.

GRIFFIN

goes to the theatre and falls asleep immediately. He's the drama critic for a local newspaper.

GRIFFITH

is an assistant to somebody important.

GROVER

isn't too sure what his plans are after college, but you can be sure whatever it is, it will have something to do with computers and the Lord.

GUNTHER

has an affection for the bygone days of aristocracy. He still uses a monogrammed wax seal on all of his correspondence.

GUS

is a short-order cook. If it's a fancy restaurant, he's the maitre d'.

GUTHRIE

is penurious and always looking for ways to make money. He puts a pay phone in his car.

GUY

should be arrested.

HADLEY

wears gray suits and contributes bizarre information to conversations. Such as — "Do you know that toilet paper was the first mass-marketed consumer product and helped to launch the advertising business?"

HAKON

can sing the national anthems of five different countries in their native tongues. This skill would be much more appreciated if HAKON could carry a tune.

HAL

will play the piano at a party if anyone wants to sing. HAL will play the piano even if no one sings . . . try and stop him from playing!

HALEY

gives "good" English and earns his tuition writing other people's papers.

HALL

doesn't mean to sound arrogant, but somehow succeeds in doing just that. Fortunately, he can get away with it. He's the boss.

HAMILTON

is tight-lipped and uncommunicative. He is the public relations representative for a large northeastern university.

HANK

is tall and an artist of some kind. He grunts instead of talking.

HANLEY

has many diplomas on his office wall. When you get close enough to read them, they come from obscure universities in countries that no longer exist.

HANS

has a hat rack for a wall decoration. Hanging on it are three World War I spiked helmets.

HARCOURT

treats everything as a life or death situation. Fortunately, he ends up a mortician.

HARDY

No matter what he wears, how he cuts his hair or who he marries, HARDY's life remains predictably mainstream.

HARLAN

Everyone respects his leadership and managerial abilities, but when he's up for promotion, it always goes to someone in the office who is less threatening to management.

HARMOND

drives an old car that always has an empty beer can rolling around on the floor.

HAROLD

is somebody's friend. Probably HOWARD's. HAROLD has a nice-looking sister.

HARPER

When you have to move a piano, HARPER is the guy who comes with his partner, OWEN. They pick it up as if it weighed 10 pounds.

HARRIS

lets his wife run the show. It makes him more comfortable not to have to make decisions and, besides, she knows his life better than he does.

HARRISON

goes to the beach but doesn't swim. The only time he gets wet is when the girl he's with brings back a pailful of water and pours it on his stomach. Then he wrestles with her and gets sand in the food.

HARRY

always knows where to get more ice.

HART

is an unsuccessful politician and a full-time political science instructor at a state university.

HARVEY

is the fellow you ask to take your girl someplace when you can't get there until later.

HASKEL

is a photographer who seldom comes out of his darkroom.

HAVELOCK

assembles one of the finest lint collections in the Southwest.

HAYWOOD

is the man a woman introduces to her family so they won't know she's really going out with VITO.

HECTOR

believes in the American Dream that anyone can grow up to be President. His parents hope he can do better than that.

HENRY

still wears the eyeglasses with metal rims they gave him in the Army. HENRY is a good fellow to ask to a party. He always brings a good bottle, even though he doesn't drink.

HERB

is always looking for a better job or a cheaper apartment.

HERBERT

Three or four times a year HERBERT writes indignant letters to the newspaper complaining about the holes in the street or the bad service on the buses.

HERBIE

is the fellow you ask to wait outside in the hall when you have to go in and see someone. You're always asking HERBIE to go someplace with you, but you never take him inside.

HERMAN

loves old John Wayne and Charles Bronson movies. His "word is his bond."

HERNANDO

is an electrical wizard and runs a TV repair shop.

HERSCHEL

is a funny kid who thinks he looks like Andy Warhol.

HILARY

straightens out the welcome mat, pours half-empty bottles of liquor into one bottle and arranges all the kitchen spices in alphabetical order . . . and that's on his first visit to your house!

HIRAM

The backwoods HIRAM wears chin whiskers and chews tobacco. The New England HIRAM's portrait hangs in the private dining room of the Board of Directors.

HOBART

is a little Irish guy who used to stutter and has almost overcome it. He marries a tiny, pretty woman and they have three beautiful, tiny children.

HOGAN

is a burly guy who has such a natural gift for acting he becomes a wrestler.

HOLDEN

thinks William Buckley is the world's greatest living human.

HOLLIS

never talks to anyone. He becomes an odd kind of writer — travel, porno, food, financial, chess.

HOMER

is the kind of guy who eats the fortune cookies in a Chinese restaurant. Sometimes he eats the fortunes, too.

HORACE

says he's going to make a long story short, but doesn't.

HORTON

is self-important and is always a generation behind the times. He listens to Supremes records and wears big, wide neckties.

HOWARD

gets through life okay. It's no strain. He lives in the suburbs, goes to PTA meetings, buys life insurance, cheats on his wife once a year and finally buys a Buick.

HOWIE

organizes the class reunions and promotes basketball games between the kids and the old-timers. HOWIE likes to talk over the PA system.

HUBERT

tries too hard. He uses antique slang, like "... the whole shootin' shebang ...."

HUDSON

lives in the past literally and figuratively. When you're in his house you wouldn't know it was the 20th century, if not for the presence of a microwave oven.

HUGH

is the guy that marries the girl you went with in high school and you can never figure out what she sees in him.

HUGHIE

used to be an athlete, but he let himself get flabby. He likes to drink beer and sing old school songs and he has eyes for very young girls. HUGHIE finally gets into some kind of trouble and no one hears about him anymore.

HUGO

is a mystery ethnic of some kind who cooks at a small continental restaurant. His specialty is unpronounceable.

HUMPHREY

worries about his pot belly and goes to the races a lot. Somehow he thinks that losing money is related to losing weight.

HUNT

spends most of his life working out his relationship with his father.

HY

is skinny and scratches a lot. He either talks your ear off or has nothing to say at all.

HYMAN

is a cantor who keeps trying to form a rock band.

IAN

is in plays that close out of town or off-off-off Broadway.

ICHABOD

???

IGNATIUS

is a former priest who met a beautiful Italian girl and decided he did not really have the calling.

IKE

performs frenzied exhibitions of break dancing in public places.

INGEMAR

does great with women. All ages, nationalities, all sizes. They like INGEMAR. He seldom disappoints them.

IRA

is sort of jerky but doesn't know it and acts like he's Sylvester Stallone.

IRVING

is always planning big deals. He winds up working for BEN.

IRWIN

carries around two-year-old newspaper clippings that mention his name.

ISAAC

always feels he has to introduce his dates to his mother the second time they go out.

ISIDORE

likes to take both sides of an argument.

IVAN

thinks there should be more jokes in *Pravda*.

IVES

isn't a name, it's a pedigree.

JACK

Before you leave town, JACK gives you a belt as a going away gift. Three years later you return home and visit JACK and the first thing he says to you is "How's the belt holding up?"

JACKSON

made a successful TV commercial when he was 12. His father invested the money in a Soul Food Cafe. Today JACKSON is a millionaire.

JACOB, JAKE

JACOB is in the garment business. JAKE is a fight manager or a security guard.

JACQUES

is the French version of IN-GEMAR but with darker hair.

JAMES

is warm and friendly and always good for a laugh and a few bucks. WENDELL hits JAMES up for money a lot.

JARED

is a hi-fi, sci-fi computer nut.

JARVIS

has straight black hair and dresses like everyone did 15 years ago.

JASON

What the masses do, JASON doesn't.

JASPER

When you ask JASPER how he's feeling, he automatically responds "The same." You feel compelled to say you're sorry.

JAY

is a compulsive check picker-upper.

JED

is an inept skier who breaks a different set of bones each time he hits the slopes. He marries SALLY, a nurse, with whom he literally fell head over heels in love . . . both legs were in traction at the time.

JEFF/JEFFREY

JEFFREY is attractive and clean cut. Some woman marries him quickly. Usually ROSA-LIND. JEFF, on the other hand, is attractive and not so clean cut. He eats, drinks and is merry with all kinds of women until he is too old to get married. Then he devotes himself to playing the horses.

JEFFERSON

is JACKSON's father. He is also a millionaire or destined to be.

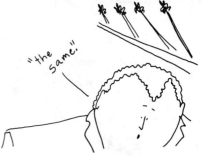

JEREMIAH

It takes four or five invitations to get JEREMIAH to the home of married friends for dinner. Around 10 o'clock he leaves explaining that he has to get up early. His friends know he has a late date.

JEREMY

has three dogs, one of which he can never housebreak. He replaces the carpet every year.

JEROME

always finishes what's left on your plate. He acts like he doesn't want to, but he's doing you a favor.

JERRY

is an energetic over-achiever who is a power in three different fields. All of which is somewhat diminished by the pieces of toilet paper covering the nicks on his face.

JESSIE

has a green thumb but lives in an apartment which faces a courtyard and is very dark. He grows mushrooms.

JESUS

The first generation JESUS is a non-union painter your miserable landlord sends to your apartment every two years. The second generation JESUS makes the dean's list.

JETHRO

is a self-made man. He should have had more help on the project.

JIM

is the one women want to marry, if they don't marry JIMMY.

JIMMY

Even in his 30s, JIMMY has the engaging look and the unblunted enthusiasm of a kid.

JOE

thinks before he says anything and speaks slowly. By the time he's 12, he knows how to fix broken toys for the younger kids. When he grows up, he never does too well in business, because he's always co-signing a bum loan or extending too much credit. He seldom leaves the town where he was born.

JOEL

is either small and cute or big and slack-jawed. The small JOEL is popular, marries well and is always changing jobs. The big one is surly, dull and very successful.

JOEY

is either a fresh kid brother who steals stuff, or a 65-year-old former comedian who lives with the son-in-law he always disapproved of.

JOHN

is a nice guy — honest, unselfish and responsible. He changes his underwear and socks every day. When he was younger, he exercised every day and talked about being an astronaut. But he got married, took a job with a big corporation and is the head of his department.

JOHNNY

is the same as JOHN except taller and slimmer and less responsible.

JONATHAN

is seldom called by his full name. His friends use his initials, such as J.B., J.G. or J.J.

JORDAN

goes to movies to escape stress, but it never works. He gets a broken seat or a kid spills soda on him or the lady next to him asks him to watch her seat and doesn't return until the movie is three-quarters over. He leaves in much worse shape than when he came in.

JOSE

In addition to his immediate family, JOSE supports four aunts, two wives and someone he thinks is a cousin.

JOSEPH

As soon as he arrives at a dinner party, usually late, he asks if he can use the phone. He stays on it for an hour.

JOSHUA

is the best nonprofessional horse handicapper you know. In any given year he almost breaks even.

JUDD

doesn't go on fishing trips until after he's married.

JULES

wears a coat with a velvet collar, drives a big black car and looks like a high-class gangster. He's an accountant.

JULIAN

is your immediate superior. He always has a middle initial and is never going to retire.

JUSTIN

marries his high school sweetheart and works all his life for a boss he can't stand. He retires and spends his last 20 years in Florida. He hates it.

KARL

marries late in life and lives with his wife and mother in the house where he grew up. Eventually the house will be his and he and his wife will move out.

KEANE

is good in bed.

KEEFE

Tennis shoes are his trademark.

KEENAN

If you are involved in a business deal with KEENAN, make sure you are on his side.

KEITH

feels he has to live up to his name. He plans to be a mountain climber or live in Acapulco or sail around the world on a 35-foot boat. He ends up in the suburbs married to CAROL.

KELLY

programs computers and goes to folk dances in the hope of meeting someone different.

KELVIN

To satisfy his unquenchable thirst for gossip, he buys and operates a singles bar.

KEN

When your girl goes to California on vacation she meets KEN and marries him.

KENDRICK

is a world class freeloader.

KENNETH

is soft-spoken and neat. He was secretly in love with LIZ; but when he was 26, his hair started to fall out, and he married JANE.

KENNY

is the fellow who helps you move. You don't really know him very well and feel guilty while he's carrying out all the boxes so you keep talking about the big housewarming you're going to have. But when you have it, you forget to invite KENNY.

KENT

goes to college on an athletic scholarship. In his third year he develops a trick knee. They drop him from the team. Because of his great looks he gets a running part in a daytime soap and, over the years, learns how to act.

KERMIT

writes a fictitious account of the true life he leads with his wife and their closest friends. The book is published, becomes a best-seller and all the couples divorce. As part of the divorce settlement, KERMIT's wife gets the royalties from the book.

KERRY

looks great, but occasionally makes grammatical mistakes.

KEVIN

is a six-year-old boy whose mother loves him.

KIM

Whenever KIM feels really good about himself he shaves off his beard. He's had it on now for about two years.

KINGSLEY

All he has to do to dominate a meeting is attend it.

KIPP

is the top-of-the-line eccentric.

KIRBY

plays bass in a trio. They work weekends in small hotels.

KIRK

is one-half of a ballet ice-skating team. At 30 he becomes a stock-broker.

KNOX

wears three-piece suits and is always pleasant. He is also always successful.

KURT

loves to return salutes.

KYLE

knows how to shop for cheese.

LAIRD

is very elegant. Or at least tries to be. But don't try to borrow anything from him.

LAMAR

is a skinny kid who works in JACKSON's Soul Food Cafe. LAMAR will never be a millionaire.

LAMONT

surprises his friends when he joins the Marines. He astonishes them when he reenlists.

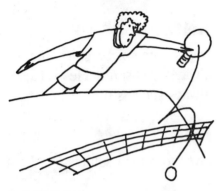

LANCE

had a strong-minded, beautiful mother and an amiable, hard-working father. He is curly haired, sort of handsome and good at non-varsity sports, i.e. ping-pong, handball, volleyball.

LANE

is a deputy sheriff in a Southwest town. He gives out a lot of tickets.

LANGDON

has a lot of nicknames. In high school he was an all-state tackle.

LANNY

Among his passions are divorced women and argyle socks. Not necessarily in that order.

LARRY

is always late to the office, but he works for himself and takes care of everybody and never wants any credit. He has only one vice — an expensive foreign car which is always in the shop.

LARS

is a big Danish carpenter who can build anything.

LAWRENCE

knows that there are two 'c's and one "r" in "occur" and that "i" comes before "e" except after "c".

LAZARUS

Maybe he will rise from the dead someday. Who knows. JOSH will make book on it, though.

LEANDER

is LEE's real name. He doesn't tell anyone.

LEE

works for his father or a successful brother. He has dinner once a week with ARTHUR. They get separate checks.

LEIF

gravitated naturally toward water, boat building, sailing, raising tropical fish.

LELAND

has trouble making decisions. Once when he went in for a pack of cigarettes the clerk asked him what brand he wanted. By the time LELAND made up his mind, he had given up smoking.

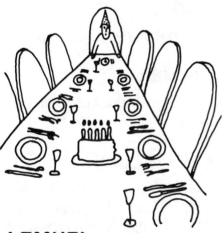

LEMUEL

is essentially lonely. Everyone likes him, but no one loves him. He pals around with STANLEY.

LEN

At parties, LEN is always in the kitchen leaning on the refrigerator holding a can of beer while he talks to some girl. Probably JUNE.

LEO

is an All-State linebacker at 18. He plays pro football for a few years and ends up with a broken nose, a trick knee and a job selling sporting equipment.

LEONARD/LEON

LEONARD and LEON are good card players. They are both successful; LEONARD because he is smart and LEON because he is able to organize other people.

LEOPOLD

has given up rock music, peace marches and girls for fatherhood. Eventually he'll go back to one of the three.

LEROY

Everybody says LEROY hasn't scratched the surface of his potential. He'd better hurry up or he'll need an icepick to do it.

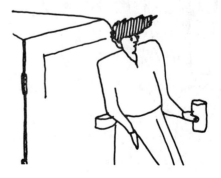

LESLIE

is PATTY's second (or third) husband. He works for GM or EXXON or AT&T, and in 17 years, he has never been late to the office.

LESTER

worries about germs. He hates to shake hands and gets mad if you breathe on him. He carries a thermometer, has memorized the phone numbers of 12 different doctors and is the only fellow around who knows what "Rx" means. His wife always has her purse filled with LESTER's pill bottles. You sometimes wonder what kind of sex life they have.

LEWIS

avoids decisions. Somehow he gets married three times.

LINCOLN

drives a foreign car.

LINDSAY

If he's a politician, he wears gray flannel. If he's a doctor, it's polyester all the way.

LINUS

does not enjoy comic strips.

LIONEL

is cold to the touch and inclined to rust.

LLEWELLYN

is an interior decorator. He and GAYLORD live upstairs and they paint their bathroom black. The neighbors are always complaining about the screaming and door-slamming late at night.

LLOYD

is worried about talking too much and listening to what others say. He calls a radio psychologist to explain his problem to her, but the show runs out of time before he finishes.

LOGAN

comes from Arkansas or West Virginia. He settles on the West Coast but never loses his accent.

LON

has heavy-lidded eyes. Girls are afraid of him . . . until he opens those eyes.

LOREN

is attractive. Everyone likes him. He is a great person to invite to parties for that reason alone. He also brings a cake.

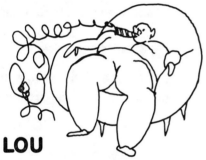

LOU

is someone's husband. He has a big stomach and chews on cigars. LOU overtips in restaurants.

LOUIE

is well-educated but is flamboyant and eccentric. Don't go chasing around town late at night with LOUIE or you'll get in trouble. LOUIE won't, but YOU will.

LOUIS

is an accountant, a lawyer or a sex surrogate you go to for a second opinion.

LOWELL

will kiwi, sushi and tofutti you to death.

LUCAS

calls everyone by a nickname which doesn't fit.

LUCIAN

says unflattering things about all the attractive women at a party so he'll be comfortable in their presence.

LUKE

belongs to a street gang as a kid. He grows up to be a U.S. Senator.

LUTHER

As soon as LUTHER is old enough he buys a homburg. He hates to be called LUTH.

LYLE

calls up and tells you he is going to commit suicide and you have to rush over and go out for coffee with him and he borrows five bucks.

LYMAN

runs some kind of retail business.

LYNDON

has a mirror in every room of his house.

LYNN

has frizzy hair and nimble fingers. He plays piano in a gay bar.

MAC

can fix anything but his marriage.

MACE

always speaks reasonably and in a modulated tone. You don't realize until you leave his office that you've had an argument with him.

MADISON

steeples his fingers, leans back in his chair, listens to what you have to say and is asleep in five minutes.

MAL

wishes he were taller. He owns a coat with funny buttons on it, and he and MICKEY are buddies.

MALCOLM

is a teacher at a big school, who makes his students buy the textbook that he and his wife wrote.

MANFRED

fixes watches and clocks in a little booth at the department store.

MANUEL

challenges the incumbent for a seat on the school board every time there's an election.

MARCEL

At least once a day, he has to return home to pick up something he forgot to bring . . . often it's his wife.

MARCUS

is kind-hearted and active in charity groups.

MARIO

plays the accordion. During the Christmas holidays, he works part-time at the post office.

MARION

works with an "800" number on television, selling great value "Tool Kits" or promising to save the souls of the afflicted.

MARK

has coffee cup stains on seven of the eight important documents on his desk.

MARLON

is startlingly original in everything he does but often behaves childishly.

MARSHALL

belongs to a group of guys who play golf early in the morning before they go to work. Every night he falls asleep watching TV with his wife.

MARTIN

is married to HORTENSE and has a lot of "get up and go." He goes bankrupt several times, but it doesn't seem to bother him. It bothers HORTENSE though.

MARTY

hangs around ranches and ski resorts with BERNIE. They don't ride or ski. But they wear the clothes and drink the Margaritas.

MARVIN

likes to sneak into reserved sections in private beaches. It takes him a long time to get out of the mail room.

MASON

joins the Rotary Club.

MATT

is the son of a minister. Matt becomes a relief quarterback in the NFL.

MATTHEW

is a handsome, bright little kid whose father is an orthodox rabbi. He ends up as editor of a pornographic magazine.

MAURICE

wears a black hat and never kids around. No one knows what business he's in, but if he wants to, he can get you expensive jewelry and good watches wholesale — but really wholesale. MAURICE doesn't try to make a penny on you.

MAX

loves to help. He always knows someone who knows someone who can take care of whatever you need or whatever went wrong.

MAXWELL

has a car accident while taking his driver's test. He strikes terror in the hearts of all the DMV officers when he returns for the second attempt.

MAYNARD

Wherever you put MAYNARD, he falls asleep.

MEL

never apologizes for burping. He says "It's a compliment to the cooking." He also drops ashes on the rug and says "It will keep the moths out."

MELVILLE

is skinny and tries to write poetry.

MELVIN

As a kid, MELVIN gets a job working for a veterinarian. He stays with it, gets a degree and now runs a fancy doggie beauty parlor.

MEREDITH

When you visit out of town, you stay with MEREDITH. It's never an imposition, he's lonely and glad to have you. Your phone calls are the only ones he ever receives.

MERLE

is either a loud hillbilly or a sissy. Or both.

MERLIN

is big. He can never buy anything off the rack. Even as a baby his diapers had to be custom-made.

MEYER

worries a lot.

MICHAEL

If you call MICHAEL "MIKE" he responds, but reluctantly. MICHAELs are fastidious, organized, make good fathers and take time-consuming showers.

MICKEY

When you have a fight with your girl at a party and walk out on her, MICKEY takes her home. MICKEY wears bow ties and everyone tries to fix him up with PATTY because she's short too. PATTY and MICKEY hate each other.

MIKE

wears a silver identification bracelet and has hairy wrists. MIKE always goes with one girl, but he never talks to her. All anyone ever hears him say at parties is "Okay, Honey, let's go home." Later MIKE marries the girl and still never talks to her.

MILES

gets an ulcer.

MILLARD

tells people he doesn't understand what all the Yuppie publicity is about. MILLARD is the epitome of Yuppiness.

MILO

played five different musical instruments as a child. Now there are days you can't even get him to hum.

MILT

is outgoing, extroverted and a prankster. He embarrasses you by pretending to be something he isn't. In a crowded elevator he's a salesman of exclusive Italian silk neckties which he pretends to have in his briefcase. Everyone gets off at the first stop. In an elegant restaurant, he becomes a foreigner who can only say "Screw you" in English. And when you take him to an "In" party, he presents himself as the world's foremost importer of Danish dental floss.

MILTON

is a rarity, a teacher who loves to teach. His boys and girls keep in touch with him throughout the years.

MISCHA

teaches piano but can't stand the lack of talent in his students. After 30 years, he abandons the profession and opens a laundromat which features classical music.

MITCH

has a couple of drinks and he wants to fight. Luckily, nobody ever takes him up on it.

MITCHELL

is always looking for a job that allows him to sleep late in the morning.

MOHAMMED ABDUL al RESCHID

is black, seven feet tall and a millionaire.

MONROE

is usually very quiet, but after a couple of drinks, he will tell you long, sad stories about his life.

MONTGOMERY

His parents chose MONT-GOMERY because they could live comfortably with the diminutive MONTY. MONTGOMERY's friends call him GUMMY.

MONTY

is a brilliant nut who is always lousing up himself and everyone else. If he comes to your house, he insults the cleaning lady or your mother.

MOOSE

was older than the other kids in his class. He got married when he was 19 and started having children, but he never stays home. He hangs around the schoolyard playing ball with the kids half his age.

MORGAN

is at every party you attend, but no one ever knows who invited him.

MORRIS

has some Israeli relatives who make him very nervous. He buys a lot of Israel Bonds because they tell him to.

MORRISON

You never know your friend HERBIE or JERRY or TEDDY's first name is MORRISON until you receive the formal invitation to the wedding.

MORT

is 5'8" or under and is good-natured. He likes girls but usually picks one he can't handle.

MORTIMER

can tell you the comparative nutritional value of breakfast cereals.

MORTON

is always trying to hypnotize everybody. The only one it ever works on is AUGIE. BERNICE pretends it works on her and talks about how "funny" she felt, but she just wants attention. MORTON doesn't come on with girls at all, but GORDIE and GIL are always trying to get MORTON to teach them hypnotism. They figure maybe someday they can get LIZ alone and . . . WOW!

MOSES

is a great jazz musician who has to take a blue collar job to make a living. But, you can catch him Monday nights at the Blue Note.

MURDOCK

plays all the angles. Somehow, he managed to live on Social Security at the age of 14.

MURRAY

has a thin, black moustache. When MURRAY dances with a girl, he drums on her back with his fingers.

MYRON

makes up terrible jokes and puns. He'll call you and say "Sorry to bother you at home, but I didn't know where else to bother you."

NAT

acts like a big man until his mother gets there. When he gets older he acts like a big man until his wife gets there.

NATE

is in business for himself. You can trust NATE.

NATHAN

has three doctorates and lives with his aunt in Brooklyn and is writing a second book on 18th Century Ceramic Chickens. He lost the first book on the subway.

NATHANIEL

writes self-help books. His private life is emotionally turbulent.

NEAL

is someone who belongs to a clique and never pays any attention to you at parties unless he's trying to move in on the girl you brought. If there's a fight, it's NEAL who gets beat up and everyone is secretly pleased.

NED

There are only a handful of people on earth that NED regards as equals. This includes some of the British Royal Family.

NELSON

has a nameplate on his desk at the office. He has another on his desk at home.

NEVILLE

didn't grow to be as big as his parents wanted him to be.

NEWTON

is proud of the fact that he never loses anything . . . except later in life, NEWTON keeps misplacing his false teeth.

NICHOLAS

When NICHOLAS speaks to the waiter in French and orders a special wine, he's not showing off. He's a big spender and a small tipper.

NICK

was a high school dropout and ran away from home after he got one of the MacGilacutty girls in trouble. He has very hairy forearms, which some women find sexy. He ends up driving a Maserati and working as a pit boss in Atlantic City.

NICKY

has curly hair and a cute smile and makes out with all the girls GORDIE lies about.

NIGEL

is English. Or if he isn't, he wants people to think that his family is.

NILES

is in the chorus of the Ice Capades.

NOAH

collects data and knows the name of the fellow who shot President McKinley. Unfortunately, it doesn't come up in conversation very often.

NOEL

is a repository of guilty pleasures.

NOLAN

is a regular in the neighborhood bar.

NORBERT

works in a soft ice cream place and always gives you more than he should.

NORM

forgets his glasses and asks if he can borrow your car and go home and get them.

NORMAN

Some girl gave NORMAN a terrific beating once and he's been afraid to get involved ever since. He keeps saying "Who needs it? I can hire a maid to do everything a wife would do and I can come and go as I please." But, he's always asking if you know any hookers.

NORRIS

Everyone thinks NORRIS is unimportant except his wife.

NORTON

will sit on anything but a couch, a chair or a bench.

OGDEN

knows that someday he'll be honored with a postage stamp.

OLAF

is big and good-natured and drinks a lot of beer. But he can handle it. Somehow he manages to stay in great shape, but his drinking buddies, SVEN, GEORGE and TOM, all get pot-bellies.

OLIN

is usually chewing on toothpicks.

OLIVER

is a writer. Or a cat.

OLLIE

calls you up late at night and tells you to come over, he's at the Playboy Club.

OMAR

reads Tarot cards, collects and mounts butterflies and can hold his breath under water for more than a minute. He seldom has a date.

ONSLOW

thinks acting is just remembering words. He wouldn't get far in the business if he weren't already a star.

ORAN

plays golf in the low 80's, unless he's playing for money, then his game goes to pieces and he invariably shoots over 100.

ORESTES

Even his mother thinks he looks better with a beard.

ORLANDO

gives the best bear hugs this side of the Rockies.

ORSON

figures intellectuals are all liberals so he becomes a big liberal in order to look like an intellectual.

ORVILLE

is superstitious about flying. He'll only go by plane if it's on company business.

OSCAR

is a CPA who wishes he were a doctor. He drops the names of famous surgeons.

OSGOOD

works for a New York publishing house and keeps talking about the novel he's going to finish one of these days.

OSWALD

started out as an actor, but everyone said he looked like a professional man, so he became a dentist . . . at least he acts like a dentist.

OTIS

wears a belt and suspenders at the same time. He blames his wife for letting him eat so much.

OTTO

rents X-rated videotapes three times a week.

OWEN

moves pianos with HARPER.

OZZIE

takes the dog for a walk as an excuse to get a last nightcap.

PABLO

likes to talk at great length about fishing, but never wets a hook.

PAGE

is not a big fellow. He plays piano in an elegant hotel bar and seduces large women.

PARKER

has a license plate that reads LUV4SALE. Actually he's tried to give it away, but no one will take it.

PASCAL

wears one earring.

PAT

doesn't like to exercise, but has read that jogging is a sure-fire way of catching up with super ladies. Every morning he gets into a jogging suit, sprinkles water over himself to give the impression he's been running and hangs out at the jogging track. The only thing he ever catches is a cold.

PATRICK

always pitches in and helps whether you want him to or not.

PAUL

is a workaholic. He invents excuses to get to the office on Sunday.

PAXTON

This is a classy name. It could get your son an interview with IBM.

PEDRO

can get you out of most kinds of trouble, some of which he got you into.

PENN

has a great deal of confidence but little right to it.

PERCY

is like LOUIE, only nuttier. When the cops come to break up the party, PERCY gets tough with them and hides their hats.

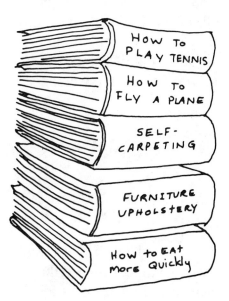

PERRY

goes by the book. If he hasn't read how to do it, he hasn't done it.

PETE/PETER

PETER is slender, rides, skis, and is an amateur artist. He dresses great and never wears anything that is polyester. Not even his underwear. On the other hand, PETE probably wouldn't even wear underwear if his wife, FLORENCE, didn't make him. PETE has what FLORENCE calls a "beer belly." He goes bowling every week with FRED, HANK and GUS.

PHALEN

You know him for years as BUZZ or CHUCK and don't discover his real name is PHALEN until he bills you for services on his office stationery.

PHIL

isn't around much. He always has something better to do. He gets married and works for his father-in-law and complains about the business which he later inherits. When he gets older, he complains about his son-in-law who is working for him.

PHILIP

is a divinity student who talks about religion as if it were basketball. He tells you frankly that he would like to be a Roman Catholic priest, but he likes girls too much; so he's going to be an Episcopalian minister. He ends up in trouble with the law.

PHILO

His ideas are good and new. Unfortunately the good ones aren't new and the new ones aren't good.

PIERCE

went to the best prep school and Ivy League college and ended up playing trumpet in a jazz band. He now owns a successful record company.

PIERRE

If you call a boy PIERRE he will either be French or lucky. Maybe both.

PITNEY

carries a thermometer with him everywhere and checks his temperature at least twice a day.

PORTER

orders some special complicated drink and makes a big scene when it isn't fixed right. In 20 years, it's never been fixed right, but he keeps ordering it.

PRENTICE

gets elected to lots of important positions in high school. But, he hates college and doesn't get good grades and quits. He starts his own software company and is bought out by IBM.

PRESCOTT

starts drinking early — or late . . . depending on what time he gets to the bar.

PRESTON

is the first to second motions at meetings.

QUASIMODO

is a bell ringer with bad posture.

QUENTIN

is 50 pounds overweight. It doesn't seem to bother him.

QUINCY

His parents were intellectuals and the only socialists in their small Midwestern town. QUINCY never talks politics.

QUINLAN

is Irish and never misses a chance to tell you so.

QUINN

is a computer technician who makes dates with female operators on his terminal screen.

RADCLIFF

wears a jacket and tie at the beach.

RAFE

is an old guy who lives in Appalachia and looks like a moonshiner. Why not? He is a moonshiner.

RALPH

has taped "The Honeymooners" on his VCR. Just once he'd like to say "Pow! Right in the kisser" to his wife, but doesn't have the courage.

RAMSAY

is someone in business that everyone calls by his initials. ("I agree with you 200%, R.J.")

RANDALL

has a passion for urban living in high style. His underwear is monogrammed.

RANDOLPH

has his hands in his pockets all the time.

RAPHAEL

reads poetry to ladies on the first date.

RAY

is the pal of the fellow who is the leader of the gang. When he grows up, he still thinks of himself that way. He carries an empty briefcase to work and back.

RAYMOND

seems tricky. People don't trust RAYMOND, but he likes it that way.

RAYNOR

sits in public places and does crossword puzzles in ink.

REECE

His parents think REECE is a big brain because he is skinny and nearsighted. They buy him computers and hire tutors but he still only manages a C + average.

REED

takes out full-page ads in second-rate newspapers announcing the publication of his book, *How To Make a Million Before You're Forty.* Readers are instructed to send $9.95 to a post office box in Scottsdale, Arizona. REED becomes a millionaire at age 37.

REGINALD

smokes Schimmelpennick cigars. He is one of the few men in the Western hemisphere who can spell Schimmelpennick.

REMINGTON

is the kind of name two television writers named MEL think up for a super-WASP hero. It catches on and becomes the 109th most popular name in a survey conducted in 1993.

RENE

is thin and overdresses. He identifies himself only in relation to women — his mother, his girl. RENE always has a girl but he doesn't get married until he's 44 years old. The marriage only lasts a week.

REUBEN

is a pessimist. He makes out his will when he's 25.

REX

wears bow ties and was a hipster back in 1953.

RHETT

changes the message on his answering machine twice a day. After six, it becomes suggestive.

RICHARD

is almost always called DICK or RICKY or RICHIE. All of these fellows start out life pretty good. DICK was voted "Most Likely to Succeed" but didn't. RICKY was "Most Popular" and the star of the drama club. Later he became a male model and the last anyone heard, he was a bartender in Chicago. RICHIE was Valedictorian and President of the senior class. Fifteen years later he calls you up and you are flattered that he still remembers you — but he is trying to sell you insurance. However, if your peers call you RICHARD when you are 17, you will become a partner in a prestigious law firm and end up in Washington as a Presidential advisor or Cabinet member.

RILEY

is a 14-year-old kid who wants to be an astronaut.

ROBERT

If he is called ROBERT by people other than his parents, he tends to straighten pictures on walls, empty ashtrays, and wash his hands a lot. BOB doesn't do any of that stuff. BOBBY is someone else entirely. Never lend money to BOBBY.

ROBIN

Girls like guys named ROBIN and vice versa.

ROCKY

No one can be as sexy as ROCKY looks.

ROD

is tall, quiet and good-looking. He has a moustache but no sideburns. He likes guns and television. He marries a girl who smokes a lot.

RODNEY

left college but college has never left him. RODNEY joins the alumni association, buys season tickets to the football games, has the family wear varsity T-shirts and has the two cars in the garage painted in the school colors.

ROGER

wore glasses when he was nine which made him look studious. He became the teacher's pet and made the best grades in school. All the girls' mothers liked ROGER.

ROLAND

has something to do with publishing, but no one knows what.

RONALD

is an IRS agent who lives exceptionally well. Some friends do believe him when he says his wife has money.

RONNIE

is a charmer and girls fall for him because he cries. He plans to get married as soon as his psychoanalyst tells him it's okay.

RORY

If you can't take it out, send for it or boil it in a bag, RORY doesn't eat it.

ROSCOE

is a good soul who can easily be mistaken for a used car salesman.

ROSS

knows everything. He can settle bets about whether DiMaggio or Williams had the best overall average of runs batted in.

ROVER

should stay off the sofa.

ROY

There are two kinds of ROYs: the big city ROY and the small town ROY. The big city ROY has a fat face and his ambition is to be the best used car salesman in town. He's always standing out front next to the lemon they have on the platform as the "Daily Special" and jingling the coins and keys in his pocket. The small town ROY has a big Adam's apple and hollow cheeks. He's the one who buys the "Daily Special" from the other ROY.

ROYCE

has business cards with only his name on them.

RUDY

doesn't own a pair of shoes without holes in the soles.

RUDOLPH

is a small man who dates giant women or is an unusually gangly man married to a short-waisted wife.

RUDYARD

shocks his family by taking it upon himself to earn a living.

RUFUS

belongs to a lodge which has a secret handshake.

RUPERT

finds ways to make quick, substantial and untraceable money.

RUSS

Things happen to RUSS. He's always having a wreck or breaking his big toe, or getting his shirt caught in his zipper.

RUSSELL

takes 10 minutes to tell a lousy joke that you've heard eight times before.

RUTHERFORD

never can find a place that serves a decent piece of meat.

RYAN

is on an endless quest for a cologne that attracts women who like Mozart and pizza.

SALVATORE

sings arias in the shower.

SAM

Everyone in the world is named SAM. They just don't know it.

SAMUEL

does not like all the normal social amenities that people from all walks of life like. The last time he went out for an intimate lunch, the coffee was 10 cents and the waiters were pleasant.

SANCHO

is serving his fifth term as head of the Chamber of Commerce in a southwestern state and says he will not run again. He's been saying that for 20 years.

SANDOR

is a psychiatrist, a wrestler or a brand name for sandpaper.

SANFORD

always has something in need of repair . . . his car, his teeth, his life.

SAUL

SAUL's father sold things well. SAUL sells them even better. His son becomes an incredible salesperson.

SAWYER

is a wunderkind of marketing who constantly worries about being replaced by next year's wunderkind.

SCHUYLER

will be an astronaut . . . unless his mother says "No you won't."

SCOTT

has musical ambitions and buys a synthesizer at a discount from BENNIE. Then he blames BENNIE because he can't learn to use it.

SEAMAN

has a nickname. Or should have.

SEAN

goes to the beach on workdays.

SEBASTIAN

talks a lot but people like to listen to him.

SELIG

goes to computer camp and later, computer training classes. He ends up repairing computers.

SETH

is a scrawny, bespectacled kid with a high IQ.

SEYMOUR

Anyone who is constantly called SEYMOUR is in trouble.

SHANE

is a good name if you liked the movie.

SHAWN

is always talking to someone else's wife.

SHEA

goes to self-realization meetings, attends encounter groups and takes awareness training until he's collected enough slogans to justify the way he leads his life.

SHELDON

takes papers home from the office to work on over the weekend. The papers are never seen again.

SHELLEY

wonders whether or not he should grow a beard.

SHEPARD

is okay. He's sort of a hip HOWARD.

SHERMAN

chews on pencils.

SHERWIN

is a committed hypochondriac who will someday chair the "Disease of the Month Club."

SHERWOOD

responds with "What you're trying to say . . ." and then repeats exactly what you just said.

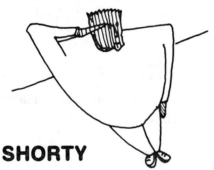

SHORTY

is either 5'3" or 6'8".

SID

would love to have the courage to cheat on his wife . . . but he would have to get married to do that. He doesn't have THAT much courage.

SIGMUND

manages to click his heels even when wearing sneakers.

SILAS

has show business instincts which serve him well in the ministry.

SIMON

has a way of smiling out loud.

SINCLAIR

stages campy dance numbers.

SMILEY

is a guy who has a scar running from his right ear to the left side of his chin. He was named SMILEY after he got the scar.

SOCRATES

Only a dominating or frustrating father could give a child an outrageous name such as SOCRATES, or ALGERNON or ARISTOTLE. This child will do badly in school and wind up being presented with a gold watch after working 25 years at the same unimportant job — unless, of course, he happens to be a Greek. Then SOCRATES is an okay name, and when the child grows up he will, no doubt, continue to be a Greek. As to being important — there is no such thing as an unimportant Greek.

SOLOMON

makes dumb decisions.

SORRELL

was brought up by two maiden aunts. He was overweight at the age of 10 and never looked back.

SPAULDING

has 73 sweaters, no two alike.

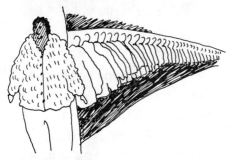

SPENCER

doesn't go out much. He is working on some mysterious project that no one has ever seen.

STACY

has ambitions to become the best in the world at what he does. He just doesn't know what it is that he does.

STAN

talks a lot about Ferraris and Alfa Romeos and Porsche 928's, but he drives a 1972 Chevy.

STANLEY

believes that a really smart operator can take an idea and parlay it into a million bucks. By the time STANLEY is 30 years old, the only thing he is really big at is smoking.

STEPHEN

has a long-time live-in girl friend following his divorce.

STERLING

is a writer born married and under contract.

STEVE

must have the latest in electronic gadgets. He is loaded with computers, VCRs, cordless telephones, compact discs and credit card balances that rival the national deficit.

STEWART

buys one good suit.

STUART

buys one good suit and has copies made in Hong Kong.

SULLY

is almost great looking. He ends up seducing second-rate girls and working at a second-rate job.

SUMNER

is a writer who is constantly searching for a precise word buried in the back of his mind. To clear his head, he goes for long walks. He never finds the word, but ends up in great shape.

SY

Girls are always teaching SY to dance. He smiles a lot, never loses his temper and doesn't look tough. But he had a good combat record in Viet Nam. SY likes PATTY, but she thinks he's not going to amount to anything and ignores him. Later, when SY is very successful, PATTY keeps telling her husband, who isn't, how SY was crazy about her and wanted to marry her.

SYLVESTER

remarries his second wife.

TAD

never fails to use the paper seat covers in public toilets.

TAYLOR

makes out detailed laundry lists and checks the mailbox twice a day.

TED

is husky and nice-looking and girls think he is deep because he doesn't talk much — but it's really because he can't think of anything to say. He marries the girl he took to the senior prom and they both don't say much.

TEDDY

is your girl's 16-year-old brother who wears preppie clothes and treats you as if you were a Russian spy with halitosis.

TERENCE

is a poet, a psychic, an astrologer and a numerologist but has no sense of what to do with his life.

TERRY

There are two TERRY types. One TERRY goes to a hair-stylist, still wears fringed leather vests and wide belts. The other TERRY wears a three-piece suit and is an investment counselor, a lawyer or a salesman in a conservative men's store which features three-piece suits.

THADDEUS

works for a publisher and writes book jacket copy such as "Only she could have written this towering, deeply compassionate novel . . . ." He has yet to open one of these books.

THEOBALD

will never commit himself. He qualifies every answer with phrases such as "To my way of thinking" or "To the best of my knowledge." It takes him several hours to make a snap judgment.

THEODORE

If you are called THEODORE and not TEDDY or TED, you are undoubtedly a person of importance.

THOMAS

is a City Attorney who never loses a case until a week before he's to run for nomination as Mayor. The party nominates SPENCER.

THORNTON

is high up in the hierarchy of a multinational corporation.

TIM

is a bartender and a friend of AGGIE. About once a month he closes up an hour early and goes home with AGGIE. For the next week, AGGIE doesn't come in the place.

TIMOTHY

wishes he were born in another time. He can't handle a generation of lowered expectations.

TINY

is a fat man with a little nose and little feet and a lot of hair.

TITUS

has a box in the attic labeled "pieces of string too short to do anything with."

TOBY

is anxious to please. He laughs before you get to the punchline of a joke.

TODD

plays an electric guitar. He wants to form a rock band but can't come up with a name.

TOM

is a solid citizen. He is dependable and makes a fine husband and father. His only problem is a tendency toward hyperacidity as he gets older.

TOMMY

figures the world owes him a living and he's clever enough to collect it. He lets his hair fall over his forehead, wears cashmere jackets, borrows money and plays tennis. His attitude toward women is predatory. He brings them little gifts and eventually marries an older woman who has something put aside.

TONY

There is a dark, fat TONY and a tall, blond TONY. Both of them are only interested in Number One.

TRAVIS

can quote the villain's dialogue in any of Shakespeare's plays.

TRENT

knows what kind of hook, lure, fly or bait will catch trout, striper, sand bass or catfish. He's always yelling "Break their necks!"

TREVOR

wears a blue suit with brown shoes and tries to use an English accent.

TRISTAN

is an artist who is very happy with his work until he sobers up in the morning.

TROY

is full of mind-boggling trivia that no one has ever been able to verify.

TRUE

No matter where you run into him, the fern bar, the croissant shop or the ice cream parlor, he frets about maintaining his grade point average.

TRUMAN

writes Southern novels, even though he was born in Michigan.

TY

chews tobacco and whistles a lot.

TYRONE

is a giver and not a taker, which would be admirable, if we weren't talking about advice.

ULRIC

is a name for someone who raids coastal cities and sacks churches.

ULYSSES

tries to invest everything he reads with philosophical meaning, even graffiti.

UPTON

is always against something.

VAL

manages the careers and business affairs of many successful people, but needs a lot of help with his own life.

VALENTINE

does not care very much for holidays.

VAN

says things like "This is the best corned beef I've ever tasted — and I don't like corned beef."

VANCE

has a bouffant hairstyle and always carries a comb.

VAUGHN

goes to a crisis counselor. If he doesn't, he is one.

VERNON

sits in the park and plays checkers with WILL.

VICTOR

always impresses you when you see him. He looks shrewd, tough, intelligent and efficient. When you have to go to court for anything, VICTOR is always the other fellow's lawyer. Your lawyer is a cousin of HERBIE's who still has the same briefcase he used in college.

VINCE

gives the impression he's wearing a shoulder holster.

VINCENT

has all of his clothes tailor-made and makes terrible puns.

VIRGIL

lives in a rural community. He's the stepfather of either CORA, DEBORAH or MARY ELLEN.

VITO

is shocked that his kids don't get misty-eyed when he tells them how rough it was when he was going to school.

VLADIMIR

sought political asylum in Toledo, Ohio.

VOLNEY

marries the best-looking blonde in the eastern part of the state.

WADE

knows how to throw a spitball.

WALDO

is a dude. He wishes it were still okay to wear pointed yellow shoes and double-breasted vests.

WALLACE

hangs around museums because he figures he can meet lonely, out-of-town girls. It worked once.

WALLY

used to save stamps, but now he has a lathe in the basement and does woodworking. He reads science-fiction and *Popular Mechanics* and likes to get on mailing lists.

WALT

is chunky and wears glasses and hangs around drinking with ALFRED, NICHOLAS and MIKE. WALT does well in the world but does badly with women. He likes them, but when he gets around a first-class girl, he kicks his feet and tells dumb jokes.

WALTER

There are several different kinds of WALTERs. The only thing they have in common is that none of them are WALT or WALLY.

WARD

has seen *Casablanca* 53 times. When WARD toasts a girl, he says "Here's looking at you, kid." It works.

WARNER

Whenever he is photographed at a social function he is always identified in the newspaper as "an unknown guest."

WARREN

When WARREN takes a girl out he is thoughtful, considerate, reserved, never makes a suggestive remark and gives the impression that he has a large private income. The girl thinks she has struck gold, but on the third date, all of a sudden he turns into a sex-crazed monster.

WAYLAND

His necktie is a record of what he's eaten for the past week.

WAYNE

doesn't look like he knows what he's doing until you read the small print in the contract you signed with him.

WEBSTER

is a news commentator or an editorial writer who has a nodding acquaintance with facts.

WELLS

doesn't get many dates because he's described to women by his friends as bright, kind and sweet. Sweet is the killer word.

WENDELL

is never doing as well now as he used to.

WERNER

They are still looking for WERNER in East Germany.

WES

is organized. He has a place for everything and everything is in its place. His home maintenance list includes the names of three back-up plumbers and an all-night roofer.

WESLEY

runs for class officer each and every term. In his senior year, he's elected "Most Persistent."

WHIT

does devastating impersonations of his friends.

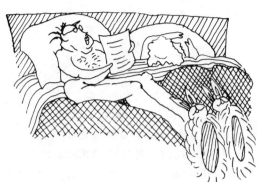

WHITEY

His father used to drink a lot. And then he disappeared. WHITEY's mother works as a waitress in a coffee shop.

WHITNEY

His idea of a good time is to put on his slippers and pore over financial reports until late at night.

WILBUR

hangs around chain drugstores and when girls stop to look at the paperbacks he sidles up to them and says "Say, I bet you like to read a lot." He often gets arrested.

WILFRED

exaggerates about everything in his life. He becomes a most successful copywriter for an ad agency.

WILL

is the same as WILLIAM only WILL tends to drink more.

WILLIAM

gives endowments to a hospital, a library or a curvaceous blonde in the typing pool.

WILLY

is fast on his feet. When he's a kid, he's always running up and down the block. When he gets older, he becomes a famous athlete.

WINSTON

is a consulting specialist in economics and finance. He can never balance his checkbook.

WINTHROP

is a very private person. He even sings duets alone.

WOODROW

At 20 WOODROW is the Valedictorian who wants to hitchhike around the world and doesn't care about becoming rich. At 30, he begins to be compulsively goal oriented. At 40, he shifts interests, grows up and does something that makes him feel good . . . possibly marriage.

WORTH

has a lot of opinions and signs petitions a lot, but never has the courage to sign his real name.

WYATT

is deeply patriotic. He even stands when they sing "America the Beautiful."

WYLIE

will come to your house unannounced after midnight, and when you come to the door in your pajamas, he says "Hey, I didn't know you were asleep," and keeps talking about how sorry he is "to have gotten you up" until you are wide awake.

XAVIER

is hemmed in literally and figuratively. He has seven sisters.

YALE

carries in his wallet a clipping of a letter to the editor he wrote which was published ... 15 years ago.

YANCY

After a couple of drinks, his nose becomes red enough to stop traffic.

YUL/YULE

is in charge of programming for a religious music station.

YVES

pays palimony in two different countries.

ZACHARY

buys into an all-night supermarket so he'll have some place to hang out after work.

ZANE

is into body-building and muscle toning. His handshake is a lethal weapon.

ZEKE

manages to chew tobacco and a toothpick simultaneously.

"Every man has three names: one his father and mother gave him, one others call him, and one he acquires himself."

Ecclesiastes

SIGN
OFF!

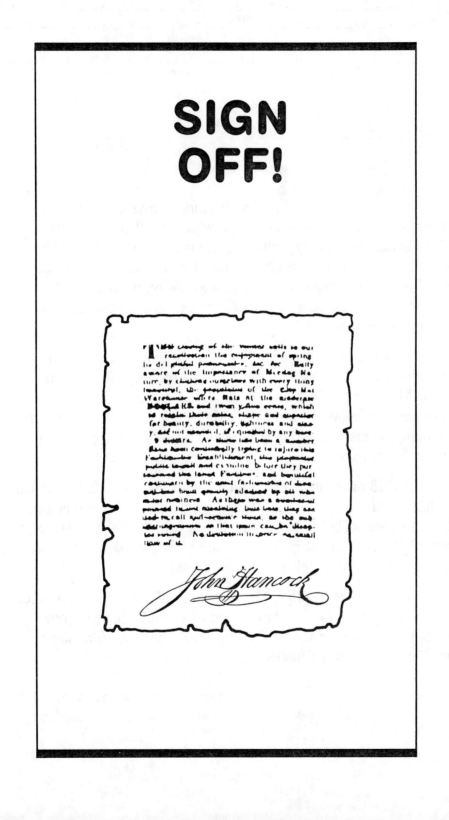

In handwriting analysis, a signature represents the writer's outer facade while all other pen strokes show actual personality traits. Napoleon's signature looked like the rest of his writing, which means it was easier to know the real "Bonie." His aggressive nature was always apparent and most people didn't want to play Pinochle with him because he was such a poor loser.

His signatures exemplify how writing may deteriorate in legibility over time. They became even more illegible after he died. Mr. Napoleon's distorted "n's" (1794 sample) show his mommy didn't love him. But he didn't stoop to whine for approval as many others with his configuration do — he just grabbed the world by its axis.

In 1808 messy ink blobs (which later influenced Mr. Rorschach) obliterate his signature underlining, which means he was getting a bit obnoxious. The diagonal underlinings from 1794 to 1813 point out his innate leadership flair. But after his "vacation" on Elba, we see he no longer felt so sure of himself.

We know his health suffered because of secretly administered one-a-day arsenic tablets. This, of course, would make anyone irritable, and we see his writing ultimately diminish into subway graffiti just before he finally packed it in.

Anne Silver-Conway, M.S., M.A.
Graphologist

1794, Brigadier General

1796, Commander,
Army of Italy

1798, Commander,
Army of Egypt

1803, First Consul

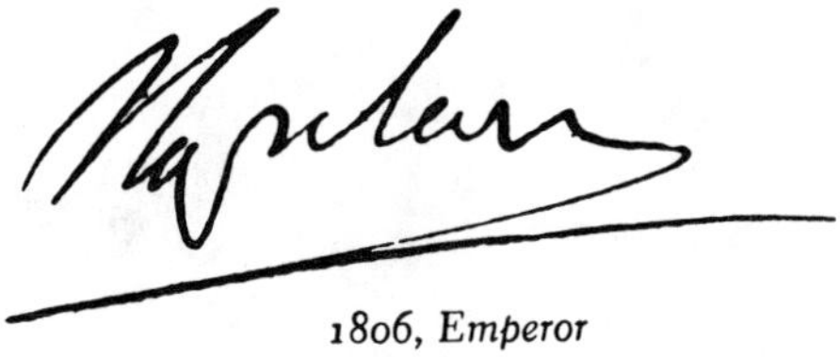

1806, Emperor

1808, Emperor

1810, Emperor

1813, Emperor

Variant signatures of Napoleon I

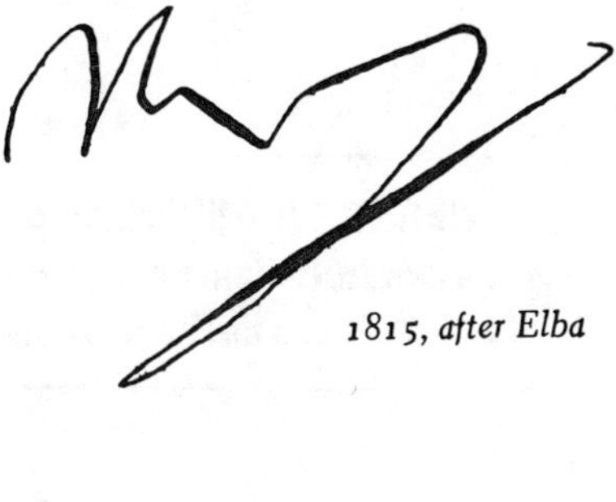

1815, after Elba

WINFRED EUGENE HOLLEY, a Los Angeles man who played Santa Claus at many charity functions over the years, had his name legally changed to **SANTA CLAUS** in 1982.

HOW TO CHANGE YOUR NAME

W hy do people change their names?
The reasons are probably as varied as the names they choose.
Sometimes parents change their minds or realize that their child,
as they get to know him or her better, doesn't fit the original
choice.

A name may be changed because of adoption or other
alteration of the family unit. Merged families and single parent
families are becoming a larger portion of our society and with
such new households come new affiliations.

Adults and teenagers often change their names because they
didn't feel comfortable with them in the first place. In business,
fictitious names are fairly commonplace. Sometimes they are used
to protect the privacy of an individual who doesn't want to be
bothered with work-related issues at home. We are all familiar
with the show business names used to disguise real names that
were too cumbersome, too dull, too ethnic-sounding or even too
funny for the marquees.

There are also those who wish to hide their identities:
criminals, those trying to hide from civil actions and those with
shady pasts.

The two separate bodies of law which relate to names are
common law and statutory or written law.

Common law is the unwritten law of the courts and comes
from a tradition handed down to us from the earliest days.

It is every bit as binding as statutory law. In most states a
person can simply use a new or different name without going
through any legal process as long as there is no fraudulent or
criminal intent. A simple change in spelling (say from JEFFREY
to GEOFFREY) would probably be best accomplished in this
easy way.

As with all legal matters, however, caution is the rule. A legal document may be contested if the name shown differs from the name used by the person. Such important papers as wills, deeds and insurance policies may be disputed if any identity is in question.

Most states make it quite easy to use the statutory method, but regulations vary from state to state. It is best to check with the authorities (usually the County Clerk's office) before proceeding. A petition is usually filed with the court stating the exact name you have chosen and the reasons for the change. Some states require the petition to be published in a local newspaper for a certain period of time (usually once a week for a month). Some states simply grant the name change after the filing, but many require a hearing before a judge. If third parties object to the name change, for whatever reason, the court will hear their objections and then make a decision.

Many states require that the petitioner be a resident and some have substantial time restrictions on residency.

A child's petition must be signed by a parent or guardian and if the child is over a certain age (generally from 11 to 14), the child must also be present to attest that he or she actually wants the change of name.

It is generally believed that the law requires a woman to assume her husband's name, but, in fact, this is merely custom. A woman who chooses not to take her husband's name may simply go on using her maiden name. An announcement of the choice may help alleviate any confusion. Similarly, if a woman or a couple wish to hyphenate the two last names, that can also be done by simply using the new double name.

The value of changing your name can be minimal or vast. Psychologists tell us that people who dislike their names often dislike themselves. Surely, in some cases a new name is like a new lease on life. It costs less than a face lift or a nose job and can make you feel like you are finally yourself, the self you've always felt you were.

Actors often change their names, but not always for the reasons you might suspect. The Screen Actors Guild doesn't allow two actors to have the same name. TIM CONWAY, the wonderful comedian and author, was born TOM CONWAY, but when he joined the Actors Guild they already had a member named TOM CONWAY so the future star of stage and screen became TIM. The TOM CONWAY who was then a member of the S.A.G. was really not TOM CONWAY, either. He was the brother of the great actor, GEORGE SANDERS!!

A fellow by the name of JOHN COHN once legally changed his name to JACK ROY, but he decided, as he's been saying ever since, "If you're going to change your name, CHANGE it!" He is now known to the world as RODNEY DANGERFIELD.

ARNOLD GEORGE DORSEY seems to have learned Mr. Dangerfield's lesson. He changed his name to GERRY DORSEY first, but when his singing career still went nowhere, this Welshman decided to call himself ENGLEBERT HUMPERDINCK.

Even politicians change their names. One presidential hopeful whose name change is thought by many to have hindered his political career is Senator GARY HART, whose real last name was HARTPENCE. Interestingly, three of our United States presidents *have* changed their names and in each case they did it by dropping their first names. GROVER CLEVELAND dropped his first name of STEPHEN. CALVIN COOLIDGE left off his given name, which was JOHN, and WOODROW WILSON was really named THOMAS. What does dropping one's first name have to do with becoming Commander in Chief? Who knows, but it didn't hurt these gentlemen!

Authors don't really have to change their names because they can assume a NOM DE PLUME or PEN NAME:

Samuel Langhorne Clemens = MARK TWAIN

Frederic Dannay *and*
Manfred Bennington Lee = ELLERY QUEEN

Charles Ludwidge Dodgson = LEWIS CARROLL

Mary Ann Evans = GEORGE ELIOT

Salvatore A. Lombino = HUNT COLLINS
EVAN HUNTER
ED McBAIN
RICHARD MARSTEN

Henry Wadsworth Longfellow = JOSHUA COFFIN
HANS HAMMERGAFFERSTEIN

Frank Morrison = MICKEY SPILLANE

William Sidney Porter = O. HENRY

Hector Hugh Munro = SAKI

Nathaniel Wallenstein Weinstein = NATHANIEL WEST

Singers and musicians change their names just as other public figures do.

Frank Castelluccio = FRANKIE VALLI

Henry John Deutschendorf, Jr. = JOHN DENVER

Norma Egstrom = PEGGY LEE

Eleanora Fagan = BILLIE HOLIDAY

Vincent Damon Furnier = ALICE COOPER

Stevland Morris = STEVIE WONDER

Robert Zimmerman = BOB DYLAN

These days few actors change their names for the sake of the marquee. CHARLES BRONSON is a notable exception. His name used to be CHARLES BUCHINSKY. Some of the names that sound as if they must have been made up for stardom's sake, like CHEVY CHASE and RIP TORN, turn out to be real. For many years when the Hollywood star system was at its height, actors and actresses had their names changed routinely. Sometimes it is pretty obvious why. Can you picture a meteoric rise to stardom for EUNICE QUEDENS or ISSUR DANIELOVITCH DEMSKY? Those two turned into EVE ARDEN and KIRK DOUGLAS!! Here are some other name changes, Hollywood style:

Rosita Dolores Alverio = RITA MORENO

Frederic Austerlitz = FRED ASTAIRE

Norma Jean Baker = MARILYN MONROE

James Baumgarner = JAMES GARNER

Nathan Birnbaum = GEORGE BURNS

Reginald Cary = REX HARRISON

Margarita Casino = RITA HAYWORTH

Stefania Federkiewcz = STEPHANIE POWERS

Roy Fitzgerald = ROCK HUDSON

Joyce Penelope Frankenburg = JANE SEYMOUR

John Freund = JOHN FORSYTHE

Arthur Gelien = TAB HUNTER

Edna Rae Gillooly = ELLEN BURSTYN

Emanuel Goldenberg = EDWARD G. ROBINSON

Michael James Vijencio Gubitosi = ROBERT BLAKE

Frances Gumm = JUDY GARLAND

Natasha Gurdin = NATALIE WOOD

Diane Hall = DIANE KEATON

Annemarie Italiano = ANNE BANCROFT

Carol Diahann Johnson = DIAHANN CARROLL

Melvin Kaminsky = MEL BROOKS

Allen Stewart Konigsberg = WOODY ALLEN

Cherilynn LaPierre = CHER

Archibald Leach = CARY GRANT

Lucille Le Sueur = JOAN CRAWFORD

Patsy McClenny = MORGAN FAIRCHILD

Maurice Micklewhite = MICHAEL CAINE

Joan Molinsky = JOAN RIVERS

Krekor Ohanian = MIKE CONNORS

Michael Orowitz = MICHAEL LANDON

Betty Joan Perski = LAUREN BACALL

Michael Igor Peschkowsky = MIKE NICHOLS

William Henry Pratt = BORIS KARLOFF

Shirley Schrift = SHELLEY WINTERS

Bernie Schwartz = TONY CURTIS

Sofia Villiani Scicolone = SOPHIA LOREN

Frances Octavia Smith = DALE EVANS

Raquel Tejada = RAQUEL WELCH

Here are a few assorted name changes from the worlds of sports, fashion, journalism and even psychology:

Ferdinand Lewis Alcindor = KAREEM ABDUL-JABBAR

Roy Halston Frowick = HALSTON

Margaret Hookham = DAME MARGOT FONTEYN

Leslie Hornby = TWIGGY

Harold Caspar Frederick Kaplan = CARLTON FREDERICKS

Esther "Eppie" Pauline Friedman Lederer = ANN LANDERS

Edson Arantes Do Nascimento = PELE

Pauline "Popo" Esther Friedman Phillips = ABIGAIL

VAN BUREN

"DEAR ABBY"

Jack Rosenberg = WERNER ERHARD

With a name like yours, you might be any shape, almost.

Through the Looking Glass
Lewis Carroll

One Plus One
Equals You
NUMEROLOGY
AND
YOUR NAME

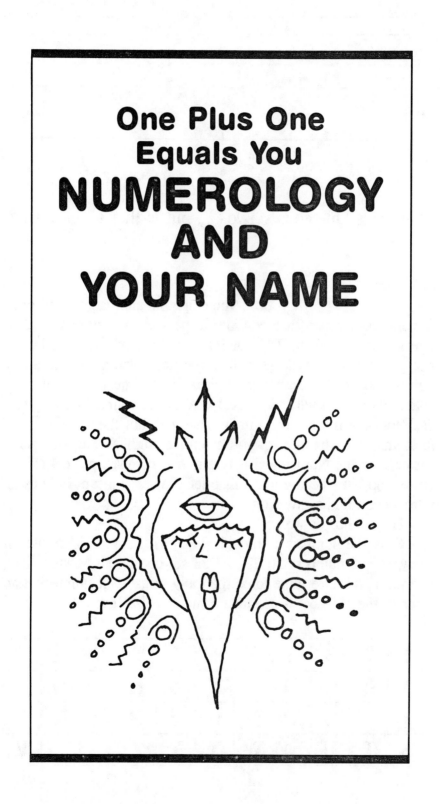

One plus One equals Two ... but is that all it equals?

Numerologists are practitioners of an ancient craft, which they consider to be a science, started by the Greek mathematician, PYTHAGORAS. They believe that the time and place of your birth, as well as the name you are given, are not matters of chance, but of choice. These indicators can be analyzed and can tell you a great deal about yourself and your life. Not only is your given name analyzed, but the various nicknames and diminutives you acquire along life's way are also subjects for the Numerologist. It is a very complex process for those who truly believe and this brief chapter is meant only as an introduction and a diversion.

Here is how it works:

Only the numbers 1 through 9 and 11, 22 and 33 are used in analysis. The numbers 11, 22 and 33 are considered Master Numbers and have more force than any single digit numbers. Each letter of the alphabet is assigned a number like this:

1	2	3	4	5	6	7	8	9	11	22
A	B	C	D	E	F	G	H	I		
J		L	M	N	O	P	Q	R	K	
S	T	U		W	X	Y	Z			V

To analyze your name, first assign each letter with its appropriate number and than add them all together. Next, do the same for all the vowels and then for all the consonants. Now you have a three digit number and can consider the import of each digit.

Since no double digit number can be considered unless it is one of the three Master Numbers, you will need to add the two digits of any double digit number together to come up with a single digit number ($15 = 1 + 5 = 6$). Use that single digit result in your analysis. Here are some samples to show you how it works.

L	A	U	R	A				
3	1	3	9	1	=	17 (1+7=8)	*8*	name
	1	3		1	=		*5*	vowels
3			9		=	12 (1+2=3)	*3*	consonants

LAURA is an 8 - 5 - 3

J	A	M	E	S				
1	1	4	5	1	=	12 (1+2=3)	*3*	name
	1		5		=		*6*	vowels
1		4		1	=		*6*	consonants

JAMES is a 3 - 6 - 6

Each number exhibits specific characteristics, but in general the even numbers indicate a more active and participatory personality and the odd numbers show one who leans more toward introspection. All numbers are said to have both positive and negative "vibrations" and a person who studies Numerology and reads the numbers could write extensively about you and your name. Here is a brief breakdown of the positive and negative aspects of each number.

1 + Independence, initiative and leadership
  − Selfish, weak and tyrannical

2 + Loving, helpful and outgoing
  − Timid, moody and cynical

3 + Creative, talkative and upbeat
  − Vain, prideful and inconsiderate

4 + Pragmatic, dependable and hard-working
  − Boring, small-minded and strict

5 + Flexible, adventurous and good character judge
  − Overly self-indulgent, irresponsible and forgetful

6   +   Domestic, nurturing and just
       −   Depressed, mistrustful and interfering

7   +   Intelligent, scholarly and self-confident
       −   Snobbish, rude and misanthropic

8   +   Ambitious, zealous and discriminating
       −   Anxiety-ridden, materialistic and nasty-tempered

9   +   Just, compassionate and selfless
       −   Egocentric, vague and crass

11   +   Intuitive, powerful and idealistic
       −   Adrift, stingy and over-zealous

22   +   Analytical, adventurous and wise
       −   Criminal, full of hot air and unsure of himself

33   +   Spiritual, patient and extremely able in any area
       −   Very mistrustful, moody and self-destructive

You may never become a true believer in Numerology, but at the least it can provide an amusing party game.

WHAT'S IN A NICKNAME?

Well-known baseball manager Tommy Lasorda believes in the power of the nickname. He started calling his well-educated, soft-spoken pitcher Orel Hershiser BULLDOG, hoping to inspire him to pitch with a ferocity not native to his personality.

PUT
YOUR NAME
TO WORK
Best Names
For Chosen
Professions
And
Occupations

RUSSELL? IVAN? JANET? CRAIG?

EDWARD? DONALD?

ELLEN?

$\mathcal{C}$ertain names seem better suited to some professions than others. For instance, in 1980 Standard and Poors directory of corporate officers listed *eight* ROBERT ANDERSONs as either president or chairman of major American companies. This name far outpaced any other common name in the listings. Here are some of the most popular names for a variety of careers. If you want a head start in any of these fields of endeavor, choose one of the following first names.

MASCULINE CAREER NAMES

DOCTOR
David
William
Allan
Sheldon

CORPORATE PRESIDENT
Robert
John
Henry
Junior

LANDLORD
Ebenezer
Slade
Sharkey

LAWYER
Michael
Stephen
Edward
William

WRITER
William
Robert
John

COMEDY WRITER
Mel
Mel
Mel

FEMININE CAREER NAMES

DOCTOR
Irene

Anne

Margaret

ACCOUNTANT
Diane

Patricia

Elizabeth

ROMANCE WRITER
Barbara

Anne

Patricia

PUBLISHING EXECUTIVE
Katherine

Barbara

Judith

LAWYER
Elizabeth

Katherine

Judith

MARTYR
Bernadette

Joan

Mother

LETTER PERFECT
ANAGRAMS AND YOUR NAME

Have you ever noticed the letters of your name are also the letters of another word, a word that may be funny or somehow oddly appropriate? ANAGRAMS may not always spring to mind when you look at a word or name, but they can have either a comforting or a disquieting subconscious effect upon the reader. Some of the name anagrams that jumped off the page at us as we compiled this book made us laugh and some of them made us wince!

BASIL—Bails	LEE—Eel
BRIAN—Brain	LIN—Nil
CEIL—Lice	LISA—Sail
CHESTER—Retches	LOIS—Soil
CLARE—Clear	NAOMI—I Moan
DEAN—Dane	NEIL—Line
DON—Nod	NEVA—Vane
EDGAR—Raged	NICO—Coin
ERIC—Rice	PAM—Map
EVAN—Vane	RENA—Near
GARY—Gray	THOM—Moth
KAY—Yak	TOD—Dot
LANA—Anal	VERA—Rave

HISTORICAL ORIGINS AND DEFINITIONS OF NAMES

N̶ames in America, like our language itself, evolved from the two language groups known as Indo-European and Afro-Asian. The Indo-European languages break down like this:

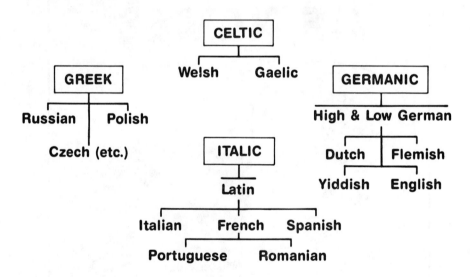

From the Afro-Asian group we get Hebrew, Persian and the Aramaic languages. Some people believe that Hebrew names have a link to other Indo-European names but this is generally not an accepted theory. The Hebrew languages grew up independently.

Briefly, the various influences on our modern language, and hence on our modern names, occurred chronologically like this: The Celts invaded England in 1000 B.C. from lower Germany. Other Celts were driven to settle in England in 55 B.C. because Caesar and the Romans were attacking them. They brought their

language and it evolved into Welsh and Irish Gaelic and Scottish. The Celts came under Roman rule in England shortly after this time and the Romans remained in power for almost 500 years. In 410 A.D. when the Romans left to defend Italy the Anglo-Saxon period first began. Old English was spoken in England for the next 600 years. It is essentially a Low German tongue and was spoken by the Angles, Saxons and Jutes who arrived from the Continent around 500 A.D. Low German and Anglo-Saxon were not the languages of aristocrats, but were considered rather vulgar and low.

The Norsemen, principally the Danes, waged war on England and finally took power in 1017. The Danish influence on English is the result of this association. In 1066 the Norman invasion brought a strong German influence which also carried with it a tradition of speaking French among the upper classes. French was the dominant language at court and among the literate English for quite some time and by the time English reemerged as a language for use in literature it had gained a great deal from French. The dominance of English began sometime around the 12th century.

What follows is a catalogue of given names listed by their origin and with their historical meanings.

FEMININE NAMES OF OLD AND MIDDLE ENGLISH

ADA Prosperous, happy.

ADELINE Noble, kind.

ALBERTA Noble, strength.

ALDITH Old in battle.

ALDORA Noble birth.

ALEXA Protector of men.

ALFREDA Little elf.

ALICE Of noble birth.

ALICIA Truth, noble.

ALISON Son of Alice.

ALVINA Noble, friend.

ALYS Noble birth.

ANNE Gracious.

ANNICE Gracious.

ARDITH Prosperous, happy.

ARLISS To pledge, oath.

ARLYNN To pledge, oath.

ASHLEY Ash tree meadow.

AUDRA Noble, strength.

AUDREY Noble, strength.

AVERELL April born.

AVERY Elf ruler.

AVIS Refuge in battle.

BAILEY Fortification.

BEATRIX A blessing.

BEVERLY Beaver's mother.

BILLIE Strong willed, resolute.

BIRD Like a bird.

BLAZE Aflame.

BLISSE Joyous.

BLOSSOM A flower.

BLYTHE Joyous.

BREE A broth, soup.

BRENDA Firebrand.

BRETT From Brittany.

BROOKE From a brook.

BROWN Brown colored.

BRYDNE Strong, lofty.

BRYNN/BRYNNA Strong, valiant.

BUNNY Small rabbit.

CALLAN To shriek.

CARLA Strong, womanly.

CARLINE Strong, womanly.

CASEY Strong, valorous.

CHANNING Knowing, wise.

CHELSEA A port of ships.

CHITA Kitten.

CICELY Blind one.

CLEVA From a cliff.

CLOVER Clover blossom.

COLE Black farm.

CORLISS Cheerful, good-hearted.

COURTNEY From court.

CYD A public hill.

CYR A kernel of corn.

DALE Of the valley.

DARA Courageous, daring.

DARLA Loved one.

DARYL Loved one.

DAWN Sunrise.

DEVON/DEVONA An English shire.

DILLIAN/DILLIANA An idol.

EARLENE Noble birth.

EARTHA Of the earth.

EASTER Easter born.

EDITH Rich, gift.

EDLYN Small, noble.

EDREA Prosperous.

EDWINA Prosperous friend.

EGBERTA Noble, strength.

ELFREDA Elf ruler.

ELLA Light, elf.

ELLEN Light.

ELMIRA Noble, famous.

ELVA Elf ruler.

ELVINA Little elf ruler.

ETHEL Noble birth.

FAITH   Fidelity.

FARRAH   Pleasant one.

FAWN   Friendly one.

FERN   A soft plant.

FILOMENA   Lover of spring.

FORSYTHIA   Yellow spring
flower.

GAIL   Happy, gay.

GAINELL   To profit.

GARNET   Red gem.

GENEVIEVE   White wave.

GEORGIANA   Farmer.

GEORGINA   Farmer.

GILDA   Gold covered.

GISELLE   Bright, pledge.

GLEANA   Small glen.

GOLDIE   Golden.

HADLEY   Heath.

HALE   Health, hero.

HAPPY   Merry, joyous.

HARLEY   Planted meadow.

HARTE   A deer.

HAYLEY   Hero.

HAZEL   Hazelnut.

HEATHER   Heather plant.

HOLLACE/HOLLIS   Hero.

HOLLY   Holly tree.

HONEY   Sweet one.

HOPE   Hope.

IDA   Prosperous.

IVY   Vine.

JAIME   The supplanter.

KELLY   Warrior, ship.

KENDALL   Clean river.

KENDRA   Knowledgeable.

KENNA   Knowledgeable.

KIM Ruler.

KIMBERLY Castle on a meadow.

KIRBY Church.

LANA Light, torch.

LEALA Legal, loyal.

LEANA Lovely meadow.

LEE Meadow.

LEIGH Meadow.

LELAND Meadow land.

LEVINA Bright, shining one.

LINDSAY Camp near a stream.

LOGAN A felled tree.

LOLA Alluring one.

LONDON Fortress of the moon.

LORNA Solitary, alone.

LUELLA Elf, sprite.

LYNNE Waterfall.

MAIDA Maiden.

MAISIE Meadow, field.

MARDELL Valley of lakes.

MARIGOLD The flower.

MAY Daisy, the month.

MELVA/MELBA Friend, mill worker.

MERCY Compassion.

MERRY Gay, joyous.

MILDRED Gentle counselor.

MISTY Obscured, fogged.

NARA Near by.

NEDDA A retreat.

NEDRA Under the earth.

NELDA Elder tree cottage.

NOLA Famous.

NORRIS House of a northerner.

ONA/OONA From the river.

PAIGE Small child.

PERNELL A rock.

PERRY Pear tree.

PIPER   Pipe player.

QUANDA/QUENDA
Companion, friend.

QUEENIE   Queen.

QUENBY   Castle of the queen.

QUINN   Queen.

RAE   Female deer.

RANDALL   Shield, protector.

RANDY   Shield, protector.

RAYMONDA   Protector.

READE   Red-haired.

ROBERTA   Bright fame.

ROBIN   Robin bird.

ROSEMARY   Rose of Mary.

ROWENA   Well-known, famous.

RULA   Ruler.

SCARLETT   Red.

SELBY   Sheltered home.

SHELBY   Sheltered home.

SHELLEY   High meadow.

SHIRLEY   Bright meadow.

SIBLEY   Sister, sibling.

SIDNEY   From St. Denis.

SPENCER   Steward, dispenser.

STOCKARD   Wooden enclosure.

STUART   Caretaker.

SUMMER   Summer.

SUNNY   Bright, happy.

SYDELL   From St. Denis.

TATE/TATUM   Cheerful one.

THORNE   Thorny place.

TRACEY   Brave, valorous.

TRILBY   Soft hat.

TUESDAY Tuesday born.

TWYLA Woven double thread.

TYBALLA Holy place.

TYNE A river.

VANA High, lofty.

VELVET Velvet fabric.

WALLIS Wales, a fort.

WANDA Slender young tree.

WENDY White, pale.

WESLEY Western meadow.

WHITNEY White island.

WILHELMINA Determined protector.

WILLOW Willow tree, free.

WILONA Desired one.

WINSLOW Victory on a hill.

WINTER Winter.

WORTH Estate.

WYNDHAM Enclosure on a path.

YETTA Ruler of home.

FEMININE NAMES OF FRENCH ORIGIN

ADELLE Noble, kind.

ADOREE Adorable one.

ADRIENNA Dark one.

ANNETTE Gracious.

ANTOINETTE Priceless.

AURELIE Golden.

BELLE Lovely one.

BERNADINE Bold as a bear.

BLANCHE White, pale.

BONNIE Pretty one.

BRIGITTE Resolute, strong.

CARLOTTA Strong, womanly.

CAROLINE Strong, womanly.

CHARLOTTE Strong, womanly.

CHER/CHERIE Dear one.

CHERYL Strong, womanly.

CLAIRE Bright, clear.

CORINNE Maiden.

COSETTE Victorious.

DARCY Dark one.

DARLENE Little darling.

DARRELL Little dear one.

DELLA Noble birth.

DENISE From Dionysius.

DESIREE Desired one.

DIXIE Tenth child.

DOMINIQUE Of God.

DORE Golden.

EGLANTINE Woodbine rose.

ELAINE Light.

ELISE God's oath.

ELISSA   God's oath.

ELITA   Chosen one.

ELOISE   Warrior woman.

ESTELLE   A star.

FAWN   Young deer.

FAY   Elf.

FERNANDE   Bold, courageous.

FLEUR   Flower.

FONDA   To melt.

FRANCINE   Free one.

FRANCOISE   Free, French.

GABRIELLE   God is my strength.

GARLAND   Wreath of flowers.

GARNER   Martial, war-like.

GAY   Happy one.

GERALDINE   Mighty one.

GERMAINE   From Germany, a bud.

HARRIET   Home ruler.

HELOISE   Warrior woman.

HENRIETTE   Home ruler.

ILA   Island dweller.

ISABEAU   Consecrated of God.

JACQUELINE   Supplanter.

JANET   God is gracious.

JEAN/JEANNE/JEANNETTE   God is gracious.

JEWEL   Precious gem.

JOANNA   God is gracious.

JOLIE   Pretty one.

JOSCELINE   Merry one.

JOSEPHINE   He shall increase.

JULIENNE/JULIET   Soft-haired.

LAVERNE   Spring-like.

LEONORE   Light.

LIANA   Climbing vine.

LILA   Lily flower.

LINETTE Flaxen.

LORRAINE From Lorraine.

LOUISE Warrior woman.

MARCELLA Martial, war-like.

MARGOT A pearl.

MARGUERITE A pearl.

MARIE/MARIETTA Bitterness, sorrow.

MARILYN Bitterness, sorrow.

MARION Bitterness, sorrow.

MARJORIE A pearl.

MARLENE From Magdala.

MAUDE Mighty one.

MAVIS Songbird.

MERLE Black bird.

MYRA Song.

NADINE Hope

NOEL Christmas born.

ORALIE Golden.

OTTILIE Small, wealthy.

PATIENCE Enduring, awaiting.

PRUNELLA Plum colored.

RENEE Reborn.

RITA A pearl.

RIVA Riverbank.

ROCHELLE Little rock.

SOFIE Wisdom.

STEPHANE Crowned one.

SYDNEY St. Denis.

THERESE Reaper.

VALARIE To be strong.

YVETTE The archer.

YVONNE The archer.

FEMININE NAMES OF GERMAN ORIGIN

ADELAIDE   Noble, kind.

ALDA   Wise, rich.

ALFONSINE   Noble, prepared.

AMELIA   Hard worker.

ARNOLDA   Strong as an eagle.

BATHILDA   Commanding woman.

BERTHA   Shining, bright.

BRUNHILDA   Warrior woman.

CHRISTIANA   Christian.

CLOTILDA   Battle woman.

CONRADINE   Bold counselor.

DOROTHEA   Gift of God.

DRUELLA   Elf.

EDELA   Noble one.

ELSA   Noble birth.

EMMA   Nurse, caretaker.

ERNESTINE   Sincere, resolute.

ETTA   Small.

FERNANDA   Bold, adventurer.

FREDERICA   Peaceful ruler.

FRIEDA   Peaceful one.

GALIENA   Lofty one.

GERTRUDE   Warrior woman.

GILBERTA   Trusted one.

GRETA   A pearl.

GRETCHEN   A pearl.

GRISELDA   Warrior woman.

HEDDA Strife.

HEIDI A star.

HILDEGARDE A fortress.

HOLDA Concealed, hidden.

HUBERTA Brilliant mind.

ISA Strong-willed.

JARVIA Sharp spear.

KARLA Strong, womanly.

KARLOTTE Strong, womanly.

KATARINA Pure, unsullied.

KLARA Bright, illustrious.

LEOTA Woman of the people.

LORELEI Alluring one.

LUDOVIKA Famous warrior.

LURLINE Siren, singer.

MADLEN From Magdala.

MARELDA Famous warrior.

MARTHE Lady.

MATHILDE Warrior woman.

MILLICENT Industrious.

NORBERTA Brilliant heroine.

NORDICA Northerner.

ORDELLA Elf-spear.

RODERICA Famous ruler.

ROLANDA From famous land.

ROSAMOND Famous guardian.

SIGFREDA Victorious.

SOLVIG Victorious.

THEOBALDA Of the people.

TRUDA Loved one.

UDA Prosperous, happy.

ULA Estate owner.

ULRICA Ruler.

VALA Chosen one.

VERENA Defender.

WALDA Ruler.

WINIFRED Peaceful friend.

ZELDA Warrior woman.

MERCEDES

ACADIA Thorny tree.

ADENA Noble, adorned.

AGATHA Good, kind.

AGNES Pure.

ALCINA Intelligent, willful.

ALEXANDRA Helper of humankind.

ALEXIS Helper of humankind.

ALTHEA Healing, wholesome.

ANASTASIA Resurrection.

ANDREA Strong, courageous.

ANGELA Angel, heavenly.

ARETHA The best one.

BERNICE Light bearer.

BERYL A green gem.

CALANDRA Lark.

CALLA Beautiful.

CANDACE Incandescent, white.

CASSANDRA Disbelieved by men.

CATHERINE Pure.

CELANDINE The swallow.

CELIOSA A burning.

CHARISSA Loving.

CHLOE Verdant, youthful.

CHRISTINA Christian.

CLARA Bright.

CLEMENTINE Merciful.

CLEOPATRA Father's fame.

CLIANTHA Flower.

CLYTIE   Beautiful one.

COLETTE   Victorious in battle.

CORA   Maiden.

COSIMA   Harmony of nature.

CYBIL   Soothsayer.

CYNTHIA   Of the moon.

CYRENA   From Cyrene.

DACIA   From Dacia.

DAPHNE   Laurel tree.

DARIA   Wealthy, queen.

DELFINE   Delphinium flower.

DELIA   From Delos.

DEMETRIA Of the fertility goddess.

DESDEMONA   Ill-fated.

DIONNE   Divine queen.

DOLLY   Gift of God.

DORA   Gift.

DORIS   From the sea.

DOROTHY   Gift of God.

ECHO   Echoing sound.

EDE   Generation.

ELEANOR   Light.

ELECTRA   Shining brightly.

ELYSIA   Blissful.

EUGENIA   Well-born.

EUNICE   Happy victory.

EVANGELINE   Bringer of good news.

HAIDEE   Honest.

HALLIE   Sea thoughts.

HELEN   Light.

HERMIONE   Earthly, mortal.

HYACINTH   Flower.

IANTHA   Violet-colored.

ILLANA   From Ilion.

IOLANTHE   Purple flower.

IRENE   Peace.

IRIS   Rainbow.

KALIKA   Rosebud.

KATE   Pure, unsullied.

KATHERINE   Pure, unsullied.

KORA   Maiden.

LACEY   Cheerful one.

LARISSA Cheerful one.

LOIS Good, desirable.

LOTUS Flower.

LYDIA From Lydia.

LYSANDRA To free.

MADELINE From Magdala, high tower.

MAGDA From Magdala, high tower.

MALINDA Gentle one.

MALVA Soft, slender.

MARGARET A pearl.

MEGAN Great one.

MELANIE Dark appearance.

MELBA Soft, slender.

MELINDA Dark, beautiful.

MELISSA A bee.

MELODY A song.

MONA Solitary, alone.

MYRNA Myrrh.

MYRTLE Myrtle tree.

NERISSA From the sea.

NICOLE People's victory.

NYSSA Beginning.

ODESSA Odyssey, long trip.

OLYMPIA Goddess.

OPHELIA Serpent.

PAMELA Honey, sweet.

PANDORA Gifted one.

PENELOPE Weaver.

PHEDRA Bright one.

PHILLIPA Horse lover.

PHOEBE Shining light.

PHYLLIS Leaf.

RHEA A stream.

RHETA Orator.

RHODA Flower, from Rhodes.

ROSE Flower.

SAPPHIRE Blue gem.

SELENA Moon.

SIBYL Prophetess.

SIRENA A siren, singing maiden.

SOPHIA Wisdom.

STACY Resurrection, spring.

STEPHANIE Crowned one.

SYNA Together, side by side.

TALIA Blooming.

TERESA Reaper.

TESSA Fourth child.

THADDEA Courageous.

THALIA Blooming.

THEA Healing, wholesome.

THELMA Infant, young one.

THEODORA Gift of God.

THEONE God's name.

THYRA Shield bearer.

TIMOTHEA Honors God.

TITANIA Giant.

TOBY God is good.

VANESSA Butterfly.

VILLETTE Country estate.

VOLETA Flowering veil.

XANTHE Yellow colored.

XENIA A guest, stranger.

YOLANDA Violet colored.

ZELIA Zeal, fervor.

ZENOBIA A sign, symbol.

ZETA The letter "Z".

ZOE Life.

FEMININE NAMES OF HEBREW ORIGIN

ABIGAIL Father of joy.

ABRA Mother of multitudes.

ADINA Voluptuous.

ANNE Graceful.

ARDITH Meadow of blossoms.

ARIEL Lioness of God.

BETH/BETSY/BETTE
God's oath.

BEULAH Married one.

DANIELLE God is my judge.

DAVIDA Beloved.

DEBORAH A bee.

DENA Vindicated.

DINAH Judgment.

EDEN Delight, adornment.

EDNA Delight, desired.

ELIZABETH God's oath.

EMMANUELLE God is with us.

EVE Life.

GABRIELLA Person of God.

HANNAH Graceful.

ILANA Big tree.

JANE God is gracious.

JEMIMA Dove.

JESSICA Wealthy, happy.

JETHRA Riches, abundance.

JOAN God is gracious.

JOSEPHINE He shall add.

JUDITH From Judah.

LEAH Weary.

LIBBY/LISA/LIZA God's oath.

MAHALIA Affection.

MARA Bitterness, sorrow.

MICHELLE Who is like God?

MIRIAM Bitterness, sorrow.

MITZI Bitterness, sorrow.

NANCY Gracious.

NAOMI Pleasant.

NATHANIA Gift of God.

NITA Graceful.

ODELIA I praise God.

RACHEL Female sheep.

RAPHAELA God has healed.

REBECCA Bound.

ROCHELLE Female sheep.

RUTH Friend of beauty.

SABRINA Thorny cactus.

SADA Princess.

SADIE Princess.

SALLY Princess.

SALOME Peace.

SAMARA Ruled by God.

SARAH Princess.

SEMIRA Heaven's height.

SERAPHINA Ardent one.

SHARON A plain.

SIMONA One who hears.

SUSAN Lily flower.

TAMARA Palm tree.

TAMMY Perfect one.

TOBY God is good.

VIDA Beloved one.

YAFFA Beautiful.

YEDIDAH Friend, beloved.

YEIRA Light.

YIGALA God will redeem.

YONAH A dove.

YENTAL

ZAKA Pure, clear.

ZEHARA Shining, light.

ZEHIRA Guarded one.

ZEPHIRA Morning.

ZETA Olive tree.

ZEVIDA A gift.

ZILLAH Shade, cool place.

ZIMRA Song of praise.

ZIPPORAH A bird.

ZIRA Gathering place.

FEMININE NAMES OF IRISH ORIGIN

AIDAN Little fire.

AILEEN Light carrier.

ALANNA Beautiful, fair.

ARLEEN/ARLEN Pledge, oath.

BARRIE Spear, pointed.

BLAINE Thin, lean one.

BLAIR From the plain.

BRENNA Raven haired.

BRETT From Brittany.

BRIANNA/BRIANNE Strong.

BRIDGET Resolute, strong.

CAITLIN Pure, unsullied.

CALEY Thin, lean one.

CARA Friend.

CARRICK Rocky land.

CASEY Brave one.

CASSIDY Clever, quick one.

COLEEN A girl.

COREY Near a pool.

DARBY Free woman.

DARON Great one.

DERRY Red-haired.

DIERDRE Sorrows.

DOREEN Sullen one.

DUANA Little dark one.

EDANA Little fiery one.

EILEEN Light.

ERIN Peace, Irish.

FIONA Fair, lovely.

FIONNULA Fair, lovely.

FLANNA Red-haired.

GAYNOR Blond man's child.

GENA Queen.

GLENDA From the valley.

ITA Thirst.

KATHLEEN Pure, unsullied.

KEELY Beautiful.

KELLY Warrior woman.

KERRY Dark one.

MACKENZIE Son of a wise ruler.

MALVINA Chief.

MAUREEN Little Mary.

MEARA Happiness, mirth.

MOIRA Bitterness, sorrow.

MOLLY Bitterness, sorrow.

MURIEL Of the sea.

NEALA Champion.

NORA/NOREEN Respect.

ODELA Melody, song.

QUINLAN Strong one.

RHONDA Powerful river.

SHANNA God is gracious.

SHANNON God is gracious.

SHEENA God is gracious.

SHEILA Maiden, girl.

TARA Rocky cliff.

TRACEY Battler.

TULLIA Peaceful.

VEVAY White wave.

VEVILA Harmonious one.

FEMININE NAMES OF ITALIAN ORIGIN

AIDA   Prosperous, happy.

ALESSANDRA   Protector of man.

ALESSIO   Protector of man.

ANTONIA   Flourishing.

BAMBALINA   Child-like.

BENADETTA   Blessed one.

BIANCA   White, pale.

CAMEO   Carving.

CARLITA   Strong, womanly.

CARLOTTA   Strong, womanly.

CARMINA   Vineyard of the Lord.

CAROLINA   Strong, womanly.

CHARITO   Grace, beauty.

DANIELA   God is my judge.

DANITA   Lasting, durable.

DONNA   Woman, lady.

EDA   Poetry.

ELISABETTA   God's oath.

ENRICHETTA   Home ruler.

FRANSESCA   Free woman.

GELSEY   A flower.

GRAZIA   Grace.

LEONARDA   Strong as a lion.

LIA   Weary, tired.

LISETTINA   God's oath.

LUISA   Famous in battle.

MARIA   Bitterness, sorrow.

MARIETTA   Of Mary.

MIA   My own.

PAGE   Attendant.

POALINA   Small one.

RAFFAELLA   God has healed.

RICARDA   Powerful, rich ruler.

ROMA   Daughter of Mars.

ROMY   Daughter of Mars.

ROSA   The rose.

VALENTINA   Healthy, strong.

VALONIA   An acorn.

ZOLA   Of earth.

FEMININE NAMES OF LATIN ORIGIN

ADORA   Adorable one.

ADRIA   Dark one.

ALMA   Soul.

AMANDA   Worthy of love.

AMY   Beloved.

APRIL   To open.

ARABELLA   Beautiful, holy place.

ARDEN   To burn, ardent.

ARIANA   Holy one.

AUGUSTA   Majestic one.

AURELIA   Golden.

AURORA   Dawn.

AUSTIN   Majestic.

AVA   Bird.

BARBARA   Stranger, guest.

BEATA   Blessed one.

BEATRICE   Bringer of joy.

BELINDA   Beautiful one.

BRITTANY   Of England.

CAMILLE   Unblemished virgin.

CANDIDA   Bright white.

CARI   Strong.

CAROL   Strong, womanly.

CECILIA   Blind.

CEIL   Blind.

CELESTE   Heavenly.

CHARITY   Sisterly love.

CHARMAINE   Singer.

CLARA   Bright, shining one.

CLARISSA   Most shining one.

CLAUDIA   Lame one.

CLEMENTIA   Calm, merciful.

CLORINDA   Beautiful.

CONSTANCE   Constant, consistent.

CORNELIA   Color of horn.

CRYSTAL   Clear, glass.

CYRELLA   Lordly.

DEANNA   Divine.

DELICIA   Delightful.

DELILAH   Gentle.

DIANA/DIANE   Divine.

DOCILA   Calm, quiet.

DULCIE   Sweet.

EMILIA   Flattering.

EMILY   Industrious.

EUSTACIA   Tranquil, abundant.

FALINE   Cat-like.

FELICE   Happy one.

FIDELITY   Faithful.

FLORA   Flower.

FLORENCE   Blooming.

FLORIDA   Blooming.

FORTUNA   Fate.

FRANCES   Free one.

GEORGIA   Farmer.

GILLIAN   Young child.

GINGER   Ginger spice, flower.

GLORIA   Glory.

GRACE   Grace of God.

HILARY   Cheerful.

HONORIA   Honorable.

HORTENSE   Gardener.

IMOGENE   A likeness.

IRMA   Noble.

ISADORA   Gift of Isis.

JILL   Young child.

JINX   Charm, spell.

JOCELYN   Happy one.

JOY   Joy.

JOYCE   Joyous.

JULIA/JULIE   Youthful.

JUNE   The month of June.

JUSTINE   Just, fair.

LAURA Laurel crown.

LAVINA Purified.

LEONA Lion.

LETITIA Joy.

LILLIAN Lily flower.

LILY Lily flower.

LORETTA Laurel crown.

LUCILLE Light.

LUCRETIA Riches, reward.

LUCY Light.

MABEL Lovable.

MAGNOLIA Magnolia flower or tree.

MARANDA Admirable, extraordinary.

MARCIA/MARCIE Martial, war-like.

MARINA Of the sea.

MARTINA/MARTINE Martial, war-like.

MARY Bitterness, sorrow.

MAXINE Greatest one.

MAY Great one.

MIRA Wonderful.

MIRANDA Admirable, extraordinary.

MONICA Advisor, trusted.

NATALIE Christmas born.

NOLA Small bell.

NORMA Peaceful one.

NYDIA From the nest.

OCTAVIA Eighth child.

OLIVE/OLIVIA Olive tree.

ONA/OONA Unity.

ONDINE Small wave.

ORALIA Golden.

ORIANA Golden dawn.

PATRICIA Noble birth, patrician.

PAULA/PAULINE Small one.

PEARL Pearl.

PERDITA Lost one.

PERSIS Persian.

PETULA Seeker.

PLACIDA Peaceful one.

POLLY Small one.

PORTIA Offering.

PRISCILLA Ancient one.

PRUDENCE Intelligence.

QUINN Fifth child.

REGINA Queen.

RENATA Born again.

REVA Strength regained.

RISA Laughter.

ROSEMARY Rosemary herb.

RUBY Red gem.

SABINA Woman from Sabin.

SABRINA From the boundary.

SIDRA Starry, glittering.

SIGNA Signer.

STELLA A star.

SYLVIA Forest, sylvan.

TANSY Persistent.

TERTIA Third child.

TIFFANY The Trinity.

TITA Honored.

TRISHA Patrician.

TRISTA Melancholy.

UNDINE A wave.

URSULA Little bear.

VALENTINA Healthy, strong.

VERA Truth.

VERNA Like spring, truth.

VERONICA Truth.

VICTORIA Victorious.

VIOLET Violet flower.

VIRGINIA Pure, virgin.

VITA Life.

VIVIAN Alive.

ZINNIA Zinnia flower.

FEMININE NAMES OF NORSE AND SCANDINAVIAN ORIGIN

ALVA Wise one.

ANDRA A breath.

ASTRA/ASTRID Divine strength.

BRYNJA Strong one.

DAGMAR Bright, sunny day.

DAHLIA From the valley.

DANA From Denmark.

DAVIN Bright, shining one.

DENBY From Denmark.

DISA Lively one.

EDDA Poetry.

ELSEBIN God's oath.

ELVA All wise.

ERICA Eternal ruler.

FREYDA Noble, a goddess.

GERDA Enclosure.

GUDRUN Friend in war.

HALDANA Half Danish.

HARALDA Army leader.

HELSA God's oath.

IDONEA Laborer.

ILSA God's oath.

INGRID Daughter of a hero.

JADA/JADE An old horse.

KAREN Pure, unsullied.

KELDA A fountain, spring.

KELSEY Ship, island.

KIRSTEN Christian.

KRISTEN Christian.

LINNEA Lime tree.

NISSA Brownie, sprite.

NORNA Goddess of fate.

OLGA Holy one.

OTTALIE Wealthy, prosperous.

RAN Mighty power.

RONA Mighty power.

SELMA Protected by God.

SIGRID Victorious.

SONIA Wise one.

SYLVI Forest dweller.

TANGYE Dagger.

THORA Thunderer.

THORDIS The spirit of Thor.

VALDA Mighty ruler.

FEMININE NAMES OF PERSIAN AND ARAMAIC ORIGIN

ALMA Learned.

ALMIRA Princess, exalted one.

ALTAIR A bird.

AMBER Yellowish-brown stone.

AZURA Blue sky.

BETHANY House of poverty.

BIBI Lady.

DARIA Queen.

DICKLA Palm tree.

ESTHER A star.

IDRA Flag, fig tree.

ILLIT The best one.

KALILA Beloved one.

KIRA Sun.

LILAC Lavender color.

LILITH Of the night.

MARTHA Lady.

MURIEL Myrrh.

RAZILI My secret.

ROXANNE Dawn.

SABA Old, aged.

SADIRA A constellation.

SAMANTHA Listener.

SAMIRA Entertainer.

SIMA Treasure.

TAMATH To walk about.

TELI Lamb.

VASHTI Beautiful.

VEGA The falling.

ZADE Lucky one.

ZENA/ZENANA Woman.

FEMININE NAMES OF RUSSIAN ORIGIN

ALENA Light.

ALEXSHA Protector of man.

ANYA Gracious one.

DANICA Morning star.

EKATERINA Pure, unsullied.

FANIA Free one.

GALINA Light.

ILKA Industrious one.

JARA Adored warrior.

KASIMIRA Commanding peace.

KATRINA/KATRINE/ KATRINKA Pure, unsullied.

LUDMILLA Beloved by the people.

MAGDA From Magdala.

MARIKA Sorrow, bitterness.

MARYA Sorrow, bitterness.

NADIA Hope.

NAIDA Hope.

NASTASIA Resurrection.

NATASHA Born Christian.

NEDA Sunday born.

NIKA Victory of the people.

PETRINA A rock.

RADINKA Active, busy one.

TABITHA Gazelle.

TANYA Giant, fairy queen.

TATIANA Giant, fairy queen.

THEODORA Divine gift.

VALESKA Glory.

VANYA God is gracious.

VELIKA Great one.

FEMININE NAMES OF SCOTTISH ORIGIN

AINSLEY Private meadow.

ALAMEDA Poplar tree.

ANNOT Gracious.

CAMERON Bent nose.

CHRISTAL Christian.

DONALDA World ruler.

EDIE Prosperous, happy.

EDINA From Edinburgh.

EIRIC Ruler of home.

ELSPETH God's oath.

GREER Vigilant one.

JANA God is gracious.

JEAN God is gracious.

KYNA Kin, relative.

LESLIE Meadow lands.

LILLIAS Lily flower.

LOGAN From the valley.

MAIRGHREAD A pearl.

MAIRI Bitterness, sorrow.

MOIRE Bitterness, sorrow.

MORAG Princess.

MORBEAL Lovable one.

NAIRNE Alder tree by the river.

PAYTON Patrician, noble.

SEONAID God is gracious.

SILEAS Youthful one.

SINEAD God is gracious.

SIUSAN Lily, graceful.

FEMININE NAMES OF SPANISH ORIGIN

ALEJO Protector of man.

ALTA Tall one.

ANITA Gracious.

BENITA Blessed one.

BLANCA White, pale.

CALIDA Warm, loving.

CARMEN Vineyard of the Lord.

CHIQUITA Little girl.

CLARITA Clear, bright.

CONSUELA Consolation.

CREOLA Dark-skinned.

DANUTA Little noble woman.

DOLORES Sorrows.

ELDORA Gilded one.

ELVIRA Elf-counsel.

ESMERALDA Emerald stone.

ESTRALITA Little star.

EVITA Little life giver.

FELICITE Happiness.

HERMOSA Beautiful.

INEZ Pure, unsullied.

ISABEL Consecrated to God.

JUANA God is gracious.

LINDA Beautiful.

MANUELA God is with us.

MARJORIE A pearl.

MERCEDES Mercies.

NEVA Snow.

NINA Graceful, child.

PALOMA A dove.

PEPITA God will add.

PILAR Water basin.

QUERIDA Beloved, sympathetic.

RAMONA Wise priestess.

RAQUEL Ewe, female lamb.

ROSALINDA Beautiful rose.

SENALDA A sign, symbol.

TOMASA A twin.

VENTURA Good fortune.

FEMININE NAMES OF WELSH ORIGIN

ARDRA The high one.

BARRIS Child of Henry.

BINNIE Receptacle, bin.

BLODWEN White flower.

BRIANNE Strong one.

BRICE Warrior woman.

BRONWEN White flower.

CAREY Rocky island.

CORDELIA Jewel of the sea.

CYMBALINE Lord of the sun.

DAVINA Beloved.

DEE Dark one.

DEVERELL River bank.

EVELYN Pleasant one.

FIONA White, pale.

GLADYS Princess.

GLENNA From a valley.

GLYNIS From the valley.

GWENDOLYN White, blessed.

GWENEVERE White ghost.

GWYNETH White, pale.

GWYNNE White, pale.

ISOLDE Fair lady.

JENNIFER White, pale.

KIMBALL Warrior woman.

KYLE Grazing hill.

LINETTE Graceful, lovely.

LYNN A brook.

MARGIAD A pearl.

MAURA Dark one.

MEGAN A pearl.

MEREDITH Protector of the sea.

MORGANA Edge of the sea.

SLOAN Great warrior.

TAFFY Beloved.

WREN Great ruler.

WYNNE Fair one.

MASCULINE NAMES OF OLD AND MIDDLE ENGLISH

ADDISON Son of Adam.

ADNEY Island dweller.

ALBERT Noble birth.

ALCOTT Cottage dweller.

ALDEN Wise one.

ALFRED Elf.

ALLARD Brave, noble.

ALTON Town or estate dweller.

ARCHER Bowman.

ARLO Fortified hill.

ASHBY Ash tree farm.

ASHLEY Ash tree meadow.

ASHTON Ash tree farm.

ATHERTON Spring farm.

AVERELL April born.

AVERY Elf king.

BAILEY Fortification.

BARCLAY From birch meadow.

BARNABY Son of a prophet.

BARRETT Bold as a bear.

BARTON Barley farm.

BAXTER Baker.

BAYARD Auburn haired.

BELDEN Valley lost in dreams.

BENTLEY From the moor.

BERKELEY From the birch meadow.

BLAINE Source of a river.

BLAKE White, fair.

BOND To bind.

BOOKER Beech tree.

BOURKE From a brook.

BRADFORD/BRADLEY From broad meadow.

BRANDON Raven, firebrand.

BRETT From Brittany. ✓

BREWSTER Brewer.

BRODERICK Rich, flat land.

BROOKE A stream.

BUCKLEY Deer meadow.

BURTON A fortress.

CALDER The brook.

CALDWELL Cold spring.

CARTER Driver, carter.

CASEY Valorous, strong.

CEDRIC War-chief.

CHAD Warrior.

CHANCE Fortune.

CHANNING Knowing, wise.

CHARLTON Father's town.

CHAUNCEY Church official.

CLAY/CLAYBOURNE/ CLAYTON
  From a place of clay.

CLIFF Cliff.

CLIFFORD River near a cliff.

CLIFTON Town near a cliff.

CLINT/CLINTON Hill town.

CLIVE Cliff.

CODY A cushion.

COLBERT/COLBY/COLE
  Black farm.

CONAN Intelligent.

CRANE A hoarse cry.

CRAWFORD A stream near crows.

CREIGHTON Town on a creek.

CROSBY Sign of the cross.

CROWELL Victory cry.

DALE Valley.

DALTON Valley estate.

DAVIS Son of beloved.

DELBERT Bright as day.

DENTON Valley estate.

DENVER Edge of the valley.

DERWARD Deer warden.

DIRK Famous ruler.

DREW Sturdy.

DUDLEY From the meadow.

DWIGHT Blond, fair.

EARL Earl's land.

EDGAR Riches, wealth.

EDMUND Prosperous protector.

EDWARD Prosperous protector.

EDWIN Prosperous friend.

EGBERT Bright sword.

ELDRIDGE Old fort.

ELLERY From the elder tree.

ELLIOTT Elijah.

ELMER Noble, famous.

ELTON From an old estate.

ERWIN Friend of the sea.

EWING Friend of the law.

FARLEY A wayside place.

FARNHAM From a farm.

FIELDER/FIELDING Field worker.

FORD Road or passage.

FRANKLYN Free holder.

FREEMAN Free man.

FULTON Field near a town.

GALT Steep hill.

GARDNER Gardener.

GARFIELD Triangular field.

GARRICK Oak spear.

GARY Spear carrier.

GEOFFREY Gift of peace.

GILFORD River ford near woods.

GORDON Pasture land.

GRANT Great one, to assure.

GRANTLAND Deeded estate.

GRAYSON Earl's son.

GROVER Tree grower.

HADLEY Heath.

HALE Hero, health.

HALEY Healthy, hero.

HALL Manor home.

HALSEY Hal's island.

HAMILTON Home lover.

HAMPTON Town.

HARLAN Strand of flax.

HARLEY Planted meadow.

HARMON Soldier.

HAROLD Army leader.

HARRISON Son of Harry.

HARRY Home.

HARTE A deer.

HARTLEY Deer field.

HAYWOOD Hay field.

HERBERT Bright, excellent.

HOLLIS Holly grove.

HOWARD Watchman.

HOYT A ship.

HUGH Intelligence, spirit.

HUNT/HUNTER To hunt, hunter.

HUNTINGTON Town of the hunt.

HYLAND From a high place.

HYMAN From a high place.

JAMES The supplanter.

JEFFREY Gift of peace.

JENNINGS Descendant of John.

KEANE Sharp.

KELLY Warrior, ship.

KENDALL Clear river.

KINGSLEY King's meadow.

KIP From pointed hill.

KIRBY A church.

KIRKLAND Church's land.

KNOLL Small hill.

LANE Narrow path.

LANGFORD From a long river.

LANGSTON Town near a long river.

LEE Meadow.

LELAND Sheltered place.

LESTER Protected camp.

LEWIS Famous in battle.

LINCOLN Camp near a stream.

LINDSAY Linden tree island.

LOGAN A felled tree.

LONDON Fortress of the moon.

LONGFELLOW   Tall person.

LONSDALE   Londe's valley.

LOWELL   Beloved.

LUKE   Light.

LYNDON   Linden tree.

MANLEY   Hero's meadow.

MARSHALL   Steward of horses.

MARVIN   Sea lover.

MELBOURNE   Brook near a hill.

MELVILLE   Town near a hill.

MELVIN/MELVYN   Mill worker.

MENDEL   To repair.

MILBURN   Mill near a brook.

MILLER   Miller.

MILTON   Town near a mill.

MONTGOMERY   Hill, mountain.

MORRIS   From a moor.

MORTON   From the sea.

NAYLOR   Sailor.

NED   Happy protector.

NELSON   Son of Neil.

NEVIN   Middle, hub.

NORRIS   House of the northerner.

NORTON   From the north.

OAKLEY/OAKLEIGH   Field of oaks.

OGDEN   Oak valley.

OLIN   Ancestor.

OSBORN   Divinely strong.

OSWALD   Forest god.

OTIS   Prosperous, hears well.

PALMER   Palm carrier.

PARKER   Protector of parks.

PARNELL   A rock.

PERRY   Pear tree.

PIERCE   A stone.

PINKERTON   To perforate.

POTTER To swell.

PRESCOTT Priest's home.

PRESTON Priest's home.

PRICE Value.

PROCTOR Manager, director.

RADCLIFFE Red cliff.

RALPH Fearless advisor.

RALSTON Ralph's estate.

RAMSAY Ram's island.

RANDALL Shield.

RANDOLPH Fearless advisor.

RAYMOND Protector.

REED Red haired.

REEVES Steward, caretaker.

REMINGTON Raven's estate. ∫

RIDER Clear land.

RIDLEY Meadow land.

ROBERT Bright fame.

RODNEY Cleared land.

ROONE Counsel.

ROSS Woods, meadow.

ROWLAND Rugged land.

ROYAL King, kingly.

RUTHERFORD River crossing of red stones.

SANFORD Sandy river crossing.

SAWYER Works with a saw.

SCOTT From Scotland.

SEAMAN Sailor.

SEDGEWICK Saw-shaped leaf.

SELBY A sheltered home.

SEYMOUR Sea marsh.

SHELBY Sheltered home.

SHELDON Protected hill.

SHEPHARD Sheep tender.

SHERIDAN Head of shire.

SHERMAN Shearer.

SHERWIN Friend, neighbor.

SHERWOOD A district.

SIDNEY From St. Denis.

SIMPSON Son of Simon.

SPENCER Steward, dispenser.

STAFFORD From the landing.

STANLEY Stony meadow.

STANTON   From a rocky place.

STROUD   From the thicket.

STUART   Caretaker.

SUMNER   One who calls.

TAYLOR   Tailor.

THORNE   Thorny place.

THORNTON   Thorny place.

TODD   A fox.

TOLLAND   Owner of a taxed estate.

TRUMAN   Faithful.

TUCKER   Cleans and thickens cloth.

TURNER   Lathe worker.

TYLER   Maker of tiles.

UPTON   Upper town.

VANCE   Thresher.

WADE   At river crossing.

WAKEFIELD   Wet field.

WALCOTT   Enclosed cottage.

WALKER   Cleans and thickens cloth.

WALLACE   Welshman.

WARD   Guardian, keeper.

WAYLAND   Came by road.

WAYNE   A way or meadow.

WEBSTER   Weaver.

WELBY   Village near willows.

WELDON   Willow place.

WELLS   Willows.

WESLEY   Westerner.

WHITNEY   Island place.

WHITTAKER   Small acre.

WILBUR   Willow.

WINSLOW   Victory on a hill.

WINTHROP   Victory, crossroads.

WOODROW   Path in a woods.

WORTH   Estate.

WYLIE   Charming.

WYNDHAM   Enclosure on a path.

YUL   Christmas season.

MASCULINE NAMES OF FRENCH ORIGIN

ALGERNON Bearded one.

ANDRE Courageous, valiant.

ANTOINE Priceless.

ARMAND Strong as an eagle.

AUBREY Blond ruler.

BEAUMONT Beautiful mountain.

BEAUREGARDE Handsome, lovely.

BELTON Beautiful town.

BENNETT Little blessed one.

BONAIRE Kind, gentle.

BOYCE From a forest.

BURGESS Shopkeeper.

CHANDLER Candle maker.

CHARLES Manly, strong.

CHARLTON Charles' town.

CHASE Hunter.

CHESTER Knight, noble.

CLARK Scholar, clerk.

CORNELL Horn colored hair.

CURTIS Courteous.

DARCY Dark one.

DARRELL Little beloved.

DEAN Leader, church official.

DELANO Near a nut tree.

DELMER From the sea.

DESMOND Worldly, traveled.

DRURY Darling one.

ETIENNE Crowned.

FARRAR Blacksmith.

FLETCHER Arrow.

FORTUNE Lucky, fateful.

FRANCHOT Free, French.

FRANCOIS Free, French.

FRANK Free, Frank.

FRAZER Charcoal maker.

GARETH Watcher.

GARLAND Wreath of flowers.

GARNER Martial, war-like.

GARRISON Troops, army fort.

GASCON From Gascony.

GAYLORD Brave, valiant.

GERARD Spear, sharp.

GERMAIN German, a sprout.

GISCARD A manner, behavior.

GRANVILLE Great town.

GUILLAUME Resolute protector.

GURNEY To grunt.

HEWETT Little Hugh.

HILAIRE Cheerful one.

HUGO Bright mind, spirit.

JACQUES The supplanter.

JARVIS Battle spear.

JAY Crow.

JEAN God is gracious.

JUSTIS Just, fair.

LANCE Attendant, follower.

LAURENT Laurel crown.

LEON Strong as a lion.

LEONARD Strong as a lion.

LEROY The king.

LEVANT To rise.

LIONEL Lion-like.

LISLE Islander.

LOUIS Famous in battle.

LUNDY Monday born.

MARCEAU Martial, war-like.

MARCEL Martial, war-like.

MARION Sorrow, bitterness.

MARLON Falcon, of the sea.

MASON Stone worker.

MATHIEU Gift of God.

MERCER Textiles dealer.

MERLE Blackbird.

MICHEL Who is like God?

MICHON Who is like God?

MONTAGUE Mountain.

MORTIMER Lives by the sea.

NEVILLE New village.

NOEL Christmas born.

NORMAN Norse man.

NORRIS Northerner.

OLIVIER Olive tree.

ORVILLE Golden city.

PERCIVAL Pierce the valley.

PERCY Pierce the valley.

PHILLIPPE Horse lover.

PIERRE A rock.

PURVIS Food seller.

QUINCY Fifth child.

RAY Kingly, lordly.

RENAUD Wise one.

RENE Reborn.

ROBART Bright fame.

ROY The king.

RUPERT Bright fame.

RUSSELL Red-haired.

SABIN Juniper tree.

SARGENT Officer, attendant.

SAVILLE Estate with willows.

SERGE To serve.

SILVAIN From a forest.

TRAVIS Crossroads.

TROY Curly haired one.

TYSON Son of a Teuton.

VALENTIN Valorous, strong.

WYATT Little warrior.

YANCY Englishman.

MASCULINE NAMES OF GERMAN ORIGIN

ABELARD Resolute, noble.

ADALARD Noble, brave.

ADLER Eagle.

ADOLPH Noble one.

ALARIC Highest ruler.

ALDO Old, wise.

ALPHONSE Eager one.

AMORY Famous ruler.

ANSEL Helmet of God.

ARCHIBALD Very bold one.

ARNOLD Strong as an eagle.

ATTILIO Little father.

AXEL Father of peace.

BALDRIC Bold ruler.

BALDWIN Bold friend.

BERN Like a bear.

BERNHARD Like a bear.

BERTHOLD Bright ruler.

BERTRAM Illustrious one.

BOGART Strong bow.

BRUNO Brown one.

BUBBA Boy.

BUCK Male deer.

BYRON Cottage.

CARL Farmer.

CONRAD Honest advisor.

DEDRICK Ruler, lordly.

DEREK Ruler, lordly.

DEWITT White, pale.

DUSTIN Warrior.

EDEL Noble, well-born.

EMERY Industrious ruler.

EMIL   Ruler, lordly.

EMMET   Ruler, lordly.

ERHARD   Strong, resolute.

ERNEST   Sincere.

EVERETT   Wild boar.

FERDINAND   Bold, courageous.

FRANZ   Free man, French.

FREDERICK   Peace, gift.

FREMONT   Noble, free.

GERALD   Spear, sharp.

GILBERT   Trusted one, famous.

GODDARD   Divinely strong.

GODFREY   Divinely peaceful.

GREGOR   Vigilant.

GUS   Staff of the Goths.

GUY   Warrior.

HARDY   Bold one.

HARVEY   Army battle.

HENRY   Home lover.

HERMAN   Army man.

HOBART   High, brilliant.

HODGES   Famous spear, warrior.

HORST   Thicket.

HOWE   High, illustrious.

HUBERT   Bright mind, spirited.

HUMBERT   Bright Hun.

HUMPHREY   Peaceful Hun.

INGLEBERT   Heavenly, bright.

JAKOB   Supplanter.

JOHANNES   God is gracious.

KARL   Manly, strong.

KASPAR   Treasure guard.

KONRAD   Honest advisor.

KURT   Courteous.

LEONHARD   Strong as a lion.

LEOPOLD   Bold, free man.

LINDBERT   Linden tree hill.

LOCKE   A hole.

LOEB   A lion.

LORENZ   Laurel crown.

LUDWIG   Famous warrior.

LUTHER   Famous warrior.

MANDEL   Almond.

MANFRED   Man of peace, free.

MANHEIM   Servant's home.

MAYNARD   Strong, manly.

NORBERT   Heavenly, bright.

OBERT   Prosperous, bright.

OTTO   Wealthy one.

PENROD   Famous warrior, ruler.

PETRUS   A rock.

PHILLIP   Horse lover.

RAYMOND   Mighty protector.

REGAN   Wise one, ruler.

REGINALD   Wise one, ruler.

REINHART   Courageous one.

REYNARD   Courageous one.

RICHARD   Powerful ruler.

RITTER   Judge.

ROGER   Famous warrior.

ROLAND   Fame of the land.

RUDOLPH   Famous wolf.

RUTGER   Famous warrior.

SAXON   Sword, knife.

SAYER   Victory.

SELIG   Blessed one.

SIEGFRIED   Victory, peace.

SIGMUND   Victory, protection.

THEOBALD   Of the people.

THEODORIC   Ruler of the people.

ULRIC   Wolf, ruler.

VALDEMAR   Famous ruler.

WALDO   Ruler.

WALFRED   Peaceful ruler.

WALTER   Powerful warrior.

WARNER   Preserver.

WARREN   Defender.

WEBER   Weaver.

WENDELL   Wanderer.

WERNER   Defending army.

WILBUR   Resolute, bright.

WILLIAM   Resolute guardian.

WILMER   Resolute one.

WOLFGANG   Advancing wolf.

YALE   Producer.

ZOLA   Toll, duty.

MASCULINE NAMES OF GREEK ORIGIN

ALEXANDER Protector of men.

AMBROSE Immortal one.

ANATOLE Rising of the sun.

ANDREW Courageous, valiant.

ANTHONY Flourishing.

ARGUS Vigilant, watchful one.

BALTHASAR God protect the king.

BARNABAS Son of a prophet.

BERYLE Green stone, gem.

CASTOR Diligent, beaver.

CHRISTIAN Christian.

CHRISTOPHER Christ bearer.

CLEON Famous one.

COSMO Universe.

CRONAN Companion.

CYRIL Lordly, noble.

DAMIEN Divine power.

DEMAS Well-liked.

DEMETRIUS Of the fertility god.

DEMOS The people.

DENNIS Of Dionysius.

DORIAN From the sea.

ERASMUS/ERASTUS Lovable.

EUGENE Lucky, well-born.

GEORGE Farmer.

GILES Goat skin.

GREGORY Vigilant, dutiful.

HECTOR Anchor, steadfast.

HOMER A hostage.

HORACE To see, knower.

IGNATIUS Fiery, lively.

ISIDORE   Gift of Isis.

JASON   Healer.

JASPAR   Semi-precious gem.

LEANDER   Lion-man.

LEX   A word.

LINUS   Flaxen colored.

MENELAUS   Spartan king.

MINOT   A son of Zeus.

MYRON   Fragrant, sweet smelling.

NESTOR   Wise old person.

NICHOLAS   People's victory.

ORESTES   Mountain man.

PARIS   King of Troy.

PETER   A rock.

PHILMORE   Sea-lover.

RING   A ring.

SEBASTIAN   Venerable.

STEPHEN   Crowned one.

THADDEUS   Courageous.

THEODORE   Gift of God.

TIMON   Honor, reward.

TIMOTHY   Honoring God.

TOBIAS   God is good.

TYRONE   Sovereign, king.

ULYSSES   Wrathful, war-like.

ZENO   Sign, symbol.

ZEUS   Living one, immortal.

MASCULINE NAMES OF HEBREW ORIGIN

AARON Exalted, shining one.

ABEL Breath, vapor.

ABNER Father of light.

ABRAHAM Father of the multitude.

ABRAM Father of the multitude.

ADAM Man, earth.

AMOS Life's burden.

AREL Lion of God.

ARI Lion.

ASA Healer.

ASHER Happy one.

BARTHOLOMEW Farmer's son.

BEN Son.

BENJAMIN Son of my right hand.

BENSON Son of Ben.

BETHEL House of God.

BEZALEL In the shade of God.

CAIN Possessed.

CALEB Bold, dog.

CHAYIM Life.

DAGAN Corn, grain.

DANIEL God is my judge.

DAVID Beloved of God.

DAVIS Son of David.

DAWES Son of David.

DEUEL Knowledge of God.

DOVEV To speak, whisper.

EBENEZER Rock of help.

EDEN On high.

ELIHU/ELIJAH/ELISHA Lord is my God.

ELLIS Lord is my salvation.

EMMANUEL God is with us.

EMMET Truth.

ENOCH Dedicated, educated.

EPHRAIM Fruitful, productive.

ETHAN Strength of God.

EZEKIEL Strength of God.

EZRA Helper.

GABRIEL Man of God.

GIDEON Warrior, maimed.

GILI My joy.

GURI Young lion.

GURIEL God is my lion.

GURION Strong as a lion.

HASKEL God is my strength.

HILLEL Praised one.

HIRAM Most noble.

ICHABOD Without glory.

IMMANUEL God is with us.

IRA Descend.

ISAAC God is salvation.

ISRAEL Prince of God.

ITIEL God is with me.

JEDIDIAH Beloved of God.

JEPHTAH He will open.

JEREMIAH Appointed of God.

JEREMY Appointed of God.

JESSE Wealthy, gift.

JESUS God will help.

JETHRO Riches, abundance.

JOCK God is gracious.

JOEL God is willing.

JOHN God is gracious.

JONATHAN God is gracious.

JORDAN The descender.

JOSEPH God will add.

JOSHUA Lord is my salvation.

JOSIAH Fire of the Lord.

LABAN White.

LEMUEL Devoted to God.

LEV A heart.

LEVI Attendant.

LOTAN To envelop.

MATTHEW Gift of God.

MEIR One who shines.

MENACHEM Comforter.

MICHAEL Who is like God?

MICHAH Who is like God?

MITCHELL Who is like God?

MORDECAI Martial, war-like.

MOSES/MOISHE/MOSHE
Child, son.

NATHAN Gift of God.

NEHEMIAH Comforted of
the Lord.

NISSAN Emblem, sign.

NISSIM Miracles.

NOAH Wandering, peace.

NOY Beauty.

NURIA Fire of God.

OBADIAH Servant of God.

PINCUS Dark one.

RACHMIEL God is my comforter.

RAPHAEL God has healed.

REUBEN Behold the Son.

REUEL Friend of God.

REUVEN Behold the Son.

SAMSON Sun, shining.

SAMUEL God has heard.

SAUL Borrowed.

SETH Appointed, substitute.

SHALOM Peace.

SHAMIR Diamond.

SHLOMO His place.

SIMCHA Joy, happiness.

SIMON Hearing one.

SOLOMON Peaceful one.

THOMAS Twin.

TOBIAS The Lord is God.

URI Flame of God.

URIAH Flame of God.

YAAKOV Supplanter.

YAPHET Beautiful.

YASHAR Upright, honest.

YEHIEL May God live.

YEHORAM God will exalt.

YEHUDAH Praise.

YEHUDI From Judah.

YEMIN Right hand of God.

YIGAEL God will redeem.

YITZAK Isaac, God is salvation.

YOAV God is father.

YOEL   Joel, God is willing.

YONA   A bear.

YORA   To teach.

YORAM   God is exalted.

YOSEF   Joseph, He will add.

YUDAN   Law.

ZACHARY   God has remembered.

ZALMAN   Solomon, peaceful one.

ZEDEKIAH   God is righteous.

ZERAH   Seed, kernel.

ZEV   Wolf.

ZIA   To tremble.

ZIVI   To shine.

ZOHAN   Brilliance, shining.

ZVI   To shine.

MASCULINE NAMES OF IRISH ORIGIN

AHERN   House owner.

AIDAN   Little fiery one.

AL   Harmony.

ALAN   Cheerful, harmonious.

ALASTAIR   Protector of the people.

ALROY   Red-haired boy.

ARLEN   Pledge, oath.

BALFOUR   From the meadow.

BANNING   Little blond one.

BARD   Minstrel, poet.

BARRY   Spear, pointed.

BENROY   Mountain peak.

BLAINE   Thin, lean.

BLAIR   From the plain.

BOWIE   Yellow-haired.

BOYD   Yellow-haired.

BRADY Spirited.

BRENDON Fire-brand, lively.

BRENT Raven, dark one.

BRIAN Strength, virtue.

CALEY Thin, lean.

CARRICK Rocky land.

CARROLL Champion, leader.

CASSIDY Clever, quick one.

CAVAN Handsome.

CLEARY Educated one.

COLIN Victorious child, dove.

CONLAN Hero.

CONWAY Meadow dog.

COREY Near a pool.

COYNE Battle follower.

CULLEN Handsome.

DALLAS Wise, from a valley home.

DARBY Free man.

DARREN Small, rocky hill.

DEMPSEY Proud.

DERMOT Free man.

DERRY Red-haired.

DEVIN Poet, singer.

DEVLIN Valorous.

DUFF Dark one.

DUGAN Dark one.

DWAYNE Small, dark one.

ENNIS One choice.

FAGAN Little fiery one.

FARRELL Most valiant.

FERGUS Manly, strong.

FINLEY Fair, blond.

FINN Fair, blond.

FLYNN Son of a redhead.

FORBES Prosperous.

GALLAGHER Foreign helper.

GAYNOR Son of a blond man.

GERMAN Small blue-eyed one.

GUTHRIE Windy place.

HOGAN Youthful, boy.

HYMAN Mountaintop.

INGE Island.

IRVING Handsome one.

IRWIN Handsome one.

KANE   Tribute, honor.

KEEFE   Well-being.

KEELY   Handsome.

KEENAN   Ancient one.

KELLY   Handsome one.

KELVIN   Stream, brook.

KENYON   White-haired.

KERMIT   Free man.

KERWIN   Gentle, lovable.

KEVIN   Handsome.

KYLE   Handsome.

MACKENZIE   Son of wise king.

MAGEE   Son of a fiery one.

MANUS   Great one.

MELVIN   Chief, ruler.

MURPHY   Of the sea.

MURTAGH   River.

NEAL   Champion.

NOLAN   Noble, famous.

ODELL   A melody, song.

QUINLAN   Strong one.

RAFFERTY   Prosperous one.

RILEY   Valiant.

RORY   Ruddy one.

RYAN   Strong, little king.

SCANLON   Little trap, endearing one.

SEAN   God is gracious.

SHAMUS   God is gracious.

SHANAHAN   Wise one.

SHANE   God is gracious.

SHANLEY   Ancient hero.

SHANNON   Little ancient hero.

SHAWN   God is gracious.

SHEA   Mighty, great one.

STRUTHER   From the brook.

SWEENEY   Little hero.

TAGGART   Son of a church official.

TEAGUE   Poet, singer.

TIERNAN   Noble, lordly.

TORRANCE   From the knolls.

TREVOR   Prudent, wise.

TROY   Foot soldier.

WATKINS   A river ford.

MASCULINE NAMES OF ITALIAN ORIGIN

ALBERTI/ALBERTO   Noble birth.

ALBINO   White, pale.

ALESSANDRO   Protector of man.

ALFREDO   Elf.

ALPHONSO   Noble, lordly.

ANGELO   Messenger of God.

ANTONIO   Flourishing.

ARMAND   Great warrior.

BAMBINO   Small child.

BASILIO   Royal, kingly.

BELLINI   Beautiful.

BENITO   Well-spoken of, blessed.

BONAVENTURE   Good luck.

BONI   Good, lucky.

CARLO   Strong, manly.

CARMINE   Vineyard.

CLAUDIO   Lame one.

DANILO   God is my judge.

DANTE   Durable, lasting.

DARIO   Small, rock-like.

DENO Leader.

DINO Little sword.

EDUARDO Protector.

EMILIO Industrious.

ENRICO Home lover.

ENZIO Mine.

ERNESTO Sincere, resolute.

FICO Fig.

FRANCO Free, French.

GERARDO Great warrior.

GIACOMO The supplanter.

GILBERTO Trusted one, famous.

GINO God is gracious.

GIORGIO Farmer.

GUIDO A guide.

GUILLERMO The guardian.

GUSTAVO Staff of the Goths.

HORATIO Behold.

JACOPO The supplanter.

JUSTINO Just, fair.

LAURO Laurel crown.

LEONARDO Strong as a lion.

LORENZO Strong as a lion.

LUCIANO Light.

MARCELLO Martial, war-like.

MARIO Sorrow, bitterness.

MAURIZIO Dark skinned.

NUNCIO A messenger.

PAOLO Small one.

POMPEYO Young shoot.

PRIMO First child.

RAFFAELLO God has healed.

RENALDO Wise one.

RICCARDO Powerful ruler.

ROBERTO Bright fame.

RODOLPHO Courageous advisor.

ROLANDO Fame of the land.

ROSSANO Of the forest.

SALVATORE Savior.

SEBASTIAN Venerable.

SERGIO To serve.

SILVIO Of the forest.

STEFANO A crown.

UMBERTO Color of earth.

VALENTINO Strong, valorous.

VINCENTE Twenty.

VITO Life.

VITTORIO Conqueror.

WILFREDO Wish, desire.

ZAN A clown.

ZERO A cipher.

MASCULINE NAMES OF LATIN ORIGIN

ADRIAN Rich, wealthy.

ALBAN Fair one.

ALOYSIUS Famous warrior.

ALVIN White, pale.

ARDEN To burn, ardent.

AUGUST Majestic.

AUGUSTINE Of August.

AURELIUS/AURELIO Gold, golden.

AUSTIN Majestic.

BASIL Kingly, majestic.

BENEDICT To bless, speak well of.

BONIFACE Well-doer.

BOONE Good.

BRANCH Extension of a tree.

BREVARD Short, brief.

CAESAR Long-haired one.

CALVIN Bald.

CANUTE   White-haired.

CARDEN   To comb, brush out.

CASH   Vain one.

CASSIUS   Vain one.

CECIL   Blind one.

CLARENCE   Bright, famous.

CLAUDE   Lame one.

CLEMENT   Gentle one.

CONSTANTINE   Constant, resolute.

CORNELIUS   Color of horn.

CORY   Helmet.

COURTNEY   Enclosed place.

CURT/CURTIS   Court, enclosure.

CYPRIAN   From Cyprus.

DAMON   Demon spirit.

DEXTER   Skillful.

DURANT   Enduring.

ELROY   The king.

EMIL   Flattering.

EUSTACE   Tranquil one.

FABIAN   Bean grower.

FAUST   Fortunate, fated.

FIDEL   Faithful.

FORREST   Woods, sylvan.

FRANCIS   Free man, French.

GALLOWAY   A Gaul.

GENTILE   Of the same clan.

GILROY   King's servant.

GRADY   A ranking.

GRAM   Grain, kernel.

GRIFFIN   Mythical beast.

HASTINGS   A spear.

HILARY   Cheerful one.

HOMER   A hostage.

HORTON Gardener.

IVOR Ivory.

JANUS Gateway.

JEROME Holy name.

JOYCE Merry one.

JUDAH/JUDD/JUDE Praise.

JULIAN Of Julius.

JULIUS Light-haired.

JUSTIN Just, fair.

JUVENTINO Youthful.

LALO Lullaby singer.

LANCE Light spear.

LAWRENCE Laurel crown.

LEO Lion.

LESTER Camp of the army.

LOREN Crown of laurels.

LUCIAN Bringer of light.

LUCIUS Bringer of light.

MAGNUS Great one.

MANUEL God is with us.

MARCUS Martial, war-like.

MARIN Of the sea.

MARK Martial, war-like.

MARLIN/MARLON/MARLOW Of the sea.

MARTIN Martial, war-like.

MAURICE Dark skinned.

MAXIMILLIAN Most excellent.

MELCHIOR King.

MILES Warrior.

MILFORD Warrior.

MILLARD Mill keeper.

NIGEL Dark one.

NOBLE Well-known, high-born.

OCTAVIO/OCTAVIUS Eighth child.

OLIVER Olive tree.

ORAL From the mouth.

ORLANDO Golden yellow.

ORSON Like a bear.

OVID Egg shaped.

PATRICK Patrician, noble.

PAUL Small one.

PAXTON Town of peace.

PENN Quill, writing implement.

PERVIS   Through the way.

PIUS   Devoted to God.

PLACIDO   Quiet.

PORTER   Gate keeper.

PUTNAM   Gardener, pruner.

QUENTIN   Fifth child.

QUINN   Fifth child.

REX   King.

RIP   River bank.

RIPLEY   Meadow by a river.

RIVERS   Stream of water.

RUFUS   Red-haired.

SEXTUS   Sixth child.

SILAS   To borrow.

SILVANUS   Of the forest.

SYLVESTER   From the forest.

TELFORD   Shallow river.

TERENCE   Smooth, gentle, gracious.

TYRUS   From Tyre.

URBAN   City.

URSEL   A bear.

VALENTINE   Strong, healthy.

VERNON   Flourishing.

VICTOR   Conqueror.

VINCENT   Conqueror.

VIRGIL   Flourishing, strong.

VITO   Life.

MASCULINE NAMES OF NORSE AND SCANDINAVIAN ORIGIN

ALVIS   Wise one.

ANDERS   Courageous one.

BJORN   Bear-like.

BOOTH   Temporary home.

BORG   From the castle.

BRANDER   Sword, fire-brand.

CANUTE   Knot.

CARR   From the marsh.

CORT   Short one.

CROSBY   Shrine of the cross.

DAG   Day.

DANA   From Denmark.

DAVIN   Bright, shining Finns.

DELLING   Very bright one.

DENBY   From Denmark.

ELVIS   All wise.

ERIC   Honor, valiant.

GAMEL   Old one.

GARTH   An enclosure.

GILBY   Pledge, oath.

GUNNAR   Warrior.

GUNTHER   Warrior.

GUSTAVE   Staff of the Goths.

HALDAN   Half Danish.

HANS   God is gracious.

HARLOW   Army leader.

HAROLD   Army leader.

HARPER   A spear grip.

HAVELOCK   Contest at sea.

HOBART   Bart's mill.

IGOR   Hero.

INGEMAR   Famous son.

INGER   Son's army.

IVAR   Archer, bowman.

KAREL   Strong, manly.

KELL   Spring, brook.

KELSEY   From a ship, island.

KIRBY   Church village.

KIRK   From the church.

LAMONT   Lawyer, friend of the law.

LANG   Tall man.

LARS   Laurel crown.

LEIF   Beloved.

LUNT   From the grove.

MEREDITH   Sea defender.

MERLIN   Sea fort.

MIKEL   Who is like God?

NIEL   People's victory.

ODBERT   Otter.

ODIN   Chief god.

OLAF   Ancestor.

OLEG   Holy one.

ORMAND   Serpent

OSCAR   Divine hunter.

RAYNOR   Great army man.

ROSCOE   Deep forest.

SCHUYLER   Hide, sulk.

SKIP   Ship's master.

SUTHERLAND   From the south.

SVEN   Youthful one.

THURSTON   Thor's son.

TURPIN   Thunder-Finn.

WYBORN   Bear of war.

WYCK   Village dweller.

WYCLIFFE   Village near a cliff.

YORICK   Farmer.

YVES   Archer, bowman.

MASCULINE NAMES OF PERSIAN AND ARAMAIC ORIGIN

ABBA A father.

ABBOTT A father.

AHMED Most highly praised.

ANWAR Light.

BILGAI Joy, happiness.

CASPAR Treasure keeper.

CYRUS The sun.

DARIUS/DARIA/DARIAN A king.

DAUD Beloved.

DEKEL Palm, date tree.

DEVIR Holy place.

DURWARD Porter, doorkeeper.

EMIR To command.

GASPAR Treasure holder.

GILEAD Hump of a camel.

GUNI Reddish black.

HAMAN To rage.

HUSSEIN Small, handsome.

JED Hand.

KAHIL/KAHLIL Friend, lover.

KAREEM Noble, exalted.

MOHAMMED/MUHAMMED Most praised one.

MUHTAR Village leader.

NADAR Opposite of zenith.

NAHIR Light.

NASSER Victorious one.

NIV Speech.

OMAR Long life.

RAZIEL God is my secret.

REGEM A friend.

SAADIAH God's help.

SAGI Strong, mighty.

SALIM Whole, flawless.

SAMI Lofty.

SHAFER Beautiful one.

SHERAGA Light.

SHERIRA Strong one.

TABOR A drum.

TALIA Young lamb.

TALMAN Oppress, injure.

TAVI Good, gracious.

TAZ Shallow cup.

XAVIER Bright one.

XERXES The king.

ZEIRA Small one.

ZOLTAN The sultan.

MASCULINE NAMES OF RUSSIAN ORIGIN

ALEKSEI   Protector of men.

ARKADY   Very bold.

BORIS   Great warrior.

DMITRI   Of Demetrius.

FEDOR   Divine gift.

FYODOR   Divine gift.

ILYA   He is my God.

IVAN   God is gracious.

JAROSLAV   Spring grain.

JASCHA   The supplanter.

KAROL   Strong, manly.

LADIMIR   World prince.

LEONID   Strong as a lion.

LEOPOLD   Lion-like.

MIKHAIL   Who is like God?

MIROSLAV   Beautiful slave.

MISCHA   Who is like God?

NIKITA   People's victory.

NIKOLAI   People's victory.

OSIP   He shall add.

PETR   A rock.

ROZER   Noble warrior.

SACHA   Protector of men.

STANISLAV   Glory of the group.

VASSILY   Kingly, magnificent.

VIKTOR   Conqueror.

VLADIMIR   World prince.

YVAN   God is gracious.

MASCULINE NAMES OF SCOTTISH ORIGIN

ADAIR   Oak tree near a river.

ANGUS   Unique strength.

BAIRD   Minstrel, poet.

BEARNARD   Like a bear.

BEATHAN   Son of my right hand.

BIRK   Birch tree.

BRUCE   Of the woods.

BURNIS   Little stream.

CALDER   Stony river.

CAMDEN   Bending valley.

CAMERON   Bent nose.

CAMPBELL   Bent mouth.

CRAIG   Cliff, crag.

DONALD   World ruler.

DOUGLAS   Gray, dark warrior.

DUNCAN   Dark warrior.

DUNMORE   Fortified hill.

ERSKINE   Tall cliff.

FYFE   From Fifeshire.

GEMMEL   Old one.

GEORDIE   Farmer.

IAN   God is gracious.

KENNETH   Handsome one.

LAIRD   Landed gentleman.

LEE   Meadow.

LOGAN   From the hollow.

MALCOLM Servant of St. Columbia.

MONROE Wheel, carter.

MURRAY Sailor.

PAYTON Patrician, noble.

REYNOLDS Wise one.

RONALD Wise one.

RUDYARD Red enclosure.

SAWNEY Helper of men.

WYNDHAM Windy road.

MASCULINE NAMES OF SPANISH ORIGIN

AMADIS Love of God.

ANASTASIO Resurrection.

ANDRES Valiant, manly.

ANGEL A messenger of God.

ARMANDO Great warrior.

BENIGNO Well spoken of, blessed.

BERNARDO Bold as a bear.

BLAS Flat-footed.

BOLA Ball, round one.

BOLIVAR Strong, war-like.

BONARO Friend of many.

BRONCO Brown colored.

CARLOS Strong, manly.

CARMEN Vineyard.

CHICO Frenchman.

CID Lordly, noble.

CONSUEL Consolation.

DAGO The supplanter.

DIABOLITO Little devil.

DIEGO The supplanter.

EDWARDO The protector.

ELIGIO He is my God.

ELIO He is my God.

ENRIQUE Home ruler.

ERNESTO Sincere resolute.

ESTABAN Crowned.

ESTES The tide.

EUGENIO Well-born, lucky.

FELIPE Horse lover.

**FERNAND/FERNANDAS/
   FERNANDO** Courageous,
   bold.

FRANCO Free man, French.

GARCIA Spear, sharp.

GERALDO Warrior.

GONZALO Wolf.

GUILLERMO Resolute
   protector.

HERMINIO Army man.

HIRALDO Army leader.

HUMBERTO Bright home.

JACOBO The supplanter.

JAIME The supplanter.

JOACHIM Lord will add.

JORGE Farmer.

JOSE Lord will add.

JULIO Soft haired.

LISLE Strong cloth.

LUIS Famous in battle.

MANUEL God is with us.

MATEO Gift of God.

MIGUEL Who is like God?

OSWALDO A god.

PABLO Small one.

PACO To pack.

PANCHO A plume, feather.

PATRICIO Patrician, noble.

PEDRO A rock.

RAFAEL God has healed.

RAMON Wise one.

RAOUL Courageous advisor.

RICARDO Powerful ruler.

ROBERTO Bright fame.

RODRIGO Famous ruler.

SANCHEZ/SANCHO A saint.

SANTIAGO St. James.

SANTO/SANTOS A saint.

SELVA From a forest.

TEODORO Divine gift.

VALERIO Strong, valorous.

VINICIO Alder tree.

MASCULINE NAMES OF WELSH ORIGIN

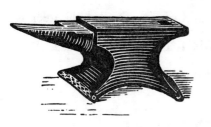

ANWELL Anvil.

ARTHUR Noble, hero.

BARRIS Son of Harry.

BRAM Raven, dark-haired.

BRICE Warrior.

CADELL Warrior.

CADMAN Warrior.

CALHOUN Warrior.

CAREY   Rock island.

CHRICHTON   Hill town.

CLYDE   Warm, gentle.

CONWAY   Head river.

CROMWELL   Winding brook.

DEVERELL   Riverbank.

DEWEY   Beloved.

DREW   Wise one.

DYLAN   From the sea.

EVAN   God is gracious.

KEITH   From the forest.

KENN   Clear water.

KENT   Bright knight.

KIMBALL   Warrior chief.

KYLE   Grazing hill.

LLEWELLYN   Lion-like.

LLOYD   Grey colored.

LYNN   A brook.

MADDOCK   Good, beneficent.

MADDOX   Son of a good man.

MALVERN   Naked hill, treeless.

MORGAN   Near the sea.

MORUS   Dark one.

OWEN   Young warrior.

POWELL   Son of Howell.

GAVIN   Little hawk.

GAWAIN   Courteous.

GILMORE   Glen near the sea.

GLEN   A valley.

GOWER   Pure.

GRIFFITH   Fierce chief.

GWYNNE   Fair, blond.

REECE   Ardent, happy man.

RENFREW   Still river.

RHETT   A stream, brook.

RHYS   Ardent, happy man.

SLOAN   Great warrior.

TADD   Father.

TRENT   Rapid stream.

TREVOR   Prudent.

TRISTAN   Noisy one.

VAUGHN   Small one.

WATKINS   A ford in the river.

WREN   Ruler, king.

WYNNE   Fair, blond.

NICKNAMES AND EPITHETS

A nickname is defined as a name added to or substituted for your real name. The word is from the Middle English, an "eke name," meaning another name. "Eke name" evolved into "nekename," which became the contemporary, *nickname.*

Nicknames can be a form of affection or admiration or ridicule and they can come from many sources. They are frequently acquired in childhood and may arise from some striking personal characteristic. Nicknames can connote social or career status or can be terms of intimacy and endearment. Like your given name, your nickname is an emblem of you and affects the way in which you are perceived by everyone you encounter.

One form of nickname is the epithet, describing physical attributes or personality traits. Homer so consistently referred to King Menelaus as the "RED-HAIRED MENELAUS" that the king will forever be thought of as one of history's great carrot-tops. You may have trouble placing Richard I in historical context but you'll never forget the great RICHARD THE LION-HEARTED!

DIMINUTIVES AND DERIVATIVES

BABS   BABETTE   BARBI

BARBARA

The wonderful thing about certain first names is that they have a great many possible derivatives and diminutives. A girl named ELIZABETH or CATHERINE, for example, could end up with one of 20 or more possible names depending upon how family and friends see her, or how she sees herself.

One modern trend in naming is to give a child a nickname (diminutive) as his or her formal name. A benefit derived from this practice is avoiding having the child end up with an undesirable diminutive later in life.

Derivatives, unlike diminutives, occur from either a foreign influence (MARY becomes MARIE, MARIA or MARIETTE) or from spelling alterations (ROBIN becomes ROBYN, ROBBIN or ROBYNE). Many American names have foreign variations. When traveling around the world a man from Duluth named LAWRENCE may find that he is called LAURENT in France, LORENZ in Germany, LORENZO in Italy and Spain and LARS in Denmark.

So, since a KATHY is a CATHY is a KIT . . . here is a thorough listing of names with their diminutives and derivations.

A

ABIGAIL
Aba
Abagail
Abbe
Abbey
Abby
Abigayel
Abra
Gael
Gail
Gale
Gayle

ACACIA
Cacia
Cacie
Casey
Casia

ADA
Adah

ADELAIDE
Ada
Adah
Adalaide
Addey
Addie
Addy
Adel
Adela
Adelaida
Adele
Adelia

Adelina
Adeline
Adell
Adella
Adelle
Alina
Aline
Del
Della
Delle
Heidi

ADELLE
Ada
Ade
Adel
Adela
Adell
Adella
Del
Della
Delle

ADENA
Ada
Adene
Adie
Adina
Adine
Dena
Dina
Ena
Ina

ADORA
Adey
Adie
Adoree
Adorna
Dora
Dore
Dorie
Dorna
Dory

ADRIENNE
Adey
Adie
Adria
Adrian
Adriana
Adriane
Adrianna
Adrianne
Adrie
Adrien
Adrienna
Adrienne
Rena
Rina

AGATHA
Agace
Agafia
Agathe
Aggie
Aggy

AGNES
Aggie
Aggy
Agnesa
Agnese
Anis
Anise
Annes
Annice
Annis
Annys
Inez
Nessa
Nessie
Ynes
Ynez

AIDAN
Adan
Aida
Aidey

Aidie
Dan
Dannie
Danny

AILEEN
Aida
Aleen
Alena
Alene
Eileen
Elena
Elene
Ileana
Ilene
Lena
Lina

AINSLEY
Ainslee
Ainsleigh
Lee
Leigh

ALAMEDA
Alley
Allie
Ally
Mada
Meda

ALANNA
Alaina
Alaine
Alana
Alane
Alayna
Alayne
Alena
Alenna
Alina
Aline
Allana
Allen

Allena
Allin
Allina
Alline
Allyn
Allyna
Allyne
Lana
Lena
Lina
Lanna
Lenna
Linna

ALBERTA
Albertha
Albertina
Albertine
Albie
Albirda
Albreda
Alby
Alie
Allie
Ally
Bert
Bertie
Berty
Bird
Birdie

ALCINA
Alcine
Alcinia
Alcyna
Alcyne
Alcynia
Elcina

ALDORA
Adora
Adoree
Alda
Alie
Alley

Allie
Dora
Dore
Dorey
Dorie

ALEXANDRA
Aleja
Alejo
Alesandra
Alessia
Alessio
Alex
Alexa
Alexandria
Alexandrina
Alexe
Alexei
Alexi
Alexina
Alexine
Alexis
Alexsha
Alix
Allesanda
Alli
Allie
Ally
Lexi
Lexie

Lexy
Sande
Sandie
Sandra
Sandy
Sondra
Zandra

ALFONSINE
Alfie
Alfonsa
Alfy
Alonza
Alphonsa
Alphonsine
Fons
Fonsa
Fonsie
Fonsy

ALFREDA
Aley
Alfie
Alfre
Alfrey
Alfrie
Alfy
Elfreda
Elfrida

Elva
Freda
Fredda
Freddie
Freddy
Freida
Freyda

ALICE
Alecia
Ali
Alicel
Alicia
Alie
Alis
Alisa
Alisha
Alishe
Alison
Alissa
Alli
Allie
Allison
Allyce
Allys
Alys
Alysa
Alyse
Alyss
Alyssa
Elise
Elissa
Elisse
Ilyssa
Ilysse
Ilsa
Lisa
Lissa
Lysa
Lyssa
Son
Sonnie
Sonny

ALMIRA
Alma
Almarine
Almera
Almeria
Almie
Almy
Mara
Mera
Mira

ALTAIR
Alta
Alto

ALTHEA
Ali
Alie
Aly
Thea

ALVINA
Ali
Alie
Alva
Alvan
Alvana
Alvania
Alvie
Alvinia
Alvy
Vina
Vinia
Vinnie
Vinny

AMANDA
Amy
Manda
Mandy

AMBER
Amberlie
Ambie
Amby

AMELIA
Amalie
Amelie
Ameline
Amilia
Emalia
Emelia
Emilia
Lia
Mel
Mellie
Mil
Millie
Milly

ANASTASIA
Ana
Anastace
Anastasie
Anstace
Nastasha
Nastasia
Nastassja
Nastenka
Stacey
Stacia
Stacie

ANDREA
Andi
Andie
Andra
Andree
Andria
Andriana
Andy

> **I would to God thou and I knew where a commodity of good names were to be bought.**
>
> **HENRY IV PART I**
> **Shakespeare**

ANGELA
Angel
Angele
Angeles
Angelica
Angelina
Angeline
Angelique
Angelita
Angie
Angy
Anjela
Anjelika

ANN
Ana
Anca
Ania
Anika
Anita
Anna
Annabel
Annabella
Annabelle
Anne
Annetta
Annette
Annice
Annis
Annot
Anusia
Anya
Hanna

Hannah
Hannie
Nan
Nancey
Nancy
Nanete
Nanette
Nannie
Nanny
Nettie
Netty
Nina
Nita
Panna

ANTOINETTE
Ann
Anna
Annie
Anny
Antonetta
Antonette
Antonia
Antonica
Nettie
Netty
Tania
Tanya
Tonette
Toni
Tonia
Tony
Tonya

ARABELLA
Arabela
Arabelle
Arbel
Arbela
Arbella
Arbelle
Orabel
Orabella
Orabelle

ARDITH
Ardie
Ardis
Ardra
Arduth
Artis
Dita

ARETHA
Arethusa
Oretha
Reta
Retha
Rita

ARIANA
Ariadne
Ariane
Oriana
Oriane

ARLISS
Arlee
Arleigh
Arlen
Arles
Arley
Arlie
Arlissa
Lee
Leigh
Liss
Lissa

ASHLEY
Ash
Ashleigh
Lee
Leigh

ASTRID
Arta
Astera
Asteria
Astra

AUDREY
Aud
Audie
Audlice
Audra
Audre
Audris
Audy

AUGUSTA
Aug
Augie
Auguste
Augusteen
Augustina
Augustine
Gus
Gussie
Gussy
Gusta

AURELIE
Aura
Auralie
Aurea

Aurelia
Aurely
Aury
Oralia
Oralie
Orelia
Orelie
Lee
Leigh
Lia

AURORA
Aura
Aurea
Aurey
Auri
Aurie
Aurore
Rora
Rorey
Rori
Rorie
Zora
Zorica

AVERELL
Ava
Avarell
Avarill
Averill
Avery
Avie
Avy

AVIS
Avice
Avie
Avise

AZURA
Azora
Azore
Azure
Zora
Zura

B

BAILEY
Baila
Baily
Bay
Bayla
Bayley
Beylah

BARBARA
Bab
Babbie
Babette
Babs
Bara
Barb
Barbe
Barbi
Barbie
Barbira
Barbra
Barby
Barra
Bobbee
Bobbi
Bobbie
Bobby
Bonnie
Bonny
Vara
Varinka
Vavara

BARRIS
Bara
Barra
Barrie

BATHILDE
Bathilda
Hilda
Hilde
Hildie
Hildy

BEATRICE
Bea
Beata
Beatrica
Beatriks
Beatrix
Beatriz
Beatrys
Bebe
Bee
Trice
Trix
Trixey
Trixie

BELINDA
Bela
Bella
Belle
Belva
Belynda
Lin
Linda
Lyn
Lynda

BENADICTA
Benadetta
Benadette
Benedetta
Benedette
Benita
Betta
Bette
Bettina
Tina

BERNADINE
Berna
Bernadeen
Bernadene
Bernadette
Bernadina
Bernadot
Bernadotte
Berne
Bernette
Bernie
Bernita
Dina

BERNICE
Bern
Berne
Berneice
Bernie
Bertrice
Bunny

BERTHA
Bert
Berthe
Berthie
Bertie
Bird
Birdie
Birdy

BERYL
Berylla
Berylle

BETHANY
Beth
Bettany

BEULAH
Lala

BEVERLY
Bev
Beva
Beverlee
Beverleigh
Lee
Leigh

BIBI
Bebe

BIRD
Birdie
Birdy
Byrd

BLANCHE
Bianca
Blanca
Blanch
Branca

BRENDA
Bren
Brenna
Brin
Brinda

BRIANE
Briana
Brianna
Brianne
Bryan
Brynja

BRIDGET
Biddie
Biddy
Birgit
Bride
Bridie
Brighid
Brigid
Brigit
Brigitta
Brigitte
Brit
Brita
Britt
Gidge
Gidget

BRITANNY
Bri
Brie
Brit
Britny
Britt
Tani
Tany

BRONWEN
Branwen
Wendie
Wendy

BROOKE
Brook
Brooks

BRUNHILDA
Brunhilde
Hilda
Hilde
Hildie
Hildy

C

CAITLIN
Cait
Cat
Catlie
Catlin
Kate
Katie
Katlin
Katy
Lin

CALANDRA
Cala
Calan
Caley
Calie

CALIDA
Cala
Cali
Calie
Lida

CALLAN
Calla
Calley
Callie
Cally

CAMERON
Camaron
Camey
Camie
Camiron
Camran
Camren
Camrin
Camron
Ron
Ronnie
Ronny

CANDACE
Candi
Candice
Candida
Candie
Candis
Candy
Candys

CARA
Carey
Cari
Carie
Carra
Carrey
Carri
Carrie
Carry

CARLOTTA
Carla
Carleen
Carlee
Carlene
Carley
Carlie
Carline
Carly
Karla
Karlotta
Lotta
Lottie
Lotty

CARMEN
Carey
Carie
Carma
Carmina
Carrie
Carry
Cary
Charmaine

CAROL
Cara
Carey
Cari
Carla
Carleen
Carlen
Carley

Carli
Carlie
Carlin
Carlotta
Carlotte
Carly
Carlyn
Carlynn
Carolin
Carolina
Caroline
Carolyn
Carolynn
Carri
Carrie
Carroll
Cary
Caryl
Kara
Karey
Kari
Karla
Lin
Linn
Linne
Lyn
Lynn
Lynne

CARRICK
Cara
Carey
Carie

Carra
Carrie
Carry
Rick
Rickie
Ricky

CASEY
Case
Cass
Cassie

CASSANDRA
Cass
Cassey
Cassie
Cassy
Sandi
Sandie
Sandra
Sandy

CASSIDY
Case
Casey
Cass
Cassey
Cassie
Cassy
Sid
Sidie
Sidy

CATHERINE
Cait
Caitlin
Caitrin
Carin
Caryn
Cass
Cassey
Cassie
Cassy
Catarin

Catarina
Cate
Caterina
Caterine
Catharina
Catharine
Cathe
Cathi
Cathie
Cathleen
Cathlene
Cathrina
Cathrine
Cathryn
Cathy
Catti
Cattie
Catty

CECILIA
Cecil
Cecile
Cecily
Ceil
Celia
Celie
Cicely
Cissy
Sissie
Sissy

CELENDINE
Cela
Celandina
Celandine
Cele
Celedina
Celie
Dina
Dine

CELESTE
Celesta
Celestina

Celestine
Celia
Celie
Celina
Cissy
Sissy
Tina

CHANNING
Chan
Chana
Chaney

CHARITY
Charissa
Charita
Charito
Charo
Charry
Cherry
Rita

CHARLOTTE
Charla
Charleen
Charlene
Charline
Charlotta
Charyl
Cher
Cheree
Cherie
Cheryl
Lotta
Lotte
Lottie
Lotty
Shaleen
Sharlee
Sharlene
Sharyl
Sherrie
Sherry
Sheryl

WHAT'S IN A NAME?

Writers often struggle long and hard to come up with the perfect name for a character. It is said that Margaret Mitchell could only begin work on GONE WITH THE WIND after considering thousands of possible names for SCARLETT and RHETT. But what admirable and successful choices. Would SCARLETT have been the same person if she had been called HENRIETTA? HENRIETTA O'HARA? Could SCARLETT have fallen for a manly hero named BERNIE BUTLER? Even HENRIETTA O'HARA would have difficulty falling in love with BERNIE BUTLER!

CHARMAINE
Charmain
Charmian
Charmiane
Charmion

CHRISTINE
Chris
Chrissie
Chrissy
Christen
Christiana
Christie
Christina
Christy
Chrystal
Kirsten
Kirstie
Kirstin
Kirsty
Kris
Krissie
Krissy
Kristen
Kristie
Kristin
Kristel
Kristy
Krystal
Krystel
Krysten
Krystin
Krystle
Tina

CLAIR
Claire
Clara
Clare
Clarissa
Clarisse
Clarita
Klara

CLAUDIA
Claude
Claudette
Claudine
Gladys

CLEMENTINE
Clem
Clemence
Clementina
Clemmie
Clemmy
Tina

CLEOPATRA
Cleo
Pat
Patra
Pattie
Patty

CLIANTHA
Clia

CLORINDA
Chloe
Cloe
Clora
Clorie
Clorin
Cloris
Clorissa

CLOTILDE
Chloe

Cloe
Clothilda
Clothilde
Hilda
Hilde
Hildie
Hildy

COLEEN
Cole
Coletta
Colette
Coline
Colletta
Collette
Collie
Colline

CONSTANCE
Connie
Conny
Constancia
Constancy
Constanta
Constantina
Constanza
Konstanze
Stanzie
Tanzie
Tanzy

CONSUELA
Connie
Conny
Consuelo
Sue

CORA
Corie
Cory
Kora
Korie
Kory

CORDELIA
Cora
Cord
Cordie
Cordy
Corey
Corie
Cory
Delia
Lia

CORINNE
Cora
Corella
Corena
Corene
Coretta
Cori
Corie
Corina
Corine
Cory

CORLISS
Cora
Corey
Corie
Corla
Corlissa
Corlisse

Cory
Liss
Lissa

CORNELIA
Cora
Corney
Cornie
Corny
Nellie
Nelly
Lia

COSIMA
Cosetta
Cosette
Cosie
Cosy
Sima

COURTNEY
Coe
Cord
Cordie
Cordy
Cort
Cortie
Cortney
Corty
Court
Courtie
Courty

CRYSTAL
Chris
Chrissie
Christal
Christy
Cris
Crissie
Cristal
Crys
Cryssie
Crystle
Krystle

CYBIL
Cibyl
Cybill
Sib
Sibbie
Sibby
Sibella
Sibelle
Sibilla
Sibyl
Sibyll
Sybil
Sybilla
Sybille

CYNTHIA
Cindi
Cindie
Cindy
Cyndi
Cyndie
Cyndy
Cynthie

DACIA
Dacie

DANIELLE
Dan
Dana
Danelle
Danica
Danice
Daniela
Danita

Danni
Dannie
Danny
Danuta
Ella
Elle

DAPHNE
Daff
Daffie
Daffy
Daph
Fennie
Phennie

DARA
Darby
Darcy
Daria
Darya

DARLEEN
Darel
Darla
Darleen
Darline
Darrel
Darrell
Darryl
Daryl
Daryll

DAVIDA
Davina
Davita
Veda
Vida
Vita

DEANNA
Deana
Deann
Deanne
Dee
Dena
Dina

DEBORAH
Deb
Debba
Debbi
Debbie
Debby
Debora
Debra
Devora

DEE
Dede
Dedi
Deede
Deedee
Deedi
Didi

DEIRDRE
Dede
Dedi
Dee
Deede
Deedi
Deerdre
Derrie
Derry
Didi

DELFINE
Dela
Delafina
Delfina
Della
Dellaphina
Delphina
Delphine

DELIA
Del
Dela
Della
Dellie
Delly
Ella
Ellie
Elly
Lia

DELILAH
Dalilah
Delila
Lila

DENISE
Denice
Deniece
Dennie
Denny
Denyce

DESDEMONA
Desmona
Mona

DEVERELL
Deva
Devarell
Devarill
Deverill
Devery
Devie
Devy

DEVON
Devan
Deven
Devin
Devona

DIANA
Deana

Deanna
Deanne
Dede
Dedi
Dee
Deedi
Di
Diane
Diahann
Dian
Dianna
Dianne
Didi
Dina
Dinah
Dyan
Dyanna
Dyanne

DILLIAN
Dill
Dillia
Dilliana
Dillie
Dilly
Lian
Liana
Lianna
Llian
Lliana

DIONNE
Dina
Dinie

Dinnie
Dinny
Nonnie
Nonny

DOLORES
Delores
Deloris
Dollie
Dolly
Lola
Lolita
Lores
Loris

DOMINIQUE
Nicki
Nickie
Nicky
Nikki

DONNA
Dona
Donell
Donella
Donelle
Donia
Donis
Donita
Donni
Donnie
Donny

DORA
Dodie
Dody

Dore
Doreen
Dorelle
Dorene
Doretta
Dorette
Dori
Dorie
Dorin
Doris
Dorit
Dory

DOROTHY
Dodi
Dodie
Dody
Doll
Dollie
Dolly
Dora
Dori
Dorie
Dorotea
Dorothea
Dorthy
Dory
Dot
Dottie
Dotty

DRUELLA
Drucilla
Druelle
Ella
Elle

DULCIE
Dulce
Dulcea
Dulcia
Dulcinea
Dulcy

EARLENE
Earla
Earleen
Earlie

EARTHA
Erda
Ertha
Herta

EDELA
Eda
Edda
Eddie
Edie
Dela

EDEN
Edan
Edana
Eddie
Eddy
Edena
Edie
Edina
Den
Dennie
Denny

EDITH
Dita
Eda
Eddy
Edie
Edithe

Edythe
Eydie

EDLYN
Eda
Edel
Edie
Edlynn
Lyn
Lynn

EDWINA
Eda
Edie
Edina
Win
Winna
Winnie
Winny

EGBERTA
Bertha
Bertie
Berty
Bird
Birdie
Birdy
Egbertha
Egbird
Egbirda

EGLANTINE
Eglan
Eglana
Eglantina
Elana
Lana
Lanie
Tina

EILEEN
Aileen
Ailene
Eilene

ONE NAME FITS ALL

There are many names that are properly used by women and men. Here is a brief sampling of unisex names.

ABBY ... ALEX ... ASHLEY ... AUGIE ... BEVERLY ... BOBBY ... CATLIN ... CHRIS ... CLAIR ... DANA ... DENNY ... DORIAN ... FRAN ... FREDDY ... GERRY ... HALEY ... JACKIE ... JAMIE ... JERRY ... JO ... KENDALL ... KIM ... LANNY ... LEE ... LESLIE ... LOU ... LYNN ... MADDY ... MARION ... MARLIN ... MATTIE ... MEL ... NAT ... NICKY ... PAT ... PAULIE ... PHIL ... RAY ... ROBIN ... SAMMY ... SANDY ... SELBY ... SHELLY ... SID ... TAYLOR ... TEDDY ... TERRY ... VAL ... WALLY ... WHITNEY ... YVES.

Names such as ANNIE-JEAN and JOE-JACK abound in the South. Today, as a reflection of the unisex trend, we may see a more adventurous pairing of names. Don't be surprised if you are introduced to a newborn named MELISSA-FRED or even STANLEY-MAY!

ELAINE
Elana
Elayna
Elayne
Ella
Lainey
Lainie
Layne
Layney

ELDORA
Dora
Dorie
Dory
Eldie
Eldy
Ellie
Ledie

ELEANOR
Elenore
Elinore
Elinor
Ella
Elle
Ellen
Ellene
Elli
Ellyn
Elora
Leanor
Leonora
Leonore
Leora

Nell
Nellie
Nelly
Nora

ELIZABETH
Belle
Bess
Bessie
Bessy
Beth
Betsey
Betsy
Bette
Bettina
Bettine
Betty
Elisa
Elisabet
Elisabeth
Elisabetta
Elise
Elissa
Elita
Eliza
Elsa
Elsbeth
Elsebin
Else
Elsey
Elsie
Elspeth
Elsy
Elysia

Helsa
Ilsa
Isabel
Lib
Libbey
Libby
Lisa
Lisabeth
Lisbeth
Lise
Lisette
Lisettina
Lissa
Liz
Liza
Lizabeth
Lizbeth
Lizzie
Lizzy

ELLA
Elle
Ellie
Elley

ELLEN
Ella
Elle
Ellie
Elly

ELMIRA
Ella
Elle
Ellie
Elly
Elma
Elmyra
Mira
Myra

ELOISE
Ella
Ellie
Elly

Heloise
Lois
Louise

ELSA
Elsie
Elsy
Ilsa

ELVIRA
Ella
Ellie
Elly
Elva
Elvena
Elvera
Elvina
Vera

EMILY
Amelia
Amy
Em
Emelda
Emelia
Emilie
Emma
Emmaline
Emmey
Emmie
Emmy

EMMA
Em
Emmie
Emmy

EMMANUELLE
Emma
Emmanuella
Manuella
Manuelle

ERICA
Eiric
Eirica
Eri
Eric
Ric
Rica
Ricci
Rickie
Ricky

ERNESTINE
Ernie
Erny
Tina
Tine

ESMERALDA
Esme
Meralda

ESTELLE
Essie
Essy
Estele
Estella
Estralita
Estrella
Estrellita
Stel
Stella

ESTHER
Essa
Essie
Ester
Ettie
Etty
Hester
Hesther
Hettie
Hetty

ETHEL
Adal
Adele
Edel
Ella
Elle
Ethella
Ethelle

EUGENIA
Eugenie
Eugene
Gene
Genia
Genie

EUNICE
Euni
Eunie
Nina

EUSTACIA
Stacia
Stacie
Stacey
Stacy

EVANGELINE
Eva
Evangella
Eve
Vangie
Vangy

EVELYN
Eva
Evaline
Evalyn
Eve
Evie
Evita
Lyn
Lynn
Lynne

FALINE
Fal
Falla
Fallah
Far
Fara
Farra
Farrah

FELICE
Felicite

FERNANDA
Ferdinanda
Ferdinande
Fern
Fernande
Fernandina
Fifi

FILOMENA
Fila
Filamena

Filamuna
Filla
Fillamena
Fillamuna
Filomina
Mena
Mina
Philomena
Philomina

FIONA
Fenella
Fennie
Fionna
Finnula
Fionnula

FLORENCE
Flo
Flora
Flore
Flori
Floria
Florie
Florida
Florinda
Florri
Florrie
Florry
Floss
Flossi
Flossie
Flossy

FORTUNA
Fortune

FRANCES
Fan
Fanci
Fancie
Fancy
Fania
Fanni
Fannie
Fanny
Fanya
Fran
Francesca
Francoise
Francine
Frank
Franki
Frankie
Franky
Franni
Frannie
Franny
Fransesca

FREDERICA
Farica
Federica
Fred
Freddi
Freddie
Freddy
Fredericka
Frederique
Rica
Ricca
Ricki
Rickie
Ricky
Rikki

FREIDA
Fred
Freddie
Freddy
Freyda

GABRIELLA
Ella
Ellie
Elly
Gabbie
Gabby
Gabrielle
Riella

GAIL
Gael
Gale
Galiena
Galina
Gayle

GAINELL
Gain
Gaina
Gainall
Gayna
Gayne
Gaynell
Gaynor
Nell
Nellie
Nelly

GELSEY
Gele
Gells
Gelsie

GENEVIEVE
Gena
Geneva
Geneveve
Genevia
Genna
Gennie
Gina
Jennie
Jenny

GEORGIA
George
Georgena
Georgette
Georgiana
Georgianna
Georgina
Georgine
Georie
Georja

GERALDINE
Deena
Dina
Geraldina
Gerhandine
Gerri
Gerrie
Gerry
Giralda
Jeri
Jerie
Jerry

GERTRUDE
Gerda
Gert
Gertie
Gerty
Truda
Trudi
Trudy
True

GILBERTA
Berta
Bertha
Bertie
Bird
Birda
Birdie
Birdy
Gil
Gilbirda
Gilby
Gilla
Gillie
Gilly

GILLIAN
Gil
Gill
Gilla
Gillie
Gilly
Jill

Jillian
Jillie
Jilly
Lia
Lian

GINGER
Ginge
Gingie
Gingy
Ginny

GISELLE
Gisela
Gisele
Gisella
Gizella
Gizelle

GLADYS
Glad
Gladie
Glady

GLENDA
Gleana
Gleanus
Glen
Glena
Glenna
Glennis
Glyn
Glynis

Glynna
Glynnis

GLORIA
Glo
Glora
Gloriana
Glorianna
Glorianne
Glorie
Glory

GOLDA
Gold
Goldie
Goldy

GRACE
Gracie
Grazia

GRETCHEN
Greta
Grete
Gretel

GRISELDA
Selda
Zelda

GUDRUN
Gudrid
Gudrin
Gudron
Guthrum

GWENDOLYN
Gwen
Gwendolen
Gwendoline
Gwenn
Gwenna
Gwenne
Gwennie

Gwenny
Gwenovere
Gwyn
Gwyneth
Gwynne
Wendi
Wendie
Wendy
Wynne

HADLEY
Hada
Hadey
Hadie
Hadlee
Hadleigh
Lee
Leigh

HALE
Haile
Hal
Haley
Halie
Halina
Hallie

Hally
Hayle
Hayley
Haylie

HANNAH
Anna
Hanna
Hannie
Hanny

HARLEY
Harla
Harlee
Harleigh
Harley
Harlie
Lee
Leigh

HARRIET
Harrie
Harriette
Hatti
Hattie
Hatty

HAZEL
Haze
Hazelle

HEDDA
Heda
Heddie
Hedwig
Hedy
Heidi

> **Good name in man or woman . . . is the immediate jewel of their souls.**
>
> **OTHELLO**
> **Shakespeare**

HELEN
Aileen
Ailene
Aleen
Eileen
Elaine
Elana
Elayne
Eleanor
Eleanore
Elena
Elenore
Elinor
Elinore
Ella
Elle
Ellen
Ellena
Elli
Ellie
Elly
Ellyn
Elora
Galina
Helena
Helene
Hellie
Ileana
Ilene
Lana
Leanora
Lena
Lenora
Lenore
Leora
Lina
Lora
Nell
Nellie
Nelly
Nora

HENRIETTA
Eiric
Eirica
Errichetta
Etta
Etti
Ettie
Etty
Hattie
Hatty
Henrie
Henrieta
Henriette
Hettie
Hetty
Yetta
Yettie
Yetty

HERMIONE
Erma
Hermina
Hermine
Herminia
Hermose
Minnie
Minny

HILARY
Hill
Hilla
Hillaire
Hillary
Hilli
Hillie
Hilly

HILDEGARDE
Hilda
Hilde
Hildi
Hildie
Hildy

HOLLY
Holda
Holdia
Hollace
Holli
Hollie
Hollis
Hollye

HONORIA
Honor
Honora
Nora
Norie

HORTENSE
Hortensia
Tensia

ILKA
Ilke
Illona
Milka

ILLANA
Ilana
Lana

IMOGENE
Emogene
Imagen
Imagene
Imajean
Imogen
Imojean

INGRID
Inga
Inge
Inger

IRENE
Erene
Ireen
Irena
Irenee
Irina
Rena
Rina

IRIS
Irisa
Irita

IRMA
Erma
Ermina
Irmina

ISABEL
Bella
Belle
Ibbie
Ibby
Isa
Isabeau
Isabela
Isabella
Isobel
Issie
Issy
Izabel

ISADORA
Isidore
Izzie
Izzy

ISOLDE
Isolda
Isolt

JACQUELINE
Jacki
Jackie
Jacquelyn
Jacqui
Jacquie

JAIME
Jaimee
Jaimie
Jamie
Jayme
Jaymie

JANE
Jan
Jana
Janel
Janelle
Janet
Janette
Janey
Jani
Janice

Janie
Janina
Janine
Janis
Janna
Jehane
Jessie
Joan
Joanna
Johanna
Juana
Juanita

JEAN
Jeane
Jeanette
Jeanice
Jeanine
Jeanne
Jeannette
Jeannine
Jene
Jenine
Jennelle

JEMINA
Jamima
Jemie
Jemma
Jemmie
Jemmimah
Jemmy
Mimi

JENNIFER
Gen
Genna
Gennifer
Genny
Jen
Jenna
Jenni
Jennie
Jenny

JESSICA
Jess
Jesse
Jessi
Jessie
Jessy

JETHRA
Jetha
Jetta

JILL
Gilli
Gillian
Gillie
Gilly
Jilli
Jillian
Jilliana
Jillie
Jilly

JOAN
Joanie
Joannie
Jodi
Jodie
Jody
Joni
Jonie

JOANNA
Jo
Jo Ann

Jo-Ann
Joann
Joanne
Johanna

JOCELYN
Jocelin
Joceline
Jocelyne
Joselina
Joseline
Josette
Josey
Josie
Joslyn
Lin
Linn
Lyn
Lynn

JOSEPHINE
Jo
Joey
Jose
Josefina
Josefine
Josephina
Josette
Josey
Josi
Josie
Josy

JOYCE
Joia
Joy
Joyous

JUDITH
Jodi
Jodie
Jody
Judi
Judie
Judy

SMACK DAB IN THE MIDDLE

This book is dedicated to the exploration of first names but middle names have a big impact, too. There are many famous folks with important and distinctive middle names. In many cases your whole image of that person depends upon the crucial middle name.

JOHN QUINCY ADAMS is a perfect name for a statesman or president but JOHN ADAMS is a name so common he could be anything at all. JOHNNIE ADAMS is probably a jockey. EDGAR ALLEN POE is a name that evokes images of scary stories told by candlelight but EDGAR POE could as easily be the fellow at your bank who handles accounts receivable. EDDIE POE is a name for a car mechanic. If you take his middle name from JOHN PAUL JONES you get a name often found on motel registration forms. And what would they have called the play and movie if MOZART's middle name hadn't been AMADEUS?! Here are some other famous names that lean toward their centers for stature.

JOHANN SEBASTIAN BACH

JEAN PAUL BELMONDO

ELIZABETH BARRETT BROWNING

WILLIAM JENNINGS BRYAN

WILLIAM CULLEN BRYANT

EDGAR RICE BURROUGHS

THOMAS ALVA EDISON

JULIA WARD HOWE

FRANCIS SCOTT KEY

HENRY CABOT LODGE

JOYCE CAROL OATES

JANE BRYANT QUINN

GEORGE BERNARD SHAW

CORNELIA OTIS SKINNER

ELIZABETH CADY STANTON

ROBERT LEWIS STEVENSON

HARRIET BEECHER STOWE

JOHN CHARLES THOMAS

MICHAEL TILSON THOMAS

WILLIAM CARLOS WILLIAMS

SMOKEY THE BEAR

JULIE
Jules
Julia
Juliann
Julianna
Julianne
Julienne
Juliet
Julieta
Julietta
Juliette

JUSTINE
Jus
Jussie
Jussy
Justin
Justina
Tina

KALIKA
Kaile
Kaley
Kali
Kalila
Kayle
Kelila
Kelula

KAREN
Cara
Cari
Carie
Carin
Carrie
Kara
Kari
Karinna
Karinne

KATHERINE
Caitlin
Caitrin
Caren
Carin
Caryn
Cass
Cassie
Cassy
Cat
Catarina
Cate
Caterina
Catha
Catharine
Cathe
Catherine
Cathi
Cathie
Cathleen
Cathrine
Cathy
Catie
Caty
Ekatarina
Ekaterina
Karen
Karena
Kari
Karin
Kass
Kata
Katalin
Katarna
Kate
Katerina
Katerine
Katey
Katha
Katharine
Kathe
Kathi
Kathie
Kathleen
Kathryn
Kathy
Katie
Katrine
Katrinka
Katya
Kay
Kaye
Kit
Kittie
Kitty

KELLY
Kelley
Kelli
Kellie

KERRY
Kerian
Kerie

KIMBERLY
Kim
Kimball
Kimmie
Kimmy

KIRA
Kireen
Kyra

KRISTEN
Kris
Krissie
Krissy
Tina

KYLE
Kile
Kileen
Kilene
Kyleen
Kylene

KYNA
Keen
Keena
Kina

L

Lorna
Lorri
Lorrie
Lorry
Lurleen
Lurlene
Lurline

LANA
Laney
Lani
Lanie
Lanney
Lanni
Lannie
Lanny

LAURA
Larissa
Laure
Laureen
Laurel
Lauren
Laurene
Lauretta
Laurette
Laurice
Laurie
Lora
Loralee
Lore
Loreen
Lorelee
Lorelei
Loren
Lorena
Loretta
Lorette
Lori
Lorie
Lorilee
Lorilei
Lorinda
Lorita

LAVERNE
Laverna
Verna
Verne

LAVINIA
Vini
Vinia
Vinie

LEANA
Ann
Anna
Leandra
Leann
Leanna
Leanne
Leona
Leone
Liana
Lianea

LEE
Leigh

LELAND
Lan
Lana
Lancha
Land
Landa
Lee
Leeland
Leelandra
Leigh
Lelandra

LEONORE
Lennie
Lenny
Lenora
Lenore
Leona
Leonarda
Leonora
Leontine
Leontyne
Leora
Letti
Lettie
Letty

LESLIE
Lee
Leigh
Les
Leslee
Lesleigh
Lesley

Lesly
Lessie
Lessy
Lezlie
Lezley

LETITIA
Leda
Leta
Lethia
Leticia
Letisha
Letti
Lettice
Lettie
Letty
Tish
Tisha

LILITH
Lil
Lili
Lilia
Lilie
Lilli
Lillie
Lilly
Lily

LILLIAN
Lil
Lila
Lili
Lilia
Lilian
Lilianna
Lilianne
Lilli
Lilliana
Lilliane
Lillias
Lillie
Lilly
Lily

LINDA
Lin
Lina
Lindi
Lindie
Lindy
Lindsay
Lindsey
Linette
Linn
Linna
Linne
Linnea
Lyn
Lynda
Lynn
Lynne
Lynnette

LOIS
Lo
Loie
Loise
Louise

LONDON
Dona
Donna
Lon
Loni
Lonni
Lonnie
Lonny

LORRAINE
Laraine
Loraina
Loraine
Lorayna
Lorayne
Lori
Lorrayne
Rainey
Rainie
Rainy

LOUISE
Alison
Allison
Aloise
Eloise
Heloise
Lois
Loise
Lola
Lolita
Lou
Louisa
Lu
Luisa
Luise
Lulu

LUCILLE
Luce
Lucey
Luci
Lucia
Lucie
Lucilla
Lucinda
Lucy
Lulu

LUCRETIA
Lu
Lucia
Lucie
Lucrece
Lulu

LUDMILLA
Lu
Ludi
Ludie
Ludmila
Lulu
Mila
Milla
Millie

LUELLA
Ella
Ellie
Lou
Louella
Lu
Luelle

Lula
Lulu

LYDIA
Lidia
Lidie
Lydie

LYNNE
Lin
Linn
Linne
Lyn
Lynn
Lynnel
Lynnelle
Lynnette

LYSANDRA
Lysa
Lyssa
Sandie
Sandra
Sandy

MABEL
Mab
Mabelina
Mabeline
Mabelle
Mai
Maibelle
May
Maybelle

MACKENZIE
Kenna
Kenza
Kenzie
Mac
Mackenza
Mackie
Macky

MADELINE
Lena
Lin
Lina
Linne
Lyn
Lynne
Mada
Madalena
Madalene
Madalina
Madaline
Madalyn
Madalynn
Madeleine
Madelena
Madelene
Madella
Madelle
Madelon
Madge
Madie
Madlen
Madlin
Magda
Magdalene
Magdaline
Mal
Mala
Malena
Malina
Marleen
Marlena
Marlene
Marlina
Marline

Maud
Mauda
Maude
Maudene
Maudie

MAGNOLIA
Mag
Maggi
Maggie
Nola
Nolie

MAHALIA
Lala
Lia
Mahala
Mahalah

MAIDA
Mai
Maidie
Maidy
May
Mayda
Maydie
Maydy

MAISIE
Mai
Maise
May
Maysie
Maysy

MALVA
Mal
Mala
Malvina

MARCIA
Mara
Marcel
Marcella
Marcey
Marci
Marcie
Marsha
Marsh
Masha

MARDELL
Dell
Della
Dellie
Mara
Maradell
Maradella
Mardella
Marelda

MARGARET
Greta
Gretchen
Madge
Mag
Maggie
Maggy

Mairghread
Maisey
Margareta
Margarete
Margarette
Margarita
Margarite
Marge
Margiad
Margie
Margo
Margot
Marguerite
Margy
Marjie
Marjorie
Marjory
Marjy
Meagan
Meagen
Meg
Megan
Megen
Meggie
Meggy
Meta
Peg
Peggie
Peggy
Rita

MARIGOLD
Mara
Maragold
Mari
Mary
Marygold

MARILYN
Mara
Maralyn
Mari
Marilee
Marilen
Marilin

TRENDSETTER NAMES OF THE 1980's

The list of most popular names at the end of the 1800's bears a rather striking similarity to that of the 1940's, '50's and even '60's. But in the last twenty years there hasn't been a MARY, MARGARET, PATRICIA or SUSAN on the feminine list. On the masculine list there isn't a JOHN, ROBERT, ANTHONY, JOSEPH or WILLIAM in sight. Here are the most popular names given in the 1980's.

FEMININE NAMES		MASCULINE NAMES	
JENNIFER	ASHLEY	MICHAEL	ADAM
SARAH	MEGAN	MATTHEW	ANDREW
JESSICA	MELISSA	CHRISTOPHER	DANIEL
AMANDA	KATHERINE	BRIAN	JASON
NICOLE	STEPHANIE	DAVID	JOSHUA

Marla
Marlena
Marlene
Marlin
Marlo
Marlon
Marly
Marlyn
Marylin
Marylyn
Meralee
Merilee
Merilen
Merilin
Merralee
Merrilee
Merrileigh
Merrilie
Merrilyn

MARTHA
Mara
Mart
Marta
Marte
Martella
Martelle
Marthe
Marti

Martie
Martina
Martine
Marty
Mat
Matti
Mattie
Matty

MARTINE
Marina
Marna
Marne
Marni
Marnie
Martina

MARY
Maira
Maire
Mairi
Mal
Mallory
Mame
Mamie
Mara
Marella

MARY *Cont.*

Maria
Marian
Mariana
Marianna
Marianne
Marie
Mariel
Mariella
Mariessa
Marietta
Mariette
Marika
Marilee
Marilin
Marilyn
Marin
Marina
Marion
Marisa
Marissa
Marita
Marla
Marlo
Marna
Marni
Marnie
Marya
Maryann
Maryanna
Maryanne
Marylin
Masha
Maura
Maure
Maureen
Maurene
Mava
Mavis
Meralee
Merralee
Merri
Merrie
Merrilee
Merrileigh
Merrilie
Merry
Mimi
Minnie
Minny
Miriam
Mitzi
Moira
Moire
Mollie
Molly
Muriel

MATILDA

Hilda
Hilde
Hildie
Hildy
Mat
Mathilda
Mathilde
Matti
Mattie
Matty
Matya
Tilda
Tilde
Tillie
Tilly

MAUDE

Maud
Mauda
Maudeen
Maudene
Maudie

MAUREEN

Mara
Maura
Maurene
Mo
Moira

MAVIS

Mae
Mai
Maiva
Maive
Maivie
Maivis
Mava
Mave
Mavie
May
Mayva
Mayve
Mayvie
Mayvis

MAXINE

Max
Maxi
Maxie
Maxime
Maxy

MAYA

Mae
Maia
Maye

MEGAN

Meagan
Meagen
Meg
Megen
Meggie
Meggy
Meghan

MELANIE

Lania
Lanie
Lannie
Lanny
Mel
Melane

Melania
Melantha
Melany
Mell
Mellie
Melly

MELBA
Mal
Malba
Malva
Melva

MELINDA
Lin
Linda
Lindy
Lyn
Lynda
Lyndy
Mal
Malinda
Malynda
Mandy
Mel
Melinde
Mellie
Melly
Melynda

MELISSA
Lisa
Lise
Lissa
Lisse
Malisa

Malissa
Mel
Melisa
Melise
Melisse
Mellie
Melly
Milisa
Milise
Milissa
Milisse
Millie
Milly

MELODY
Lody
Lotie
Lottie
Lotty
Mel
Mellie
Melly

MERCEDES
Merce
Mercey
Merci
Mercie
Mercy

MEREDITH
Meradith
Merredith
Merri
Merridie
Merridith
Merrie
Merry

MERLE
Merla
Merril
Merrill
Merryl
Meryl
Meryle

MICHELLE
Mia
Michaelene
Michaelina
Michaeline
Michele
Micki
Mickie
Micky
Midge
Shellie
Shelly

MILDRED
Mil
Mildrid
Millie
Milly

MILICENT
Mel
Melicent
Melisanda
Melisande
Mellicent
Mellie
Melly
Millicent

Millie
Milly
Mitzie
Missie
Missy

MIRANDA
Mara
Maranda
Mira
Randa
Randie
Randy

MONIQUE
Mona
Monica
Nicki
Nickie
Nicky

MORGANA
Mora
Morabeal
Morbeal
Morgan
Morrigan

MYRNA
Mirna
Morna
Myra

Natasha
Nathalia
Nathalie
Nattie
Natty
Nettie
Netty
Talia
Talie
Tallia
Tallie
Tasha

NADINE
Dena
Dina
Nada
Nadeen
Nadene
Nadia
Nadya
Nydia

NANCY
Nan
Nana
Nance
Nancey
Nanci
Nancie
Nanette
Nanine
Nannie
Nanny
Nettie
Netty

NAOMI
Nomie
Nommie
Nommy

NATALIE
Nat
Natala
Natalia
Natalina
Nataline

NEDDA
Neda
Neddie
Neddy
Nedie
Nedra
Netta
Nettie
Netty

NERISSA
Nerita
Risa
Rissa
Rita

NICOLE
Coe
Cole
Colette
Cosette
Nicka
Nicki

Nickie
Nicky
Nika
Nikki
Nikola

NISSA
Nisa
Nissie
Nissy
Nysa
Nyssa

NOEL
Noela
Noella
Noelle
Nola

NORBERTA
Berta
Bertha
Berthe
Bertie
Nora
Norbertha

NOREEN
Nona
Nonnie
Nonny
Nora
Norene
Norine
Norma

NORRIS
Nora
Norisa
Norissa
Norrie
Norrisa
Norrissa
Norry
Risa
Rissa

OCTAVIA
Tavia
Tavie
Tavy

ODELIA
Delia
Delie
Lia
Odela

ODESSA
Dessa
Dessie
Dessy
Odie

OLGA
Elga
Helga
Ola
Olie
Ollie
Olly

OLIVIA
Livia
Livie
Nollie
Nolly
Oli
Olie
Olive
Ollie
Olly

OLYMPIA
Ola
Olie
Ollie
Olly
Pia

ONDINE
Dina
Dine
Ondina

OPHELIA
Lia
Ofelia
Ophele

OTTALIE
Lee
Leigh
Ottalee
Ottilie

PAIGE
Page

PALOMA
Loma
Pal
Pali
Pallie
Pally
Papa

PAMELA
Pam
Pamelia
Pamelyn
Pammi
Pammie
Pammy

PARNELL
Nell
Nella
Nellie
Nelly
Parnella
Parrie
Pernell
Pernella
Perrie

PATIENCE
Pat
Pattie
Patty

PATRICIA
Pat
Patia
Patrice
Patrizia
Patsy
Patti
Pattie
Patty
Payton
Tricia
Trish
Trisha

PAULA
Paola
Paolina
Pauletta
Paulette
Paulie
Paulina
Pauline
Paulita
Polly

PEARL
Pearla
Pearlie
Perla
Perlie

PENELOPE
Nel
Nellie
Nelly

Pen
Pennie
Penny

PERDITA
Dita
Perda

PERSIS
Persa
Persus
Sis
Siss

PETRA
Pet
Peta
Petrina
Petrinella
Petrinelle
Petronella
Petronelle
Petronia
Petronilla
Petula
Petulia
Trina
Trinia
Tula
Tulia

PHILIPPA
Pippa
Pippie
Pippy
Phil
Phillie
Phillippa
Philly

PHOEBE
Phebe

PHYLLIS
Phil
Phillie
Philly
Phylie
Phylis
Phyllie
Phylly

PLACIDA
Placidia

PRISCILLA
Cilla
Cillie
Pris
Prissie
Silla
Sillie

PRUDENCE
Pru
Prudi
Prudie
Prue

PRUNELLA
Ella
Ellie
Elly
Pru
Prue
Pruna
Prunelle

QUEENE
Queen
Queena
Queenie
Quen
Quennie

QUERIDA
Quera
Querie
Querita
Rida
Rita

QUINLAN
Lan
Lana
Lannie
Lanny
Quina
Quinn
Quinna

RACHEL
Rae
Rachele
Rachelle
Rakel
Raquel
Raquela
Ray
Rey
Rochelle
Shel
Shelley
Shellie
Shelly

RAMONA
Mona
Rae
Ramonda

RANDALL
Randi
Randie
Randy

RAPHAELA
Rafaela
Raffaela
Raphella

RAZILI
Rae
Raza
Razi
Razie

REBECCA
Becca
Becka
Becki
Beckie
Becky
Reba
Rebeca
Rebeka
Reva
Riva
Rivkah
Rivkie

REGINA
Gina
Ginnie
Ginny
Reg
Reggie
Reggy

RENATA
Rene
Renee
Renetta
Renette
Renisa
Renise
Renita

REVA
Riva

RHEA
Rea
Ria

RHODA
Ro
Roe

RHONDA
Ro

Roe
Ron
Ronni
Ronnie
Ronny

RICARDA
Ricci
Riccie
Riccy
Ricki
Rickie
Ricky

ROBERTA
Bobbi
Bobbie
Bobby
Rob
Robbi
Robbie
Robbin
Robby
Robbyn
Robin
Robina
Robine
Robyn

ROCHELLE
Rachel
Ro
Roe
Shel
Shelley
Shellie
Shelly

RODERICA
Rica
Ricci
Rod
Roddie
Roddy

A ROSE BY ANY OTHER NAME . . . MAY BE HARD TO PRONOUNCE!

"A rose by any other name would smell as sweet." Okay. That's conceded. But, would it sound as sweet? Would it be as easy to pronounce? Would it scan? What can you rhyme with skulnick? Is it romantic to send your loved one a dozen long-stemmed skulnicks? Would Carmen be as alluring with a skulnick between her teeth? Can you imagine growing prize winning American Beauty skulnicks?

ROLANDA
Lana
Landa
Landie
Landy
Laney
Lani
Lannie
Lanny
Rollie
Rolly

ROMA
Romi
Romie
Romy

RONA
Rhona
Roni
Ronie
Rony

ROSALIND
Lin
Linda
Lyn
Lynda
Ros
Rosa
Rosalina
Rosalinda
Rosaline
Rosalyn
Rosalynd
Rosalynda
Rose
Roselina
Roselinda
Roseline
Roselyn
Roselynd
Roselynda
Rosie
Roz
Rozalin
Rozalina
Rozalind
Rozalinda
Rozalyn
Rozalynd
Rozalynda
Rozie
Rozy

ROSAMOND
Rosa
Rosamonda
Rosamund
Rosamunda
Rose
Rosemond
Rosie

ROSE
Rosa
Rosie

ROSEMARY
Marie
Mary
Rosa
Rosalie
Rose
Rosemarie
Rosetta
Rosette
Rosie

ROWENA
Rena
Ro
Row
Rowe

ROXANNE
Anna
Anne
Ros
Rosana
Rosanna
Rosanne
Roxana
Roxane
Roxanna
Roxi
Roxie
Roxina
Roxine
Roxy

RUTH
Ruta
Ruthe
Ruthie
Ruthy

SABRINA
Brie
Brin
Brina
Bryn
Bryna
Ina
Rina
Saba
Sabryna

SADIRA
Dira
Sada
Sadi
Sadie

SALOME
Sal
Salley
Sallie
Sally

SAMANTHA
Sam
Sama
Sami
Sammie
Sammy

SAMARA
Mara
Mira
Sam
Sama
Sami
Samie
Samira
Semira

SANDRA
Sandi
Sandie
Sandy
Sondra
Sonnie
Sonny

SARAH
Sada
Sadie
Sal
Sallie
Sally
Sara
Sarena
Sarene
Sari
Sarina
Sarine
Sarita
Shara
Sharie
Sharon
Sharrie
Sharron
Sheri
Sherie
Sherri
Sherrie
Sherry
Shery
Sydel
Sydella
Sydelle
Zara
Zarah
Zaria
Zarya

SELENA
Lena
Lina
Salena
Salina
Sal
Sallie
Sally
Selina

SELMA
Zelma

SEONID
Sinead

SERAPHINA
Sara
Sarafina
Sarafine
Saraphina
Saraphine
Serafina
Serafine

SHANNON
Shana
Shani
Shanie
Shanna
Shanni
Shannie
Shanny
Shenna

SHARON
Ron
Ronni
Ronnie
Ronny
Shar
Shara
Shari
Sharie
Shary
Sheron
Sherri
Sherrie
Sherry

SHEILA
Celia
Celie
Selia
Sheela
Sheelagh
Sheelah
Sheilagh
Sheilah
Shella
Shelli
Shellie
Shelly

SHELBY
Selbie
Selby
Shel
Shelli
Shellie
Shelly

SHIRLEY
Lee
Leigh
Sher
Sheri
Sherie
Sherri
Sherrie
Sherry
Sherl
Shirl
Shirlee
Shirleen
Shirleigh
Shirlene
Shirline

SIBLEY
Lee
Leigh
Sib
Siblee
Sibleigh

SIDNEY
Cid
Cyd
Sid
Sidell
Sidella
Syd
Sydell
Sydella
Sydney

SIGFRIEDA
Freda
Fredda
Freida
Freyda
Sig
Sigfreda
Sigfreyda
Siggi
Siggie
Siggy

SIRENA
Rena
Rina
Sara
Sarina
Sera
Serena

SONIA
Son
Soni
Sonja
Sonnie
Sonny
Sonya
Sunny

SOPHIA
Sofia
Sofie
Sophie

STEPHANIE
Stefa
Stefana
Stefane
Stefania
Steffie
Stepha
Stephane
Stephania
Stephie

STUART
Stew
Steward
Stewart
Stewie
Stu
Stuie

SUSAN
Siusan
Sue
Sukey
Suki
Sukie
Susana
Susanna
Susannah
Susanne
Susette
Susi
Susie
Susy
Suzann
Suzanna
Suzanne
Suzette
Suzi
Suzie
Suzy

SYDELL
Dell
Della
Dellie

Sid
Sidell
Sidella
Sidie
Sydella
Sydie

SYLVIA
Silvi
Silvia
Silvie
Sylvi
Sylvie

SYNA
Sina
Sine
Syne

TABITHA
Tabbi
Tabbie
Tabi
Tabie
Tabith
Tabithe

TALIA
Lia
Tali
Talli
Tallia
Tallie

Tally
Thali
Thalia
Thalie

TAMARA
Mara
Mari
Tam
Tamath
Tammi
Tammie
Tammy

TANSY
Tansi
Tansie
Tanzi
Tanzie
Tanzy

TANYA
Tan
Tani
Tania
Tanie
Tanni
Tannie
Tanny
Tasha

TATIANA
Tani
Tania
Tanya
Tati
Tatia
Tatie
Taty
Tatyana
Titania
Titanya

TERESA
Tera
Terese
Teressa
Teri
Terie
Terri
Terrie
Terry
Tess
Tessa
Tessie
Theresa
Therese
Tira
Tracie
Tracy

THADDEA
Thad
Thada
Thadda
Thaddi
Thaddia
Thaddie

THEODORA
Dora
Dori
Dorie
Dory
Ted
Teddie

FAMOUS UNNAMED PEOPLE

There was a time in history, before surnames, when some people did not even have a first name! Consequently, there are countless men and women who are utterly unknown because they were utterly nameless.

Those who spring instantly to mind are the inventor of the wheel or the discoverer of fire. Possibly the most courageous of all is that unnamed person who first determined the artichoke to be edible!

Teddy
Thea
Theadora
Theo

THEONE
Thea
Theana
Theane
Theanie
Theano
Theo
Theoni
Theonie

THORA
Thoria
Thorie
Thyra
Thyria
Tyra
Tyria

TIFFANY
Fanni
Fannie
Fanny
Taff
Taffi
Taffie
Taffy
Tiff
Tiffi
Tiffie
Tiffy

TIMOTHEA
Thea
Tim
Tima
Timma
Timmi
Timmie
Timmy

TOMASA
Toma
Tomasina
Tomasine
Tommi
Tommie
Tommy

TRACEY
Traci
Tracie
Tracy

TRUDA
Tru
Trudi
Trudie
Trudy
True

TUESDAY
Day
Toos
Tues
Tuse

TYBALLA
Balla
Bella
Belle
Tiballa
Tibella
Tibelle
Ty
Tyballia
Tybella
Tybelle

Valerie
Valery
Valeska
Valli
Vallie
Vally
Valonia
Velika

ULRICA
Rica
Ricca
Ricci
Riccie
Riccy

UNA
Ona
Oona

VALENTINA
Tina
Tine
Val
Vala
Valantina
Valantine
Valda
Valencia
Valentia
Valentina
Valentine
Valera
Valeria

VANESSA
Nessa
Nessi
Nessie
Nessy
Van
Vana
Vania
Vanna
Vannia
Vannie
Vanny
Vanya

VERONICA
Rana
Rani
Ranie
Rena
Reni
Renie
Ron
Rona
Roni
Ronie
Ronni
Ronnie
Ronny
Vera
Verana
Verena
Veronique

VICTORIA
Tora
Tori

Torie
Tory
Vic
Vick
Vicki
Vickie
Vicky
Vikki
Vitoria
Vittoria

VIOLET
Letti
Lettie
Letty
Vi
Viletta
Vilette
Voleta
Voletta
Volette

VIRGINIA
Gina
Ginni
Ginnie
Ginny

VIVIAN
Viv
Vivie
Vivyan

WALLIS
Walda
Wallace
Walli
Wallie
Wally

WESLEY
Lee
Leigh
Wes
Weslee
Weslie

WHITNEY
Whit
Whitey
Whitie
Wit

WILHELMINA
Bill
Billi

Billie
Billy
Mina
Minni
Minnie
Minny
Velhemina
Velma
Vilhemina
Vilhemine
Vilma
Wila
Wilhemina
Willa
Willamina
Willi
Willie
Willy
Wilma
Wylma

WILONA
Lona
Loni
Lonia
Lonie
Wilone
Wilonia

WINIFRED
Fred
Freddi
Freddie
Freddy
Win
Winnie
Winny

WINTER
Win
Winnie
Winny

WYNNE
Win
Winnie
Winny
Wyn
Wyneth
Wynna
Wynnie

XENIA
Xantha
Xanthe
Zena
Zenana
Zenia
Zenobia
Zinnia

YOLANDA
Lana
Landa
Landi
Landie
Landy
Lanni
Lannie
Lanny
Yolande

YVETTE
Eva
Evalyn
Eve
Evelyn
Evette
Yetta
Yettie
Yetty
Yves
Yvonna
Yvonne

ZADA
Sada
Sadi
Sadie
Zade
Zadi
Zadie

ZELDA
Selda
Selde
Zelde

ZELIA
Celia
Selia

ZOE
Zooey

ZORA
Sara
Sarah
Saria
Zara
Zarah
Zorah
Zorana
Zorania
Zorina
Zorinia

A good name is rather to be chosen than great riches.

PROVERBS

A

AARON
Ari
Arnie
Arny
Aron
Ron
Ronnie
Ronny

ABBOTT
Ab
Abbie
Abby
Abbot

ABEL
Ab
Abbie
Abby
Abe

ABELARD
Ab
Abbie
Abby
Abel

ABNER
Ab
Abbie
Abby

ABRAHAM
Ab
Abbie

Abby
Abe
Abram
Abran
Avram
Avi

ADAIR
Ad
Addie
Addy

ADALARD
Ad
Adal
Addie
Addy

ADAM
Ad
Addie
Addy

ADDISON
Ad
Addie
Addis
Addy
Son
Sonny

ADLER
Ad
Addie
Addy
Adlar
Adle

ADOLPH
Ad
Addie
Addy
Adolf
Dolf
Dolph

ADRIAN
Ad
Addie
Addy
Adrien
Hadrian

ALAN
Al
Allan
Allen
Allie
Ally
Allyn
Alyn

Call me Tom...Thomas is the
name I get whipped by!

TOM SAWYER
Mark Twain

ALARIC
Al
Alarick
Rich
Rick
Rickie
Ricky
Ulric
Ulrick

ALASTAIR
Al
Alas
Alasdair
Alistar
Alister
Allie
Ally

ALBAN
Al
Albie
Alby

ALBERT
Al
Alberti
Alberto
Albie
Alby
Bert
Bertie

ALCOTT
Al
Alcot
Cott

ALDEN
Al
Aldan
Aldie
Aldin
Aldy

Den
Denny

ALDO
Al
Aldie
Aldy

ALEXANDER
Al
Alasdair
Alastair
Alaster
Alec
Alejandro
Alek
Aleksander
Aleksei
Alex
Alexandre
Alisander
Allesandro
Alysandyr
Sander
Sanders
Sandy
Sasha
Saunder
Saunders
Xander
Zander

ALFRED
Al
Alf
Alfie
Alfredo
Alfy
Fred
Freddie
Freddy
Fredo

ALGERNON
Al
Alger
Algie
Algy

ALLARD
Al
Alar
Alard
Alerd
Allar
Allerd

ALPHONSE
Al
Alf
Alfie
Alfons
Alfy
Alonse
Alonso
Fons
Fonsie
Fonz
Fonzie

ALROY
Al
Roy

ALTON
Al
Altan
Alten
Altie
Alty

ALVIN
Al
Alvie
Alvy

ALVIS
Al
Alvie
Alvy

AMBROSE
Ambie
Ambrosio
Amby

AMORY
Amery
Amy
Mory

ANATOLE
Anatol
Anatoli
Nat
Nate

ANDREW
Anders
Andie
Andre
Andreas
Andrei

Andres
Andy
Dandy
Drew
Dru

ANGELO
Ange
Angelico
Angelos
Angie
Angy

ANGUS
Ange
Angie
Angy
Gus

ANTHONY
Antoine
Anton
Antone
Antonin
Antonio
Antony
Toni
Tony

ARCHER
Arch
Archie
Art

ARCHIBALD
Arch
Archie
Art

ARDEN
Ardan
Dan
Danny
Den
Denny

ARIEL
Ari
Arie
Aril

ARLEN
Arlan
Arlie
Arlo
Arlon
Arly
Lan
Lanny
Len
Lenny
Lon
Lonny

ARMAND
Arm
Arman
Army
Mandy

ARNOLD
Arn
Arnie
Arny

ARTHUR
Art
Artie
Arty

ASHBY
Ash

ASHER
Ash

ASHLEY
Ash
Lee
Leigh

ASHTON
Ash

ATHERTON
At
Ath
Athie
Athy
Attie
Atty

ATTILIO
Attila

AUBREY
Aub
Brey

AUGUST
Augie
Auguste
Augustin
Augustine
Augustus
Austen
Austin
Gus

AVERILL
Ave
Averell
Averil
Avi

AVERY
Ave
Avi

AXEL
Ax

BAILEY
Baily
Bayley
Lee
Leigh

BALDRIC
Bald
Balder
Ric
Rick
Rickie
Ricky

BALDWIN
Bald
Balder
Win
Winnie
Winny

BANNING
Ban
Banner

BARCLAY
Bar
Barrie
Barry
Clay

BARNABAS
Barn
Barnaby
Barnie
Barny

BARRETT
Barret
Barrie
Barry

BARTHOLOMEW
Bar
Bart
Barth
Bartholo
Bartholome
Bartholomieu
Bartlet
Bartley
Barty
Bat

BARTON
Bar
Bart
Bartie
Barty

BASIL
Basile
Basilio

BAXTER
Bax

BAYARD
Bay

BEAUMONT
Beau
Bo
Mont
Montie
Monty

BEAUREGARDE
Beau
Beauregard
Bo

Reg
Reggie

BELDEN
Bel
Beldan
Beldon
Dan
Danny
Den
Denny
Don
Donny

BENEDICT
Ben
Benedetto
Benet
Benigno
Benito
Bennie
Benny
Benoit
Bettine
Betto

BENJAMIN
Ben
Benjie
Benjy
Bennie
Benny

BENNETT
Ben
Benet
Benn
Bennie
Benny

BENSON
Ben
Bennie
Benny
Son
Sonny

BENTLEY
Ben
Bennie
Benny
Lee
Leigh

BERKELEY
Berk
Berkie
Berky
Lee
Leigh

BERN
Berne
Bernie
Berny

BERNARD
Barnard
Barney
Bearnard
Bern
Bernardo
Bernhard
Bernhart
Bernie
Berny

BERTHOLD
Bert
Bertie
Bertold
Bertolt
Berty

BERTRAM
Bert
Bertie
Berty

BLAINE
Blain
Blane
Blayne

BLAIR
Blaire
Blayre

BOGART
Bogie

BOLIVAR
Bola
Boli

BONAIRE
Bon
Bonnie
Bonny

BOOKER
Book
Bookie
Booky

BORDEN
Bord
Bordan
Bordie
Bordy
Dan
Danny
Den
Denny

BRADFORD
Brad
Ford

BRADLEY
Brad
Lee
Leigh

The first recorded personal name was "N'ARMER" in 3000 B.C. Given to Egypt's first pharoah, it means "the father of men."

BRADY
Brad
Bradey
Bradie

BRANDER
Brand
Brandy

BRANDON
Bran
Brand
Brandan
Brandy
Brant
Dan
Danny
Don
Donny

BRENDAN
Bren
Brend
Brendon
Dan
Danny
Don
Donny

BREWSTER
Brew
Bruce

BRIAN
Bri
Briant
Bry
Bryon

BRODERICK
Brod
Brodie
Derek
Derick

Rick
Rickie
Ricky

BROOKE
Brook
Brooks

BROTHER
Bro
Brud

BRUCE
Brucie
Brucy
Bruno

BUCKLEY
Buck
Buckie
Bucky
Lee
Leigh

BURGESS
Burge
Burr

BURNIS
Burn

BURTON
Burt
Burtie
Burty

BYRON
By
Ron
Ronnie
Ronny

CADELL
Cad
Dell

CADMAN
Cad
Man
Mannie
Manny

CALDER
Cal
Cally

CALDWELL
Cal
Cald
Caldie
Caldy
Cally

CALEB
Cal
Cally

CALHOUN
Cal
Cally

CALVIN
Cal
Cally
Vin
Vinnie
Vinny

CAMDEN
Cam
Cammie
Cammy
Den
Denny

CAMERON
Cam
Cammie
Cammy
Ron
Ronnie
Ronny

CARMEN
Car
Carey
Carie
Carmi
Carmine

CARRICK
Carey
Carie
Carr
Cary
Rick
Rickie
Ricky

A name is a kind of a face.

Thomas Campbell

CARROLL
Carol
Carrol
Carole

CARTER
Car
Cart
Cort

CASEY
Case
Cass

CASSIDY
Cass
Cassie
Cassy

CASSIUS
Cass
Cassie
Cassy

CASTOR
Cass
Cassie
Cassy
Cast

CEDRIC
Cad
Ced
Ric

Rick
Rickie
Ricky

CHAD
Chaddie
Chaddy

CHANDLER
Chan
Chaney
Channer

CHARLES
Carl
Carlo
Carlos
Carrol
Carroll
Cary
Chad
Chaddie
Chaddy
Charley
Charlie
Charlot
Charlton
Chas
Chaz
Chic
Chico
Chuck
Karel
Karl

CHAUNCEY
Chance
Chancey
Chaunce

CHESTER
Chet

CHRISTIAN
Chris
Chrissie
Chrissy
Christie

CHRISTOPHER
Chris
Chrissy
Topher

CLARENCE
Clare

CLARK
Clarke

CLAUDE
Claudell
Claudio

CLAYBOURNE
Born
Bourne
Clay
Clayborn

CLAYTON
Clay
Clayte

CLEMENT
Clem
Clemmie
Clemmy

CLIFFORD
Cliff
Cliffie
Ford

CLINTON
Clint

COLBERT
Bert
Bertie
Berty
Colby
Cole

COLBY
Coe
Cole

COLIN
Coe
Col
Cole
Collie
Collin

CONAN
Coe
Con
Connie
Conny

CONLAN
Con
Connie
Conny
Lan
Lanny

CONRAD
Con
Connie
Conny
Konrad
Rad
Raddie
Raddy

CONSTANTINE
Con
Connie
Conny
Costa
Stan
Stanley
Stantey

CONWAY
Con
Connie
Conny
Way

CORNELIUS
Corn
Cornell
Cornie
Corny

COSMO
Cos
Mo

COURTNEY
Coe
Cort

Court
Courtland

CRAWFORD
Craw
Ford

CREIGHTON
Craig
Cray

CROSBY
Cros
Cross
Croz

CULLEN
Cull
Cully
Len
Lenny

CURTIS
Curt
Kurt

CYRIL
Cy

CYRUS
Cy
Russ
Sy

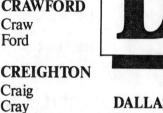

DALLAS
Dal
Dale

DALTON
Dal
Dale
Dalt

DAMION
Damien
Damon

DANA
Dane
Danna

DANIEL
Dan
Dani
Danile
Danilo
Dannie
Danny
Dante

DARCY
Darce
Darie
Darrie
Darry
Dary

DARIUS
Dari

Daria
Darian

DARRELL
Darel
Darell
Derel
Derrel
Derrell

DARREN
Daren
Darin
Darrin

DAVID
Dab
Dabney
Daud
Dave
Davey
Davie
Davis
Davy
Daw
Dov
Dow

DEAN
Deno
Dino

DEDRICK
Deder
Rick
Rickie
Ricky

DELANO
Del
Dellie
Delly
Lan
Lannie
Lanny

DELBERT
Bert
Bertie
Berty
Del
Dellie
Delly

DELLING
Dell
Dellie
Delly

DELMER
Del
Dellie
Delly
Delman
Delmar

DEMETRIUS
Dem
Demmie
Demmy

DENBY
Den
Denny

DENNIS
Den
Denis
Denny

DENTON
Den
Denny
Dent

DENVER
Den
Denny

DEREK
Der
Derrick
Derrie
Derry
Rick
Rickie
Ricky

DERWARD
Durward
Ward

DESMOND
Des
Desi
Desie

Desman
Desmon
Desmund

DEVERELL
Dev
Dever
Deveril
Deverill

DEVIN
Dev
Vin
Vinny

DEVLIN
Dev
Devlyn
Lin
Lyn

DEWITT
Dew
Dewey
Wit

DEXTER
Dex

DMITRI
Dim
Dimmie
Dimmy

DONALD
Don
Donnie
Donny

DORIAN
Dori
Dorie
Dorien
Dory

EARLY AMERICA

In 1587 in Raleigh Colony (the first English-speaking colony in America) of the 99 men and boys registered, 23 were named JOHN, 15 were THOMAS, 10 were WILLIAM and 7 each were RICHARD and HENRY.

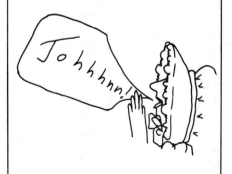

DOUGLAS
Doug
Dougie
Douglass

DOVEV
Dov
Dove

DUDLEY
Dud
Lee
Leigh

DUNCAN
Dun
Dunc
Dunmore

DUSTIN
Dust
Dustie
Dusty

DWAYNE
Wayne

DWIGHT
De Witt
Ike
White

DYLAN
Dill
Dillon
Dyl

EBENEZER
Ben
Bennie
Benny
Eban
Ebanezer
Eben
Ezer

EDEL
Ed
Eddie
Eddy

EDGAR
Ed
Eddie
Eddy
Ned
Neddie
Neddy
Ted
Teddie
Teddy

EDMUND
Ed
Eddie
Eddy
Ned
Neddie
Neddy
Ted
Teddie
Teddy

EDWARD
Ed
Eddie
Eddy
Edouard
Eduard
Eduardo
Edvard
Ned
Neddie
Neddy
Ted
Teddie
Teddy
Ward

EDWIN
Ed
Eddie
Eddy
Win
Winnie
Winny

EGBERT
Bert
Bertie
Berty
Egg
Eggie

ELDRIDGE
El
Eldredge

ELISHA
Eli
Elia
Elihu
Elijah
Lisha

ELLERY
El

ELLIOTT
El
Eliot
Elliot

ELLIS
El
Ellison

ELMER
El
Elm

ELROY
El
Roy

ELTON
El
Elt

ELVIS
El
Elvin

EMIL
Emile
Emilio
Emlen
Emlyn
Mel

EMMANUEL
Emanuel
Imanuel
Immanuel
Mannie
Manny
Manuel

EMMET
Emmett

EPHRAIM
Efram
Efrem
Ephram
Ephrem

ERHARD
Erhart

ERIC
Erik
Ric
Rick
Rickie
Ricky

ERNEST
Earn
Earnest
Ern
Erneste
Ernesto
Ernie
Ernis
Erno
Ernst

ERSKINE
Kin
Kinny

ERWIN
Er

Irwin
Win
Winnie
Winny

ETHAN
Etan

EUGENE
Eugenio
Gene

EVAN
Ev

EVERETT
Ev
Evart
Everet
Rett

EZEKIEL
Ezra
Ezer
Zeke

FABIAN
Fabi
Fabien
Fabius
Fabyan

FARLEY
Fair

Fairley
Fairleigh
Far
Farleigh
Lee
Leigh

FARNHAM
Far
Farn

FARRAR
Far
Farr

FARRELL
Far
Farr
Farral

FERDINAND
Ferd
Ferdie
Ferdy
Fernand
Fernandas
Fernande
Fernando

FERGUS
Fergie

FIELDER
Field
Fielding

FLETCHER
Fletch

FORTUNE
Fortuna
Fortunato
Fortunio

FRANCIS
Chic
Chico
Fran
France
Francesco
Franchot
Franco
Francois
Frank
Frankie
Franklyn
Frannie
Franny
Frans
Franz
Pancho

FRAZER
Fraser
Frasier
Frazier

FREDERICK
Federico
Fred
Freddie

FREDERICK
Cont.

Freddy
Frederic
Fredric
Fredrich
Fredrick
Rick
Rickie
Ricky

FREEMAN
Free
Man
Mannie
Manny

FREMONT
Free
Mont
Monty

FULTON
Fuller
Fultie
Fulty

G

GABRIEL
Gabbie
Gabby
Gabe

GAMEL
Gam
Gamal

Gamble
Gambling
Gamlen
Gamlin
Gamlon
Gemmel

GARDNER
Gar
Gardiner

GARETH
Gar
Gart
Garth

GARFIELD
Field
Fielder
Gar

GARLAND
Gar
Garlan
Garlen
Garlin

GARNER
Gar
Garn

GARRICK
Gar
Rick
Rickie
Ricky

GARRISON
Gar
Garris
Gary

GARY
Garett
Garrett

GAVIN
Gavan
Gaven
Van
Vanny
Vin
Vinny

GAYLORD
Gay
Gaylard
Gayle
Lord

GEOFFREY
Geoff
Godfrey
Jeff
Jeffrey

GEORGE
Geordie
Georg
Georges
Georgie
Georgio
Georgy
Giorgio
Goran
Jerzy
Jorge
Jorgen
Yorick
Yuri

GERALD
Garret
Garrett
Gary
Gerard
Geraldo
Gerardo
Gerhard
Gerrie
Gerry
Jerald
Jerrie
Jerry

GIDEON
Gid
Giddy
Deon
Dion

GILBERT
Bert
Bertie
Berty
Gil
Gilberto
Gilby
Gilly

GILES
Gide
Gil
Gileon
Gilles
Gilwan

GILFORD
Ford
Gil
Gilly

GILLEAD
Gil
Gille
Gilly

MOST POPULAR BIBLICAL NAMES

OLD TESTAMENT

Male	Female
ABRAHAM	DEBORAH
ADAM	EVE
BENJAMIN	HANNAH
DANIEL	JUDITH
DAVID	MIRIAM
ETHAN	REBECCA
IRA	RUTH
JACOB	SARAH
JOSHUA	
MICHAEL	
NATHAN	
SAUL	
SETH	

NEW TESTAMENT

Male	Female
JASON	ANNA
JOHN	CANDACE
JOSEPH	CLAUDIA
LUKE	DIANA
MARK	ELIZABETH
MATTHEW	JOHANNA
PAUL	LYDIA
PETER	MARY
PHILIP	MARTHA
STEPHEN	PHOEBE
THOMAS	PRISCILLA
TIMOTHY	RHODA
	SUSANNA

FUTURE TESTAMENT

Masculine	Feminine
ATARI	BINARY
DIODE	BIT
LOTUS	CHIP
MODEM	COBOL
FLOPPY DISC	FORTRAN
TANDY	PAC-MAN

GILMORE
Gil
Gilly

GILROY
Gil
Gilly
Roy

GORDON
Gord
Gordie
Gordy

GRANTLAND
Gran
Grant
Grantlan
Lan
Lanny

GRANVILLE
Gran
Grant
Gren
Grenville

GREGORY
Greg
Gregoire
Gregor
Gregorio
Gregson
Grig
Grigory
Grishca

GRIFFIN
Grif
Griffie
Griffith
Griffy

GROVER
Gro
Grove

GUNNAR
Gun
Gunn
Gunter
Gunthar
Gunther

GURIEL
Guri

GUSTAVUS
Gus
Gussy
Gustave
Gustavo
Tavio
Tavus

HADLEY
Had
Lee
Leigh

HALDAN
Dan
Danny
Hal

HALEY
Hal
Hale
Lee
Leigh

HALSEY
Hal
Hall

HAMILTON
Ham
Tony

HAMPTON
Ham
Hamp
Tony

HARLAN
Harland
Harley
Harlin
Harlow
Harry

Lan
Lanny

HARMON
Harman
Harry

HAROLD
Hal
Harry

HARRISON
Harry
Son
Sonny

HARTLEY
Hart
Harte
Lee
Leigh

HARVEY
Harve

HASKEL
Skelly

HASTINGS
Haste

HAVELOCK
Have
Haver
Lock

HAYWOOD
Hay
Hays
Wood
Woodie
Woody

HENRY
Enrico
Enrique
Enzio
Hal
Hank
Harris
Harrison
Hen
Henke
Henning
Henny
Henri
Henrico
Henrik
Henryk

HERMAN
Arman
Armand
Armant
Ermanno
Harman
Harmon
Herm
Hermann
Hermie
Hermino

HERSCHEL
Hersch
Herschie
Hersh

Hershel
Hershie
Shel
Shelley
Shelly

HILARY
Hil
Hill
Hillaire
Larry

HILLEL
Hill
Hilly

HIRAM
Hi
Hy
Hyram

HOBART
Bart
Ho
Hob
Hobie
Hoby

HOLLIS
Holl
Hollie
Hollin
Holly

HORTON
Hort
Horten
Orton

HOWARD
Howe
Howie
Ward

HUBERT
Bert
Bertie
Berty
Hubie

HUGH
Hewett
Huey
Hughie
Hugo

HUMBERT
Bert
Bertie
Berty
Hum
Humbie
Humby

HUMPHREY
Hum
Hump
Humphy
Humpie

HUNTER
Hunt

HUNTINGTON
Hunt
Hunter

HYLAND
Hy
Hylan
Lan

Land
Lanny

HYMAN
Hy
Man
Mannie
Manny

IGNATIUS
Ig
Iggie
Iggy
Ignace
Ignatz
Ignazio
Nat
Nate

INGEMAR
Inga
Inge
Inger

IRVING
Irv
Irwin
Win
Winnie
Winny

ISAAC
Ike

Isaak
Isak
Itzak
Itzik
Yitzak
Zack

ISIDORE
Dore
Dorie
Dory
Isi
Izadore
Izy

ISRAEL
Isie
Izy

ITIEL
Itie
Tiel

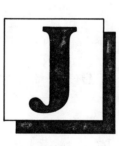

JACOB
Cob
Cobbie
Cobby
Giacomo
Jack
Jackie
Jacky
Jacopo
Jacques

Jaime
Jaimes
Jake
Jakob
Jamey
Jascha
Yaakov

JAMES
Diego
Giacomo
Jacques
Jaime
Jamey
Jamie
Jay
Jayme
Jim
Jimmie
Jimmy
Seamus
Shamus

JANUS
Jan

JASON
Jace
Jase
Jay
Son
Sonnie
Sonny

JEDIDIAH
Jed

The best name to have if you you want to win an Oscar is GEORGE. Among the GEORGEs so honored have been:

GEORGE ARLISS
GEORGE CHAKIRIS
GEORGE BURNS
GEORGE CUKOR
GEORGE KENNEDY
GEORGE SANDERS
GEORGE C. SCOTT
        and
GEORGE STEVENS

JEFFREY
Geoff
Geoffrey
Jeff

JENNINGS
Jenn
Jenner
Jenny

JEPHTAH
Jeb
Jebbie
Jebby
Jep
Jeppie
Jeppy

JEREMIAH
Jer
Jeremy
Jerrie
Jerry
Remy

JEROME
Jer
Jerrie
Jerry

JESSE
Jess

JETHRO
Jed
Jeddie
Jeddy
Jet
Jettie
Jetty

JOEL
Jo
Joe
Yoel

JOHN
Evan
Geno

Gino
Hans
Iain
Ian
Ivan
Jack
Jackie
Jacky
Jan
Jean
Jenkin
Joachim
Joannes
Jochanan
Jock
Johan
Johannes
Johnnie
Johnny
Jon
Jonathan
Juan
Nat
Nate
Nathan

Owen
Sean
Shamus
Shane
Shawn

JORDAN
Dan
Danny
Jord
Jordie
Jordy
Jory

JOSEPH
Beppo
Giuseppe
Jaska
Jessup
Jo
Joe
Joey
Jose
Josephus

Yosef
Yussif

JOSHUA
Josh

JOSIAH
Jo
Josh
Josie

JUDAH
Jud
Judd
Jude

JULIAN
Jules
Julie
Julio
Julius

JUSTIN
Just
Justino
Justus

KARL
Carl

KASPAR
Cap
Cappie

Cappy
Caspar
Casper
Cass
Gaspar

KEANE
Kean
Keen
Keenan

KELLY
Kelley

KELSEY
Kel
Kell
Kells
Kelly

KELVIN
Kel
Kell
Kells
Kelly
Vin
Vinny

KENDALL
Ken
Kendal
Kendel
Kenn
Kenner
Kennie
Kenny

KENNETH
Ken
Kenn
Kenner
Kennie
Kenny

KENYON
Ken
Kenner
Kennie
Kenny
Kenyan

KERMIT
Ker
Kerm
Kermie
Kermy
Kerrie
Kerry

KERWIN
Ker
Kerrie
Kerry
Win
Winnie
Winny

KEVIN
Kev
Vin
Vinny

KIMBALL
Kim
Kimbie
Kimby
Kimmie
Kimmy

KINGSLEY
King
Kingsleigh
Lee
Leigh

KIP
Kippie
Kippy

KIRBY
Kerby

KIRKLAND
Kip
Kippie
Kippy
Kirk
Kirklan
Lan
Land
Lanny

LAMONT
Lamie
Lamy
Mont
Montie
Monty

LANE
Lan
Laney
Lannie
Lanny
Layne

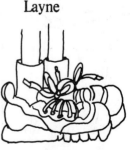

LANGFORD
Ford
Lan
Lang
Lannie
Lanny

LANGSTON
Lan
Lang
Lannie
Lanny
Lanston

LAWRENCE
Larrie
Larry
Lars
Lauren
Laurence
Laurens
Laurent
Laurie
Lauro
Lon
Lonnie
Lonny
Loren
Lorens
Lorenz
Lorenzo

LEANDER
Ander
Anders
Lee
Leigh

LEE
Leigh

LELAND
Lan
Land
Lannie
Lanny
Lee
Leigh

LEMUEL
Lem
Lemmie
Lemmy

LEON
Len
Lennie
Lenny
Leo

LEONARD
Len
Lennie
Lenny
Leo
Leon
Leonardo
Leonhard
Leonhart
Lon
Lonnie
Lonny

LEOPOLD
Lee
Leo
Poldy

Polly

LEROY
Lee
Leigh
Roy

LESLIE
Lee
Leigh
Les

LESTER
Les

LEVANT
Lev
Lever
Levy

LEWIS
Lew
Lewie
Lou
Louey
Louis
Luis

LINCOLN
Linc

LINDBERT
Bert
Bertie
Berty

Lin
Linbert
Lind
Lindie
Lindy

LINDSAY
Lin
Lindsey
Linsay
Linsey

LIONEL
El
Ellie
Elly
Lion

LLEWELLYN
Lew
Lewie
Lewis
Llewellin
Lou
Louellen
Lyn

LONDON
Don
Donnie
Donny
Lon
Londie
Londy
Lonnie
Lonny

LONGFELLOW
Fell
Fellow
Lon
Long
Longer
Lonnie
Lonny

LONSDALE
Dale
Lon
Lonnie
Lonny
Lons

LOWELL
Lovell
Lowe

LUCIAN
Luc
Luca
Lucas
Luce
Luciano
Lucien
Lucius
Luka
Lukas
Luke

LUDWIG
Lud
Luddie
Luddy
Ludgewig

LUNDY
Lun
Lund

LYLE
Lisle
Lile
Lille

LYNDON
Lin
Lindon
Linnie
Linny
Lyn
Lynd
Lyndie
Lyndy
Lynn
Lynne
Lynnie

MACKENZIE
Ken
Kenn
Kennie
Kenny

Mac
Mack
Zee

MADDOCK
Mad
Maddie
Maddox
Maddy

MALCOLM
Mal
Malc

MANFRED
Fred
Freddie
Freddy
Man
Manfredo
Mannie
Manny

MANLEY
Lee
Leigh
Mann
Mannie
Manny

MANUEL
Man
Mannie
Manny

MANUS
Man
Mann
Mannes
Mannus

MARC
Marcel
Marcello

Marcus
Mark

MARION
"Duke"
Marlon

MARLON
Lon
Lonnie
Lonny
Marlan
Marlin
Marlow

MARSHALL
Marsh

MARTIN
Mart
Martie
Marty

MARVIN
Marv

MASON
Mace
Mase
Son
Sonnie
Sonny

MATTHEW
Mat
Mateo
Matheu
Mathieu
Matt
Matteo
Matthaus
Mattia
Mattie
Matty

SURNAME means "super-name." These names were added in order to differentiate one JOHN from another JOHN. The law in England decreeing the use of the surname was passed by EDWARD IV in 1465 and instructed the people to take last names based upon a town, color, or a trade they pursued. It was a better way to be sure that taxes were collected from each and every TOM, DICK and HARRY!!

MAURICE
Mauricio
Maurie
Maurizio
Maury
Moe
Morey
Morie
Moritz
Morris
Morse
Morus

MAXIMILLIAN
Mac
Mack
Max
Maxie
Maxy

MELBOURNE
Born
Borne
Bourne
Mel

Melborn
Melborne
Melbourn

MELVILLE
Mel

MELVIN
Mel
Melvyn
Vin
Vinnie
Vinny

MENDEL
Del
Dellie
Delly
Mandel
Mannie
Manny
Mendie
Mendy

MERCER
Merce

MEREDITH
Merry

MERLIN
Marlin
Marlon
Marlow
Merle

MICHAEL
Michail
Michel
Michon
Mick
Mickey
Mickie
Micky
Miguel
Mike
Mikel
Mikey
Mikhail
Mischa
Mitch
Mitchel
Mitchell
Shell
Shelly

MILBURN
Milborn
Milbourn
Milbourne
Mill
Miller
Milly

MILFORD
Ford
Mill
Miller
Milly

MILLARD
Mill
Miller
Millord
Milly

MILLER
Mill
Milly

MILTON
Milt
Miltie
Milty

MONTAGUE
Mont
Montie
Monty
Tague

MONTGOMERY
Mont
Montie
Monty

MORRIS
Mo
Moe
Morey

Morie
Mory

MORTIMER
Mort
Mortie
Morty

MORTON
Mort
Mortie
Morty

MURPHY
Murf
Murph

MURRAY
Murr

MURTAGH
Murt

MYRON
Mayron
Ron
Ronnie
Ronny

NATHAN
Nat
Nate

NAYLOR
Nailer
Nailor
Nay
Nayle
Nayler

NEAL
Neale
Neil
Niel

NELSON
Nels
Son
Sonnie
Sonny

NEVILLE
Nev
Nevill
Newell

NEVIN
Nev
Nevan
Neven
Nevins
Niven
Vin
Vinny

NICHOLAS
Coe
Cole
Colin
Klaus
Nick
Nico
Nicol
Nicole
Nikita
Nikki
Nikolai
Nikolas
Nikolaus

NOLAN
Lan
Lannie
Lanny
Noland
Nole

NORBERT
Bert
Bertie
Berty
Norby

NORMAN
Norm
Normie
Normy

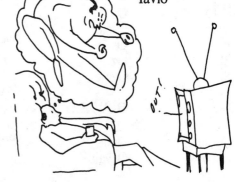

NORRIS
Norrie
Norry

NORTON
Nort

OAKLEY
Lee
Leigh
Oak
Oakleigh

OBERT
Bert
Bertie
Berty
Ober

OCTAVIUS
Octavio
Tavi
Tavio

ODELL
Dell
Dellie
Delly
Odie

ODIN
Den
Dennie
Denny
Oden
Odie

OGDEN
Den
Dennie
Denny
Ogdin

OLIVER
Nollie
Olivier
Ollie
Olly

ORSON
Son
Sonnie
Sonny

ORVILLE
Orval
Orvill
Orvile

OSBORN
Born
Borne
Bourn
Bourne
Os
Osborne
Osbourn
Osbourne
Ossie
Oz
Ozzie

OSCAR
Os
Oscie
Ossie
Oz
Ozzie

OSWALD
Os
Ossie
Osvald

Oswaldo
Oz
Ozwald
Ozzie
Wald
Waldie
Waldy
Waldo
Wallie
Wally

P

PALMER
Palm

PARKER
Park

PARNELL
Nell

Nelly
Parnel
Parry
Pernel
Pernell
Perry

PATRICK
Pad
Paddie
Paddy
Pat
Patrice
Patricio
Patsy
Pattie
Patty
Paxton

PAUL
Pablito
Pablo
Paolo
Paolus
Paulie
Paulus
Pauly
Pavel

INITIAL RESPONSE or PARDON MY ACRONYM...

Not only are you known by your name, but you are also, often, known by your initials. Many famous people, such as J.F.K. or F.D.R., are instantly known by just those three little letters. Monograms can play tricks on you, though. A former president of the American Name Society, L.R.N. ASHLEY, notes that the composer, ARTHUR SEYMOUR SULLIVAN, never ever used his initials. Consider the plight of a charming gentleman named SAMUEL OGDEN BROWN!! And SAM and ARTHUR are not alone. BRIGET URSUL GARRETT happens to be statuesque and lovely in spite of her initials and DAVID UPTON DUGAN is a real womanizer. Sometimes initials can be too revealing. RANDOLPH ALAN TYLER is thought by many to be just what his monogram implies. Sometimes parents are most mindful of the monogram when they choose a name for their little ones. JOY OLIVIA YARDLEY is a JOY no matter how you look at her name!!

PAYTON
Pay
Payt
Peyton

PENROD
Pen
Penn
Rod

PERCIVAL
Percie
Percy
Val

PETER
Parkin
Pearce
Pearson
Pedro
Peirce
Perkin
Perkins
Perry
Pete
Petey
Petr
Petros
Petrus
Pierce
Pierre
Piers
Pieter
Pietro

PHILIP
Filip
Filipe
Phil
Phillip
Phillipe
Phillipp
Phillippe
Philly

PINKERTON
Pink
Pinker
Pinkie
Pinks
Pinky

PORTER
Port
Portor
Porty

POTTER
Pot
Pots
Potsie
Potsy
Pottie
Potty

PRESCOTT
Cot
Pres
Prescot
Prez
Scot
Scott
Scotty

PRESTON
Pres
Prest
Presty
Prez

PURVIS
Perv
Pervis
Pervus
Purvus

QUENTIN
Quent

QUINCY
Quince

QUINLAN
Lan
Lannie
Lanny
Quin
Quinn

RADCLIFFE
Cliff
Cliffe
Cliffy
Rad
Radcliff
Raddie
Raddy

RAFFERTY
Rafe
Raferty
Raff

RALPH
Rafe
Ralf
Rolf

RAMSAY
Ram
Ramsey

RANDALL
Ran
Randal
Randel
Randell
Randie
Randy

RANDOLPH
Dolf
Dolph
Randie
Randy

RAPHAEL
Rafael
Rafe
Raff
Raffaelo
Ralph

RAYMOND
Ray
Raymund

RAYNOR
Rain
Rainer
Rainor
Ray
Rayner

REECE
Rees
Reese
Rhys
Rice

REEVES
Reeve

REGINALD
Naldo
Reg
Reggie
Reinhold
Renaldo
Renaud
Reynold
Rex
Ronald

REINHART
Hart
Reinhard
Reinharte

REMINGTON
Rem
Remi
Remie
Reming
Remmie
Remming
Remmy
Remy

REUBEN
Reuvin
Rube
Ben

RICHARD
Dick
Dickie
Dicky
Ric
Ricard
Ricardo
Riccard
Riccardo
Rich
Richardo
Richie
Rick
Rickie
Ricky
Ritchie
Ritchy
Rocco

RIDER
Ride

RIDLEY
Lee
Leigh
Ridleigh

RILEY
Lee
Leigh
Reilly

RIPLEY
Lee
Leigh
Rip

ROBERT
Bob
Bobbie
Bobby
Dob
Dobs
Hob
Hobs
Rip
Robart
Robb
Robbie
Robby
Roberto
Robin
Robinson
Rupert
Ruperto
Ruprecht

RODNEY
Rod
Roddie
Roddy

ROGER
Hodge
Roge
Rogerio
Rozer
Rugerio
Rutger

ROLAND
Lan
Lanny
Rolan
Rolando
Rollie
Rolly
Rowland

RONALD
Ron
Ronnie
Ronny

ROSCOE
Coe
Ross

ROSSANO
Ross

RUDOLPH
Dolf
Dolph
Rodolf
Rodolfo
Rodolph
Rodolpho
Rolf
Rolph
Rudy

RUSSELL
Russ
Russel
Rusty

RUTHERFORD
Ford
Ruther

**Three things I never lend —
my 'oss, my wife and my
name.**

Robert Smith Surtees

SALVATORE
Sal
Sallie
Sally
Salvador

SAMUEL
Sam
Sammie
Sammy
Samson
Samuels

SANFORD
Ford
Sandy

SARGENT
Sarge

SAWYER
Saw
Sawyere
Sayer
Sayers
Sayre
Saryres

SAXON
Sax

SCHUYLER
Sky
Skyler
Skyller

SCOTT
Scot
Scotty

SEBASTIAN
Bastian
Bastiano
Bastien
Sebastien

SEDGEWICK
Sedge
Sedgewyck
Wick
Wyck

SELBY
Sel

SERGE
Sergei
Sergi
Sergio

SEYMOUR
Morey
Mory
Seymore
Sy

SHANLEY
Lee
Leigh
Shan
Shane
Shaney

SHANNON
Shan
Shane
Shaney

SHELDON
Don
Donnie
Donny
Shel
Shellie
Shelly

SHEPARD
Shep
Shephard

SHERIDAN
Dan
Danny
Sher
Sherrie
Sherry

SHERMAN
Manny
Sherm
Shermy

SHERWIN
Sher
Sherrie
Sherry
Win
Winnie
Winny

SHERWOOD
Sher
Sherrie
Sherry
Wood
Woodie
Woody

SIDNEY
Sid
Syd
Sydney

SIEGFREID
Ieg
Sigfried

SIGMUND
Siegmond
Siegmund
Sig
Siggy
Sigismund

SILVANUS
Sil
Silvain
Silvan
Silvano
Silvie
Silvio
Silvy

SIMON
Si
Sim
'Simmie
Simmon
Simmons
Simons

SIMPSON
Si
Sim

In the late 1970s **DR. GEORGE McDAVID** and a group of interested scientists from Georgia State University learned that the children in the classroom with the most popular names tended to fare better than those with unpleasant or unusual names. They gave teachers an essay to grade and found that essays written by hypothetical **ELMERs** or **BERTHAs** got consistently lower grades than the exact same paper written by a hypothetical **JAMES** or **SUSAN**.

DR. THOMAS BUSSE of Temple University has also linked I.Q. and achievement test scores to the popularity or desirability of a child's name. Regardless of social or ethnic background, boys with the names **DAVID, MICHAEL, PAUL, JOHN, GARY, JAMES, RICHARD, SCOTT** or **STEVEN** do better. Girls' names which seemed to have a positive effect are **SUSAN, LINDA, BARBARA, CAROL, CINDY** and **DIANE**.

Simpie
Simpsie
Simpsy
Son
Sonnie
Sonny

SOLOMON
Sal
Salman
Sol
Solly
Soloman
Zalman

SPENCER
Spence
Spense
Spenser

STAFFORD
Ford
Staff

STANLEY
Stan
Stanislaus
Stanislaw
Stanislus

STEPHEN
Etienne
Esteban
Stefan
Stefanas
Stefano
Steffen
Steffens
Stephan
Stephano
Stephanus
Stepka
Stevan

Steve
Steven
Stevey
Stevie

STUART
Stew
Steward
Stewart
Stewie
Stu
Stuie

SYLVESTER
Silvester
Sly

TABOR
Tab
Tabbie
Tabby

TAGGART
Gart
Tag

TALMAN
Tal
Tally

TAYLOR
Tailor
Tay

TERRENCE
Terence
Terry

THADDEUS
Tad
Tadd
Taddeo
Taddie

Taddy
Thad
Thaddie
Thaddy

THEODORE
Dore
Dorey
Dorie
Dory
Fedor
Feodor
Fyodor
Ted
Teddie
Teddy
Teodoro
Theo

Theodoric
Theodoro

THOMAS
Tam
Tamas
Thom
Thoma
Tom
Tomas
Tomaso
Tommie
Tommy

THORNTON
Thor
Thorn

Thorne
Thorney

TIMON
Tim
Timmie
Timmy

TIMOTHY
Tim
Timmie
Timmy

TOBIAS
Toby

TODD
Tod

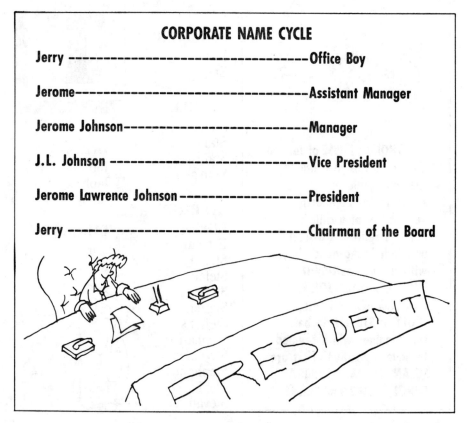

CORPORATE NAME CYCLE

Jerry --Office Boy

Jerome--Assistant Manager

Jerome Johnson--------------------------------Manager

J.L. Johnson ---------------------------------Vice President

Jerome Lawrence Johnson-----------------------President

Jerry --Chairman of the Board

TURNER
Turn

TYLER
Tiler
Ty
Tyle

TYRONE
Ty

TYRUS
Ty

Toddie
Toddy

TOLLAND
Toll
Tollan
Tollie
Tolly

TORRANCE
Torance
Torrie
Torry
Tory

TRAVIS
Trav

TREVOR
Trev

TROY
Roy

TRUMAN
Tru
True

TUCKER
Tuck

TYSON
Son
Sonnie
Sonny
Ty
Tyse

URIAH
Uri

VALDEMAR
Demar
Val
Vald

VALENTINE
Val
Valentin
Valentino

VERNON
Vern

VICTOR
Vic
Vick
Viktor
Vittore
Vittorio

VINCENT
Vin
Vince
Vincente
Vinnie
Vinny

VIRGIL
Verge
Virge

VLADIMIR
Vlad
Vladdie
Vladdy

WAKEFIELD
Field
Fielder
Fielding
Wake

WALCOTT
Cot
Wal
Wall
Wally

WALDO
Wal
Walden
Waldon
Wall
Wally

WALFRED
Fred
Freddie
Freddy
Wal
Wall
Wally

WALKER
Walk

WALLACE
Wal
Wall
Wallis
Wally

WALTER
Wal
Wall
Wally
Walt

WARNER
War
Warn
Warren
Werner

WAYLAND
Lan
Land
Lannie
Lanny
Way
Waylen
Waylon

A Minnesota man, **MICHAEL DENGLER**, tried for several years to have his name legally changed to 1069!! The courts consistently refused him even though he had acquired a driver's license and a Social Security card with the number listed as his name. In 1978 Minnesota Judge **DONALD BARBEAU** said that Dengler's request was an "offense to basic human dignity." But Dengler pressed on. In 1980, the Minnesota Supreme Court granted his name change request . . . sort of. They said he could be called "One-zero-six-nine."

WEBER
Web
Webb
Webber
Webbie
Webby

WELDON
Don
Donnie
Donny
Wel
Weld

WENDELL
Dell
Dellie
Delly
Wen
Wend
Wendy

WESLEY
Lee
Leigh
Wes

WHITNEY
Whit
Wit

WHITTAKER
Whit
Whitacker
Wit

WILBUR
Burr
Wil
Will
Willie
Willy

WILFRED
Fred
Freddie
Freddy
Fredo
Wil
Wilfredo
Willie
Willy

WILLIAM
Bill
Billie
Billy
Guillaume
Guillemot
Guillermo
Guillim
Wilhelm
Will
Willard
Willem
Willie
Willy
Wilmer
Wilmot

WINSLOW
Win
Winnie
Winny
Wins

WINSTON
Win
Winnie
Winny
Wins

WINTHROP
Win
Winnie
Winny
Wint

In England use of the term JUNIOR is non-existent. Britons who name sons after fathers use suffixes II or III and so forth. When they need to distinguish between father and son they sometimes use the expressions MAJOR and MINOR, so that you might find MR. ALFRED BRAITHWAITE, MAJOR and MR. ALFRED BRAITHWAITE, MINOR on the membership roster of a posh London club.

WOLFGANG
Wolf
Wolfie
Wolfy

WOODROW
Wood
Woodie
Woody

WYATT
Wy

WYCLIFFE
Cliff
Cliffe
Cliffie
Wy
Wycliff

WYLIE
Will
Willy
Wy
Wyle

WYNDHAM
Win
Wind
Windam
Windham
Windie
Windy
Wyn
Wynd
Wyndie
Wyndy

YANCY
Yance

YASHAR
Sharie
Shary
Yasha
Yashie
Yashy

ZACHARY
Zack

Singer, composer **FRANK ZAPPA** and his wife have a child with one of the most famous names of the 1960's. She is called **MOON UNIT**. Their three other offspring are **DWEEZIL, AHMET EMUUKHA RODAN** and **DIVA!!**

130
YEARS
OF
AMERICAN
NAMES
TO
SING

America's musical heritage is full of songs declaring love for beautiful women, admiration for heroes of war, disdain for faithless lovers and loyalty to best pals. Most of our popular songs which are directed at specific people are written to women. There is an entire chorus of MAGGIEs, ANNIEs and LIZAs. Of the many songs written to men, however, JOHNNIE's praises are most often sung.

Looking over a list of the popular name songs of the past decades we are reminded of how the times have changed and how they have remained the same. There are songs sending the JOHNNIEs off to war and songs to bring them home. In between are the songs about the exotic MARIEs and ROSIEs they met while defending foreign shores.

Our songs are not only a way to express our feelings about names but can also affect those feelings quite profoundly. Nearly everyone pictures an ethereal French beauty ever since the Beatles gave us this image of MICHELLE.

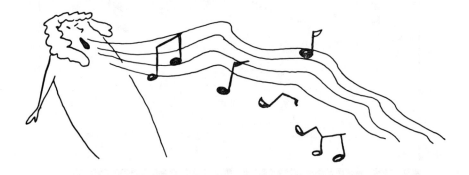

1850's

Sweet BETSY From Pike ... JEANIE With The Light Brown Hair

1860's

When I Saw Sweet NELLIE Home ... When JOHNNY Comes
Marching Home ... When You And I Were Young, MAGGIE ...
Sweet GENEVIEVE

1870's

FRANKIE & JOHNNIE ... Goodbye, LIZA JANE ... JOHN
HENRY ... Where Was MOSES When The Lights Went Out

1880's

My BONNIE Lies Over The Ocean ... My NELLIE's Blue Eyes
... JOHNNY Get Your Gun

1890's

Little ANNIE Rooney ... DAISY ... My PEARL's A Bowery
Girl ... CASEY Would Waltz With The Strawberry Blonde ...
ELSIE From Chelsea ... Sweet ROSIE O'Grady

1900's

JOSEPHINE, My JO ... BILL Bailey, Won't You Please Come
Home ... Sweet ADELINE ... Waltzing MATHILDA ...
MARY's A Grand Old Name ... So Long, MARY ... My Irish
MOLLY O ... Sunbonnet SUE ... CASEY Jones ... Has
Anybody Here Seen KELLY

1910's

Come, JOSEPHINE, In My Flying Machine ... ALEXANDER's
Ragtime Band ... Ragtime Cowboy JOE ... PEG O'My Heart
... SYLVIA Speaks ... Poor PAULINE ... REBECCA Of
Sunnybrook Farm ... Sister SUSIE's Sewing Shirts For The
Soldiers ... Since MAGGIE Dooley Learned The Hooley Hooley
... Li'l LIZA JANE ... Oh JOHNNY, Oh JOHNNY! ... Oui,
Oui MARIE ... Sweet Little ALICE Blue Gown ... IRENE ...
MANDY ... Oh! What A Pal Was MARY ... PEGGY

1920's

Mah LINDY LOU ... MARGIE ... ROSE Of Washington
Square ... My Greenwich Village SUE ... LENA From
Palesteena ... Pretty KITTY Kelly ... When FRANCIS Dances
With Me ... Dapper DAN ... MANDY 'N Me ... I'm Just Wild
About HARRY ... SALLY ... The JOHN HENRY Blues ...
GEORGETTE ... Lovin' SAM, The Sheik Of Alabam' ...
NELLIE Kelly, I Love You ... BARNEY Google ... ANNABELLE
... Raggedy ANNE ... No, No, NORA ... STELLA ...
CHARLEY, My Boy ... Hard Hearted HANNAH ... I Wonder
What's Become Of SALLY ... Oh, KATHARINA ... CECILIA
... DINAH ... Don't Bring LULU ... If You Knew SUSIE, Like
I Know SUSIE ... Sweet GEORGIA Brown ... Keep Your Skirts
Down, MARY ANN ... CHARMAINE ... MARY LOU ...
BILL ... DIANE ... RAMONA ... JEANINE, I Dream Of
Lilac Time ... MARIE ... Sweet LORRAINE ... Sweet SUE
... ANGELA Mia ... MARIANNE ... LOUISE ... Piccolo
PETE ... True Blue LOU

1930's

BETTY Co-Ed ... GEORGIA On My Mind ... Come Out Of The Kitchen, MARY ANN ... Barnacle BILL The Sailor ... I Love LUISA ... MINNIE The Moocher ... Poor PIERROT ... CORRINE CORRINA ... MIMI ... ANNIE Doesn't Live Here Anymore ... MARIE ELENA ... JIMMY Had A Nickel ... Blow, GABRIEL, Blow ... BESS, You Is My Woman Now ... JOHNNY One Note ... ROSALIE ... GEORGIANNA ... JOSEPHINE ... Just A Kid Named JOE ... Adios, MARIQUITA LINDA ... KATIE Went To Haiti

1940's

DOLORES ... JIM ... ARTHUR Murray Taught Me Dancing In A Hurry ... CONCHITA, MARQUITA, LOLITA, PEPITA, ROSITA, JUANITA Lopez ... I Came Here To Talk To JOE ... JOHNNY Doughboy Found A ROSE In Ireland ... GERTIE From Bizerte ... LILI MARLENE ... NANCY With The Laughing Face ... LAURA ... NINA ... LINDA ... CHIQUITA Banana ... STELLA By Starlight ... Open The Door, RICHARD ... Don't Cry, JOE ... MONA LISA ... Bloody MARY ... Portrait Of JENNY ... Put Your Shoes On, LUCY

1950's

Goodnight, IRENE ... SAM's Song ... WILHELMINA ...
BELLE, BELLE, My Liberty BELLE ... JEZEBEL ... ALICE
In Wonderland ... I Still See ELISA ... They Call The Wind
MARIA ... NINA Never Knew ... RUBY ... ANNA ...
Mexican JOE ... HERNANDO's Hideaway ... JOEY ... The
Crazy OTTO Rag ... Dance With Me, HENRY ...
MAYBELLINE ... JOSEPHINE ... PETE Kelly's Blues ...
Whatever LOLA Wants, LOLA Gets ... CINDY, Oh CINDY ...
JOEY, JOEY, JOEY ... Long Tall SALLY ... When SUNNY
Gets Blue ... DIANA ... MARIA ... LIDA ROSE ...
MATILDA ... PEGGY SUE ... DONNA ... GIGI ...
PATRICIA ... CHARLIE Brown ... FRANKIE ... Goodbye
JIMMY, Goodbye ... KOOKIE, KOOKIE, Lend Me Your Comb

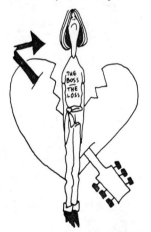

1960's

CATHY's Clown ... IRMA La Douce ... Tell LAURA I Love
Her ... Big Bad JOHN ... CORINNA CORINNA ... Hit The
Road, JACK ... Runaround SUE ... JOHNNY Angel ...
Ramblin' ROSE ... SHEILA ... SHERRY ... BOBBY's Girl ...
Hey, PAULA ... LOUIS LOUIS ... RUBY Baby ... Good Golly,
Miss MOLLY ... JUDY's Turn To Cry ... SALLY Go Round
The Roses ... Hello, DOLLY! ... DAWN ... Hush, Hush, Sweet
CHARLOTTE ... Help Me, RHONDA ... MICHELLE, Ma

Belle ... EMILY ... BARBARA ANN ... ELEANOR Rigby ...
DULCINEA ... GLORIA ... MAME ... Message To
MICHAEL ... A Symphony For SUSAN ... GEORGY Girl ...
Ode To BILLY JOE ... WINDY ... Lovely RITA, Meter Maid
... SUZANNE ... You're A Good Man, CHARLEY Brown ...
Hey JUDE ... ABRAHAM, MARTIN And JOHN ... The
Ballad Of BONNIE And CLYDE ... JULIA ... MADELEINE
... SIMON Says ... Timid FRIEDA ... A Boy Named SUE ...
JEAN ... Proud MARY ... Take A Letter, MARIA ...
GABRIELLE ... TRACEY

1970's

Cracklin' ROSIE ... CANDIDA ... Sweet CAROLINE ...
MAGGIE MAY ... Uncle ALBERT ... CLAIR ... BEN ...
BRANDY ... BRIAN's Song ... FREDDY, My Love ...
LAYLA ... Look At Me, I'm SANDRA Dee ... Me And JULIO
Down By The Schoolyard ... ANGIE ... Bad Bad LEROY
Brown ... DANIEL ... Delta DAWN ... DANNY's Song ...
LIZA With A Z ... Little WILLY ... My Sweet Gypsy ROSE
... ANGIE Baby ... ANNIE's Song ... BENNIE And The Jets
... Fly Robin, Fly ... JACKIE Blue ... MANDY ... EMMA
... Run JOEY, Run ... NADIA's Theme ... SARA Smile ...
SHANNON ... Lay Down SALLY ... ROXANNE ...
AMANDA ... My SHARONA ... CHUCK E's In Love

1980's

Little JEANNIE ... SARA ... Bella DONNA ... JESSIE's Girl
... BETTE Davis Eyes ... ARTHUR's Theme ... ELVIRA ...
JACK And DIANE ... MICKEY ... GLORIA ... ROSANNA
... CHRISTY LEE ... BILLIE JEAN ... Come On, EILEEN
... AMANDA ... BOBBY JEAN ... JOANNA ... SHEILA ...
JESSE

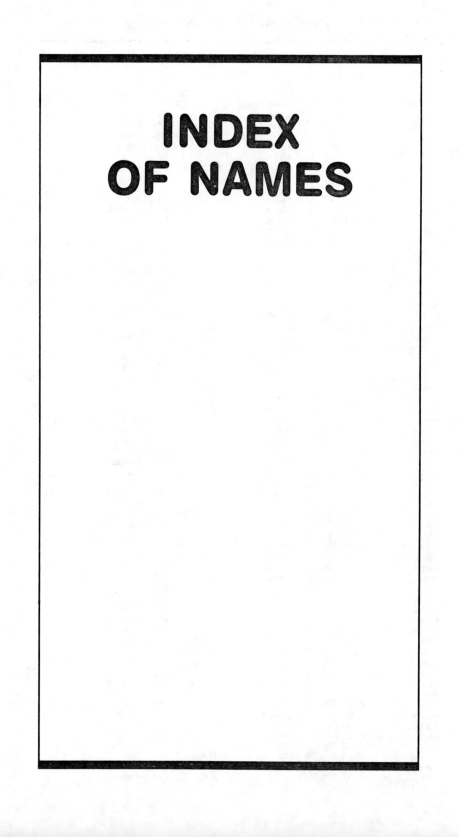

INDEX
OF NAMES

F

G

M

U

V

D

K

J

S

Z

If you have gotten this far and still haven't had your fill on the subject, we suggest these other fine books about names:

Ames, Winthrop. *What Shall We Name The Baby.* New York: Simon & Schuster, Inc., 1935.

Anderson, C. *The Name Game.* New York: Simon & Schuster, Inc., 1977.

Atkinson, Frank. *The Dictionary of Literary Pseudonyms.* London: Clive Bingley, 1982.

Bauer, Andrew. *The Hawthorne Dictionary of Pseudonyms.* New York: Hawthorne Books, 1975.

Browder, Sue. *New Age Baby Name Book.* New York: Workman Press, 1974.

Durkling, Leslie Ann. *First Names First.* New York: Universe Books, 1977.

Friedman, Flavius. *What's In A Name?* New York: Scholastic Book Services, 1975.

Kotlatch, Alfred J. *The Jonathan David Dictionary of Names.* New York: Jonathan David Publishers, 1980.

Lansky, Bruce & Vicki. *The Best Baby Name Book in the whole wide world.* Minnesota: Meadowbrook Press, 1979.

Mossman, Jennifer. *Pseudonyms & Nicknames Dictionary.* Detroit: Gale Research Company, 1982.

Nurnberg, Maxwell & Rosenblum, Morris. *What To Name Your Baby.* New York: Collier Books, 1984.

Rule, Lareina. *Name Your Baby.* New York: Bantam Books, 1963.

Shankle, George Earlie, PhD. *American Nicknames, Their Origin and Significance.* New York: H.W. Wilson Company, 1955.

Smith, Elsdon. *Treasury of Name Lore.* New York: Harper & Row, Publishers, Inc., 1967.

Stewart, George R. *American Given Names, Their Origins & History in the Context of the English Language.* New York: Oxford Press, 1979.

Tournier, Paul. *The Naming of Persons.* New York: Harper & Row, Publishers, Inc., 1975.

Webster's Dictionary of First Names. New York: Galahad Books, 1981.

Wells, Evelyn. *What To Name The Baby.* New York: Doubleday & Co., Inc., 1953.

Certain graphic materials were reprinted from these Dover Publications, Inc. books: *Men - A Dover Pictorial Archive Series,* selected by Jim Harter; *Women - A Dover Pictorial Archive Series,* selected by Jim Harter; *The Complete Woodcuts of Albrecht Durer,* Edited by Dr. Willi Kurth; *Handbook of Early Advertising Art, Mainly From American Sources,* Clarence P. Hornung; *More Silhouettes, A Pictorial Archive of Varied Illustrations,* by Carol Balanger Graston.